Edmund Rubbra Symphonist

Edmund Rubbra, photograph by C. E. Sweetland, *c.*1948

Edmund Rubbra Symphonist

LEO BLACK

THE BOYDELL PRESS

First published 2008
The Boydell Press, Woodbridge
Reprinted in paperback 2014

ISBN 978 1 84383 355 0 hardback
ISBN 978 1 84383 933 0 paperback

The Boydell Press is an imprint of Boydell & Brewer Ltd
PO Box 9, Woodbridge, Suffolk IP12 3DF, UK
and of Boydell & Brewer Inc.
668 Mt Hope Avenue, Rochester, NY 14620-2731, USA
website: www.boydellandbrewer.com

The publisher has no responsibility for the continued existence or accuracy of URLs for external or third-party internet websites referred to in this book, and does not guarantee that any content on such websites is, or will remain, accurate or appropriate

A CIP record for this book is available from the British Library

This publication is printed on acid-free paper

Designed and typeset in Adobe Myriad Pro & Adobe Warnock Pro by David Roberts, Pershore, Worcestershire

The continuous struggle over the years to bend the materials of one's art to a shape that satisfies the demands of the 'inner voice' ...

EDMUND RUBBRA

Music says it all without giving anything away.

ARNOLD SCHÖNBERG

Faith and the culture of faith have a hard time of it in the interstice between aesthetic elitism and industrial mass culture. Their position is difficult simply because art and people themselves have a hard time of it in this situation and can hardly hold their ground.

BENEDICT XVI

But the Lord was not in the fire; and after the fire a still small voice.

1 KINGS 19:12

The publication of this book was made possible
by a generous grant from the RVW Trust.

Contents

For | BENEDICT RUBBRA
    | &
    | ADRIAN YARDLEY

Preface

Some compliments turn out to be anything but. A senior BBC colleague – historian, television Head of Department, radio Network Controller and great human being – was in the habit of introducing me to people as 'a distinguished musicologist'. It wasn't worth saying so, but I always thought, 'Excuse me, that door closed fifteen years ago' (after a few unsuccessful university job applications and interviews). Co-opted into broadcasting, the most I hoped my radio programmes would do was infect others with my own love of music – and that, of course, was what made Controller-Man commend me in the first place. Musicology meant learning and analysis for their own sakes; those are very worthy things, but had little to do my imagined listeners. (Was not BBC Audience Research's typical Third Programme panellist 'a chemist's assistant in Watford'?)

So when after half a lifetime I felt a surge of interest in the music of one of my former Oxford tutors, it was frustrating to find the one sizeable book about Edmund Rubbra[1] concentrating on technical analysis at a level that must make much of it unusable for an ordinary music-lover. While offering useful information about his life and the reception of his works when first performed, it dealt with the actual music through very specific listing of just what happens to what basic intervals at what points in Rubbra's major pieces. That followed the intricate workings of the composer's mind but was not what one would recommend to engage the curiosity of Watford Chemist's Assistant's successor. Discussing the symphonies in extended programme-notes, I hope to make new friends for a deeply rewarding composer. I approach him as a symphonist, with other works accounted for as and when they bear on the main subject. A biography is needed, but would take a historian's expertise, and this is not it. (Controller-Man's successor, now a biographer though never a historian, advised me, 'It's easy – keep it simple, say what happened next.' But the problem with a major composer is that what happened next was usually 'He went off and wrote some more music'.) In this book the currently mandatory formula 'life and times' is acknowledged just enough to ring bells with the reader inhabiting a world whose problems have changed little since Rubbra was alive.

Any new study of Rubbra for music-lovers rather than fellow-composers or the writers of dissertations must bear in mind the virtual unavailability of his scores outside the academic world. They can be studied at the British Library if one is in London; some can be borrowed from public libraries; but at the time of writing not a single Rubbra symphony was to be had at the few shops stocking scores and sheet music, which were also virtually devoid of his other works. Immediately available and vivid documentation of the symphonies' musical value lies in recordings – pioneering ones reissued in the past couple of years, and the complete cycle played by the BBC National Orchestra of Wales under Richard Hickox.

To my mind – a slightly biased one since he taught me harmony and counterpoint for two years – Rubbra was a great composer, whose music the contemporary world badly needs.

An earlier book of mine found possible and actual buyers daunted by the complexity of its music examples. For this one, which has no ambitions to be a thematic catalogue, I have tried to keep them simple, reasoning that for every reader who can make sense of harmony there must be ten or a hundred who, having sung from sheet music, can follow the up and down of a melody, and its rhythm. In some cases (particularly in the latter part of the book, treating the later symphonies, whose subject matter often comes close to the Schönbergian concept of an 'idea as complex entity all of whose components are necessary if it is to make sense'), the contrapuntal nature of essential passages needed to be shown, but I have made up for it by not including an example where the material in question is so splendidly obvious that the reader-listener must be able to identify it purely from its description. That is true, as a first example, of the First Symphony's scherzo. I have included as much detail as I felt was necessary to convey a clear idea of outline and character (something that varied from work to work and even theme to theme), omitting whatever might have cluttered up the picture on the page. (Tempo indications, for example, are always close at hand within the text.)

The *Sinfonia Sacra*, with its biblical text, is left unillustrated.

A note for the benefit of readers fortunate enough to have access to scores: Rubbra's bar-numbering habits changed in the course of his career – in the first four symphonies, the Eighth and the final two he placed study figures every ten bars, while in nos. 5–7 and no. 9 (the *Sinfonia Sacra*) they were placed less regularly, mostly to coincide with structural points in the music. In either case he always regarded such numbers as part of a whole, and ran them on from movement to movement. Where I give a bar number it is the one within the movement concerned. The formula 'fig. X+1' indicates the first bar after the figure, not the second.

The text refers many times to 'Payne', meaning, with the sole exception of p. 161, the musicologist Dr Elsie Payne rather than the composer-critic Anthony Payne.

Note:

1 Ralph Scott Grover, *The Music of Edmund Rubbra* (Aldershot, 1993).

Acknowledgements

The list of people who made this book possible must begin with the name of Rubbra's younger son and artistic executor Adrian Yardley, who provided me with a wealth of material, both written and recorded, and could not have been more helpful. He also contributed most generously, from the Rubbra Estate, to the expenses involved in producing the book. I am grateful to Benedict Rubbra, son of the composer's earlier marriage, for essential biographical insights, Anthony Bennett for his thoughts on the Viola Concerto and Eighth Symphony, Piers Burton-Page for alerting me to relevant aspects of Karl Amadeus Hartmann's work, Oliver Davies and Paul Collen for valued help over Juliet Pannett's portrait of Rubbra, Lewis Foreman for allowing me to profit from his exhaustive knowledge of Rubbra's music criticism published in the *Monthly Musical Record*, Mitchell Heller for alerting me to Gary Higginson's reminiscences on the Internet, David Katz for 'draw water and hew wood', Professor Gianpaolo Romanato and the late Father Cormac Rigby for help with the theological background to Rubbra's conversion and Catholic church music, Elizabeth Watson for recollections of Maurice Loban, Anita Webber for her local knowledge of Richmond, Christopher Wintle for help in identifying quotations from Hans Keller, and Hugh Wood for alerting me to the correct version of the classic story about George VI and John Piper, also for confirming the text of a Hindemith quotation I should never have forgotten in the first place.

My special thanks are due to those who helped me keep the strength and confidence to embark on this book while fighting an at-times debilitating medical condition; I would single out Pilates instructors at the Belsize Studio in London (in particular Maika Klaukien), but also and quite specially Tisha Harrington of the Pilates Studio, Kings Cross. I am also grateful for the wise and far-seeing eye of Dr Hugh Beynon, rheumatologist extraordinary, who knew just when to slacken the steroid reins and when to keep them tight.

My thanks go to my wife, the cellist Felicity Vincent, first for letting me partner her in extraordinarily illuminating performances of Rubbra's Cello Sonata, and then for celebrating my birthday with the box of CDs containing all the symphonies recorded under Richard Hickox. Without it this book would never have been written.

My old friend and distinguished ex-BBC colleague Arthur Johnson provided indispensable help in processing the music examples; they are reproduced by kind permission of G. Ricordi & Co. (London) Ltd, who now administer the Lengnick copyrights. I am indebted to my editor, Bruce Phillips, for wise guidance at many stages in the preparation of the book, and to Caroline Palmer, Editorial Director of Boydell & Brewer, for invaluable encouragement when the book was still far short of its final state. My copy-editor, Dr David Roberts, contributed in no small degree to the final stages of this book's preparation, with his eagle eye for detail and a variety of constructive suggestions. The publication of this book was made possible by a generous grant from the RVW Trust.

Ralph Scott Grover's pioneering volume is referred to countless times in the course of this text – not always reverentially, but his thorough-going analyses can interest a music-lover once the latter has become convinced of the value of Rubbra's music and familiar with it. I hope the present book will accelerate the process, after which Grover's sedulous attention to detail can fill in my more broad-brush picture.

The more important corrections in this edition are owed principally to Rubbra's friend, the late Colin Seamarks, to whose memory the reprint is gratefully dedicated.

Abbreviations

BCI   *British Composers in Interview,* ed. Murray Schafer (London, 1963)

ERC   *Edmund Rubbra, Composer,* ed. Lewis Foreman (Rickmansworth, 1970)

Rubbra in the Third Millennium?

A composer with 164 works to his name is scarcely to be covered adequately in a single book. Ralph Scott Grover analysed the important pieces and some of the minor ones, also accounting, however briefly, for every single thing Rubbra wrote apart from the more ephemeral incidental music, and his book was no mere analytical *tour de force* but a labour of love.[1] What could act as a complement and, hopefully, bring this extraordinary composer's music a little nearer the world of that nebulous entity 'the music-lover' is an account that dares a few unashamed similes and human comparisons.[2] Rubbra, as was his good right, tended to confine comment on his own music to the kind of technicality also favoured by his first generation of apostles, so he might or might not have approved, even if this 'new testament' does its best to keep at a certain distance from a private life which he, a shy and reserved man, would have felt to be no-one else's business. What remains of him now is first and foremost his music, and it is too great to go on suffering its current neglect. It needs passionate advocates.

They may be hard to find, at least among leading performers. The best British conductor, when approached about Rubbra, confessed to me that he had never been able to enter into a relationship with his music. That is told, not in any spirit of reproach but to show the size of the problem; a whole generation has been deprived of the chance to make its mind up about him, and the desuetude into which his output fell during the decades just before and after his death might make one despair of his ever enjoying a resurrection. These things, however, work on the longest time-scale, and a substantial body of his music can now at least be heard in one's home, thanks mostly to the enterprise of the Chandos, Dutton, Naxos and Nimbus (Lyrita) record companies, backed up by Adrian Yardley's devoted and selfless stewardship of whatever income the works have produced. I once read that the average classical CD is listened to one-and-a-third times, which is not going to develop a passion in anyone, but there must always be exceptions.

This book's most glaring apparent omission needs addressing straight away. Rubbra's awareness that our music had always tended towards the miniature is reflected in most of his sixty gloriously concise choral works. The mature output for unaccompanied and accompanied choir, from the 1945 *Missa cantuarensis* to *Veni Creator Spiritus* composed just over twenty years later,[3] led to the work he considered his most personal, the *Sinfonia Sacra*. But for the most part that musical world and its procedures bear less directly on the symphonies than does, for example, his chamber-music. Martin Anderson has argued[4] that the latter 'reveals the essence of the man more directly than the larger canvasses of the symphonies', and it certainly has, above all towards the end of Rubbra's life, an intimacy and gentleness found hardly anywhere else in music apart from the work of the mature Fauré and the elderly Haydn. But Rubbra's full range, as distinct from whatever one picks on as his 'essence', must be sought in the symphony, which still stands (along with opera, where he was scarcely active) as the pinnacle of Western music. He called it 'a vehicle for the profoundest abstract statements in music … much more dramatic than a string quartet; the ideas are bolder, the texture is more variegated … [The string quartet] is like a Wordsworthian poem while a symphony is more like an entire philosophical system.'[5] His eleven symphonies composed over a period of forty-five years document the progress of an outstanding musical mind, and I hope this book may contribute to their wider and better appreciation.

Rubbra's view of 'The British Composer and the Symphony'[6] was that whereas 'the continental symphonic tradition shows an unbroken development for roughly 150 years up to 1900', so that even in opera and the Lied 'the symphony was the prime test of a composer's thinking', there had been no such developing tradition of large-scale music in England.

> Our music, even in the golden age, had always been miniature in the matter of form, if not of content. The madrigal, motet, mass were forms largely dictated by the word; but the strength of the music lay in lyrical beauty, contrapuntal daring and a feeling for long melodic lines that permeated the texture.

Rubbra took up the challenge of renewing that tradition in new terms.

Between the time of his first and last symphonies (1935 and 1979) the form, despite constant obituary notices, flourished in England, with Vaughan Williams completing his final five, Michael Tippett and Roberto Gerhard each composing their four, Havergal Brian progressing doggedly from five to thirty-two, Walton producing a second, Rawsthorne three, Malcolm Arnold seven with numbers plus one for strings and a Toy Symphony, Alan Bush two, Humphrey Searle five, Lennox Berkeley four, William Alwyn five, Benjamin Frankel eight, Malcolm Williamson five, and Robert Simpson seven. Even the avant-gardist Elisabeth Lutyens, more given to small forms, produced one, only the supreme lyricist Gerald Finzi remaining immune. From the new 'Manchester

School', Peter Maxwell Davies completed his first, while Alexander Goehr offered a full-scale symphony and the eminently touching *Little Symphony* in memory of his conductor father Walter. The Principality had Grace Williams (one symphony surviving, one 'withdrawn'), Daniel Jones (nine) and Alun Hoddinott (five), with a solitary contribution from William Mathias.

So Rubbra's eleven symphonies seem to face stiff competition, if that is what serious musical works face. All those composers excelled in some field or other, but one's automatic reaction to only a few would be 'Ah yes, memorable symphonies' – certainly Vaughan Williams in view of at least nos. 5 and 6, Simpson, probably Tippett, possibly Arnold, plus Havergal Brian by sheer weight of numbers. There is much music by all those composers to remember with pleasure or acknowledge as worth remembering, be it operas, Searle's vocal-and-instrumental *tours de force* (*Gold Coast Customs*, *The Riverrun*), Rawsthorne's irresistible *Street Corner* overture or the greater part of Walton's output, and only a very bold man would try to assess just how Rubbra compares with all of it. I can only report how he affects me, as a musician of the next generation who grew up with the traditions Rubbra knew forwards, backwards and sideways.

The unsurprising yet telling thing about the symphonies is that they represent Rubbra at a consistently maximal level of achievement. There is not one weak work among them, and though the middle four, from no. 5 to no. 8, compete for the gold medal, there is also a sense in which the older he gets the better he gets. Grover identified three middle symphonies (nos. 5, 6, 7) and then 'the last four', as much as anything on the grounds of Rubbra's declared shift of emphasis from key-contrast to contrast of intervals (see Chapter 8), whereas this book takes its cue from the processes of extreme condensation found from the Ninth (the *Sinfonia Sacra*) onward. Without being one of his short symphonies it abolishes the traditional division into contrasted movements, which is resurrected on a quite small scale in the Tenth, finally vanishing in the equally concise Eleventh.

The first attempt to pin down in words the qualities that set Rubbra apart came as early as 1950, in Wilfrid Mellers' book *Music and Society*, when there were as yet only five symphonies. Mellers wrote of the composer's broadcast introduction to the Fourth (see Appendix 1 to this book) that, given its reference to essences, i.e. 'manifestations of creative life through the medium of sound ... it should be clear that such a conception necessarily involves a religious attitude to one's experience; and I am inclined to think that Rubbra's achievement has depended on his being endowed with what is, for a man of the contemporary world, rather a peculiar spiritual make-up'. Rubbra summed up his own spirituality in a 1953 lecture:

> I'm old-fashioned enough to believe that the highest function of music is to release one from personal pre-occupation in order to know something of the Divine forces that shape all existence. To achieve this, the composer must have a faith that man is NOT the end of all things, that man is NOT unaided, the sole arbiter of his destiny, that he is an instrument, even if a weak one, of a purpose that, even if beyond our understanding, is immovably present at each point of time.

That 'unaided' could be the most significant word Rubbra ever wrote, a sign of a nature which rather than striding confidently out to conquer the world looked at all stages for a supporting hand to help him achieve his best. Without it, he could hardly live up to St Thomas Aquinas's injunction memorably set to music in one of his finest unaccompanied choral works, the 1960 *Lauda Sion*, 'quantum potes, tantum aude' – dare to do as much as you have in you. (Or, as sport more crisply puts it, 'Do what you can.')

For all the spiritual speculations and intuitions in the music and writings of Michael Tippett, with his 'move into Aquarius' standing for a new age and its hopes or illusions of a new man, there is a unique stringency about Rubbra's insight, a refusal to follow or indeed set any trend. And there, if anywhere, lies the justification for advocacy of him in a Third Millennium when so much has changed in music since his time. Despite half a century's neglect the prospects are not entirely bleak. The 'new age', for all its naïvetés, idiocies and trends, is less afflicted by the extreme tunnel-vision that obscured the view for much of the twentieth century, before 'the musical Establishment' and 'the march of History' gave way to The Music Industry; the great thing now is not how 'advanced' you are, but whether you are fly enough to stay in business through your self-marketing skills. The pretentious and over-vocal prevail in the short run, their elbows being so extremely sharp, their words so loud and plausible and their software so comprehensive and market-orientated, but a new spirit of tolerance, often sloppy but basically kindly ('anything goes') does seem to be in the air. As for any personal alienation (see p. 161), it weakens and disappears as those concerned depart this earth.

The planet badly needs men whose work reflects the humility implicit in deep religious belief, and who can communicate such inmost qualities in intelligible sounds, regardless of style or period.[7] Robert Simpson once summed up the essential quality and message of Bruckner's music as 'patience', and the greatest Rubbra, such as the slow movement of the Sixth Symphony and the entire Eighth, incorporates both the virtue of constant searching that finally brings enlightenment, and an ability to react in sound to the numinous turning-points that intervene, unsought, along the way. Near the end of his career, after 'fifty years of almost continuous writing', Rubbra penned words that could come from any true artist, telling of 'the continuous struggle over the years to bend the materials of one's art to a shape that satisfies the demands of the "inner voice" – demands that can never be stilled'.[8] In his major volume Grover named as one of two goals 'the objective study of a considerable body of music, the high quality of which should by now be obvious (I make no apologies whatsoever for my enthusiasm)'. With the minor proviso that I should probably substitute 'subjective' for 'objective', I can not improve on that and would heartily echo it.

CHAPTER 1

General Features

Rubbra's eleven symphonies from five decades represent a major journey in three distinct stages. The first four, composed before and just after the outbreak of the Second World War, and in some ways reflecting that time, made a truly striking start. There followed a period of fulfilment and highest-level achievement between 1947 and 1971, with four more, each one absolutely characteristic and fairly describable as a masterpiece. The choral Ninth Symphony (*Sinfonia Sacra*) was a one-off which meant a lot to him; it ushered in a final period in which his last two symphonies had a new conciseness.

Rubbra is not the easiest composer to classify. He sounds unmistakably mid-twentieth-century English, but with little trace of the highly chromatic, sensuous, harmonically ingenious sounds developed by post-Delius figures like John Ireland and Eugene Goossens. They were roundly deprecated by more austere colleagues, especially Vaughan Williams and Rubbra's teacher Holst (whose passion was for 'picking his music to the bare bones'). Nor does he have much if anything of the pastoral strain found in music of the inter-war years which even its devotees, turning round an expression originally meant to wound, now affectionately call 'cow-pat'. Such works reacted against both the trauma of 1914–18 and a 'modernism' aspiring to reflect the post-war world; Rubbra's mature output stands just far enough on from that clash of ways to show up as entirely new and original, though by temperament he was closer to the RVW–Holst arc. Vaughan Williams lived long enough to take in the first seven Rubbra symphonies, and found him his natural successor as a symphonist.[1]

Rubbra can be extremely vigorous, at times even tumultuous. He does not take his inspiration from folk music, in either the euphoric Percy Grainger manner or Vaughan Williams's numinous way; although he acknowledged that a vast amount of great music arose from the spirit of folk music correctly understood, he felt he was in a different tradition. In a lecture entitled 'The Contemporary Composer – Tradition and Environment', some time after the 1955 première of his Sixth Symphony, he distinguished between the two traditions. As an admirable example of a secular composer, meaning one whose work was based in the profoundest sense on the logic behind folk music, he cited Bartók, whom he respected enormously for his total integrity in taking that way of thinking further. The other tradition went back to the Middle Ages and was 'religious or even mystical'. As its two 'firmly fixed centres' he named a reliance on 'the strong and pure intervals of the 4th, 5th and octave', and the avoidance of anything suggestive of regular accents, even the 'regular irregularities' set up by, for example, complex time-signatures (so-called 'Bulgarian' rhythms) in Bartók. 'A composer who is in this [religious] tradition – it is of course purely a matter of temperament – usually dislikes using folk music in his own compositions, and even in his most secular moods tries to avoid making the bar-line significant'. An impartial observer's only possible reservation is that some of his melodies, especially in his scherzos (symphonies nos. 1, 3, 5, 6, also the latter work's finale) come close to having 'the common touch'.

Some of his characteristics look back to Bach and Beethoven,[2] and to the spirit, though seldom the techniques, found in motets and Masses by English Tudor and Elizabethan composers. There is no self-conscious harking back; as he said in *BCI*, 'I've never been conscious of selecting anything from the past in order to make use of it in my own work … When I study the music of the past, the antennae of my imagination automatically dwell on certain interesting features of the music I am studying, and later, unconsciously, some of these may find expression in my own music'. The occasional mediaevalism such as the sharpened-fourth-and-leading-note sounds in the Kyrie of the 1958 *Missa a tre* might suggest that he had become conscious of polyphonic music from the time after Machaut, where that was often the standard way to lead into a cadence; three years earlier he had composed a *Fantasia on a Theme of Machaut* for recorder, string quartet and harpsichord. Rubbra shared with 'all composers throughout history … the same problem of selecting from what was bequeathed in order to satisfy what it was necessary to express' – not for him the Stockhausen feeling of being 'the first composer'. As he also said at that time, 'the real reactionaries are the revolutionaries who react against tradition!'

Rubbra thought naturally in terms not just of melodies, *vulgo* tunes, but of several at once, something the terminology of music calls 'counterpoint'. At one point he wrote that 'melody and its concomitant, counterpoint, bring all the delights of harmony and rhythm without self-consciously showing them off'. The smoothness with which he combines his simultaneous lines shows a well-trained mind and precise aural imagination. His music's continuity and inner logic come from his total immersion in often-very-simple melodic ideas and his ability to see how they can be varied and combined. To that extent he is an easy composer to follow; the fluency and subtlety with which he derives one melody or figure from another plays a large part in the sense of inevitability given by his best music, something an uninstructed listener senses without needing to know what brought it about.

Such ability to combine self-sufficient lines had, of course, also to bear constantly in mind their effect when heard together, the harmony they created. In his youth he was greatly struck by a lively little book, *Antheil and the Treatise on Harmony* by, of all people, the poet Ezra Pound, discovered while browsing among the booths on the left bank of the Seine. He took very seriously Pound's 'perhaps frivolous' remark that 'what has hitherto been neglected in the study of harmony has been the gap *between* sounds, that is, between one sound and its successor'. In a lecture first given in the mid-1950s, shortly after the earliest performances of his Sixth Symphony, he turned to Pound's ideas, saying

> Even a silence rightly placed can lead the mind forward; harmony is an enforcement, a colouring of the passing musical moment and can never usurp the primacy of melodic flow. A piece of what looks like purely harmonic music is satisfactory only in so far as there are inward relationships between the succeeding chords, relationships that are basically melodic. Such is my standpoint, but it is one that has only gradually formulated itself in my mind through continual struggle to express *myself*, yet in terms that would link me to what we erroneously call 'the music of the past' ... As man is an individual *yet* is a member of a society, so music must be individual *yet* grounded in things, experiences and laws common to all.

In 'The British Composer and the Symphony' Rubbra summed up his thoughts on the relative importance of harmony and counterpoint in British music of his time: after the passage on 'lyrical beauty and long melodic lines' already quoted, he continued

> How could these indigenous virtues be harnessed to the modern symphonic cause? How could they become the buttresses of the strong triangular structure of symphonic form? The problem is perhaps eased by the fact that after a long period of harmonic invention, in which for the moment we seem to have reached the limits of what the ear will accept, the pendulum has naturally swung in the direction of counterpoint as offering a way out of the evolutionary impasse. Having accepted this new direction, we find that the emotional force that was once packed into harmony must now reside in the impact of significant melodic lines.

The years between 1949 and Rubbra's death saw a plethora of alternative and far more radical ways 'out of the evolutionary impasse' (or deeper into it), and that had everything to do with the decline in his fortunes in the latter part of his life.

Rubbra was commissioned by J. A. Westrup to write a short volume for a series covering music's various 'dimensions'; the resulting *Counterpoint: A Survey* (1960) proved a masterly exposition in little more than a hundred small-format pages, delightfully readable, informed and informative, covering a range of uses of the technique. The contrapuntal purity of his musical thinking can produce an open clarity but complexity such as one finds in Bach's Three-Part Inventions, though in general the sheer smoothness of his counterpoint is more Handelian – everything works as if oiled, that being in itself no guarantee that anything important is being said. A remark of his during my time as a student on the Honours Music course at Oxford was that the human ear cannot honestly claim to follow more than three real parts. Thinking it over, I realised that listening to music in more parts – four, five, six – meant a constant flickering of the attention between one part and another,[3] rather than the steady, total concentration required if one is really to take in and hear, both individually and in their sum total, three running continuously. Counterpoint is honestly followed by registering that sum total and its logic, and Rubbra's axiom depended very largely on the continuing existence of tonal harmony based on the triad, with its endless nuances and emotional overtones. For a few decades after the end of my studies with him, that infinitely ramified web of tonal relationships seemed to be becoming a thing of the past, but with the new millennium it shows signs of a new lease of life. So it is to be hoped that Rubbra's music also will.

An associated principle, which he didn't spell out to his student but expounded at about the same time in a lecture entitled 'A Symphonic Credo', was that 'at any moment there should not be more than *one* predominating line; if two or more lines are of *equal* importance the ear can find no central point to act as a core to the texture'. This he held to be 'one of the prime rules of counterpoint ... one that's rarely if ever mentioned in text books', and it offers one of the aspects in which his mind and Arnold Schönberg's, for all their immense differences, agreed; Schönberg scrupulously marked up the scores of his twelve-tone works with signs denoting main parts (*Hauptstimme*), and subsidiary ones (*Nebenstimme*), occasionally allowing himself to compromise with a bastard one marked *HN* (*Hauptnebenstimme*).

Counterpoint often culminates in fugue, at which Rubbra is an un-academic master. His slow fugues bring to mind not only Bach's '48' but the supreme

Beethoven of the opening movement of the late string quartet in C♯ minor. In *Counterpoint* he wrote that

> the adoption of fugue by Beethoven in his later works seems to have been the outcome of a deepening penetration into regions of musical thought that were increasingly 'philosophical' in the widest sense. The form for Beethoven held reserves of 'inwardness' that no other form seemed to possess: the calm assurance of its structure, its definition, made it a perfect form for his profoundest thoughts. By the force of this thought Beethoven burst the bounds of accepted fugal form and moved through it to hitherto uncharted regions.

A comparable ambition is apparent in the fugues that end Rubbra's First and Third symphonies, the 1946 Cello Sonata and the 1957 Seventh Symphony. His first major work for solo instrument and orchestra, the 1934 *Sinfonia Concertante*, ends with a Prelude and Fugue, and his very last symphonic essay, the *Sinfonietta*, also amounts to that, using as the second of its two movements a transcription of the *Fantasy Fugue* written for a young pianist a couple of years earlier. In a slow tempo his ending may be quietly elegiac (*Sinfonia Concertante*) or triumphant (Sonata), and he is even capable of desperation (Third Symphony).

When, however, he finds it in him to let counterpoint be, and 'show off' what harmony can do, as in the slow second movement of the Sixth Symphony, the result can be unbelievably beautiful. The music then takes on the freshness and purity of the best Mahler or Pfitzner, as a shining example of a historical process by which English music can lag at least a generation behind that of continental Europe and finally produce something fit to stand alongside Europe's best.[4] And yet his most vigorous, stamping dance music, like some of his passages in which simultaneous melodies each appear to have a different time-signature, can briefly seem a more sensitive English version of the mature Hindemith. His teacher Holst is there in the background of the carefree dance-like tunes in evidence from the First Symphony onward, but they rarely stay carefree for long and can become downright frantic when Rubbra's principal preoccupations recur.

In a different way he is less easy to follow: he demands great concentration. To quote his most eloquent advocate, Hugh Ottaway, he is not one of the composers who lets one 'happily drift in and out, at every "in" finding some catchy, surprising or titillating local event. With Rubbra, the continuity, the stream of thought, is everything'.[5] His most-quoted remark is that he never set out with a formal plan in mind; he was often fascinated to discover where his invention had taken him, but a feature of his mentality far less often mentioned, since it is virtually impossible to illustrate, is the extreme care he took before committing himself to begin writing a work at all. The house had to be built on firm foundations, not sand. Beethoven's way of taking the most unlikely, banal scrap of an idea and wresting from it something utterly memorable emerges vividly from his sketchbooks; Rubbra's pre-selection went on in his head, so we have nothing to show for it, but he would surely have appreciated the old joke about the Irishman asked for directions – 'If I was going there I wouldn't start here.' The great Italian writer Cesare Pavese observed in his diaries,[6] 'religion consists of believing that everything that happens in the world is extraordinarily important', and such scrupulousness before action is a small but useful pointer to Rubbra's cast of mind. In a talk for the BBC Home Service's *Music Magazine* entitled 'A Composer's Problems'[7] he said that 'if he [the composer] mistakes a path or pursues a wrong one there is every chance that progress will sooner or later be blocked, and he must go back to find out exactly where the false step was made'.

For all the spontaneity of his creative processes, Rubbra's loose-limbed aural imagination did nonetheless lead him now and then to variants of sonata form, with its contrast between initial and subsequent ideas, and between 'exposition' and 'development'. His approach is outlined on pp. 182–4. He was quite selective about when to use literal repetition and when not; bringing back something heard already, he tended to change it, heighten it and so take his argument a stage further, though there are sizeable exceptions here and there in the symphonies. Schönberg was similarly inclined, which is another curious resemblance over and above their all-consuming counterpoint. It is not a resemblance one may push too far; Rubbra was strongly critical of twelve-tone works for 'contracting music's emotional scope' and also took exception to Schönberg's alleged desire for a 'system'.[8] He expressed the latter reservation in an article 'Letter to a Young Composer' published in the BBC's periodical *The Listener* on 13 September 1956, also applying it to Hindemith. That prompted a response in the 11 October issue, 'The Tone-Row at Home', from the Schönberg apostle Hans Keller, who nevertheless praised the article as 'searching'.

The flexibility of Rubbra's thinking is well demonstrated in the 1946 Cello Sonata's first movement. An 'episode' or second subject in a different, livelier metre than that of the opening is heard for a second time towards the end, but while the piano part uses the same idea as before, setting it out at twice the length and reaching roughly the same climax in a full-blooded melody derived from it, the cello has a different tune whose immediate continuation goes elsewhere, the 'confluence' coming at the climax just mentioned. Rubbra marks the first appearance of this 'B' section 'sonoro', as if it were a hymn or a peal of bells, which the piano's climactic melody could well represent. Against it, the cello throws in some rather enigmatic pizzicato chords. Here we are in A major (the 'dominant of the dominant'). The second appearance, in the tonic major of the movement's original G minor, is marked 'giocoso', and the cello's much more enigmatic, robust triple-stops are this time played with the bow, their notes complicating the harmony in an almost perverse way reminiscent of the 'white-note atonality' identified[9] in the middle period of another favourite composer of Rubbra's, Stravinsky. This climax, which had a predecessor fifteen years earlier in the dancing coda of the Second Violin Sonata's first movement, is specifically marked *ff*, where the first, while obviously loud, has no new dynamic marking. No detail escapes Rubbra's attention. His mind generally comes much nearer to the peasant ingenuity of Haydn's, treasuring and exhausting every scrap of musical material, than to the prodigal Mozart with his melodic over-kill.

Certain passages in his work can, however, bring to mind the complaint by Mozart's quartet-playing colleague, the major violinist and very good minor composer Dittersdorf: 'He offers you one wonderful idea after another, so that in the end you can remember none of them.' And, as Mozart sometimes did, Rubbra often springs a surprise at the very end of a movement. The Cello Sonata's first movement is again a case in point; his initial position is seen from a very different angle, with the movement's two most frequently used motives combined in a surprisingly anguished emotional context: he is moving on somewhere new (though not, in fact, into anguish). The feeling of 'Where next?' at the end of an extended movement is basic to Rubbra's large-scale thought, a product of his instinct for giving an entire work, and not merely its individual movements, an overall form. It is a part of what Schönberg (apropos Sibelius and Shostakovich) called 'the breath of a symphonist'. The sudden reflective endings to the 1953–4 Sixth Symphony's bluff and joyous first movement and scherzo are outstanding examples.[10]

Another thing common to Schönberg and Rubbra is a mastery of ostinato, a musical procedure adequately suggested by its derivation from 'obstinate'. *The New Grove Dictionary of Music and Musicians* defines it as 'the repetition of a musical pattern many times in succession while other musical elements are continually changing', devoting a full page to its history and ramifications down the centuries. Rather as a talented fast bowler will have a deceptive and often lethal 'slower ball', Rubbra even commands that rarest of resources, a slow ostinato; there is one midway through the slow movement of the Fifth Symphony, and a crucial section at the heart of the corresponding movement in the Sixth has the strings organising the music around seven appearances of a descending scale, which then turns back upward. A sevenfold flute scale in the Passacaglia finale of the Seventh is another outstanding example. In their frequent derivation from themes already heard, such ostinatos work on a higher artistic plane than the straightforward melodic or accompanimental ones so often found in Holst (a point well made by Grover).

'Progressive tonality', meaning that a work begins in one key and finds a path by following which it can convincingly end in another, had developed as from Mahler's middle symphonies and is frequent in large-scale Rubbra works. The Cello Sonata opens in G minor, to end in D major, both the second and third movements gradually shifting their tonal centre from an initial key to a different one – C minor to A♭, then G major to D major. Rubbra's use of progressive tonality reflects on the largest scale a supreme virtue of his major works: he is always on his way somewhere. He has a grand command of tempo, and well-nigh instant command of tempo-change, with a way of passing from section to contrasting section without a caesura.[11] His metronome markings are surprisingly frequent and detailed; rather like Bartók's extraordinary to-the-second timings for short subsections, they are a reliable guide to tempo-relationships even when the vicissitudes of concert-giving preclude literal adherence. In the Cello Sonata's scherzo, varied landscapes seem to flash past at a breathless pace; a recording of a 1959 BBC Third Programme broadcast preserved in the National Sound Archive shows Rubbra himself performing it at a tempo reminiscent of those in one or two of Beethoven's almost impossibly fleet middle movements – and in general his metronome markings have to be taken seriously. The one for the sonata's finale could well be thought a mistake, with a minim replacing his intended crotchet, and the music would still make sense at the quicker tempo. It makes far deeper sense, however, if the metronome marking is respected! Some further implications of this are considered on pp. 95–6.

In his later music Rubbra achieved sudden but amazingly inevitable-seeming changes of tempo and mood; he stands at the opposite end of the time-scale from Wagner, who could make a transition last anything up to a quarter of an hour. Rubbra can achieve instant transformation, as if in a film dissolve[12] or a dream, the Sixth Symphony containing transitions of amazing instantaneity, particularly in its finale.

Recollections of the young Rubbra by his fellow-student Maurice Jacobson (*Monthly Musical Record*, February 1935) spoke of 'an inner dynamic demon quite out of keeping with his normal gentle manner', and he had indeed a demonic side, not in the sense of anything evil but in Goethe's sense of an enormously enhanced and concentrated vital energy able to find vigorous and positive expression.[13] Schönberg is perhaps the supreme 'demon composer'. The 'inner demon' plays its part in the dancing quality of some of Rubbra's quick movements, which cover the range from charmingly balletic through assertive to downright menacing. Perhaps one English composer in each recent generation has been able to make his music dance; Rubbra's successor in that, Hugh Wood, prefaced one of his string quartets with lines spoken by the demoniacally jealous King Leontes in *The Winter's Tale* – 'My heart dances – but not for joy, not joy.' In both composers there is joyful dancing music and very ominous dancing music; ecstatic movement, is after all, part of forms of worship practised in various parts of the world, for example by the whirling dervishes. As we shall see when we come to the scherzo of the Second Symphony, the demon also takes on other equally legitimate artistic forms. What Jacobson called 'an effect … very near that of a pagan frenzy' in the original finale of the First String Quartet is rarely present later, but much that is strongly argumentative can be found, for example in the scherzos of the Second, Seventh and Eighth symphonies. The 1951–2 Second String Quartet's 'polymetric' scherzo goes some way beyond its initial late-Beethoven fleetness, and in the first section of the 1956 *Cantata Pastorale* Plato's tree-nymphs footing it round the God Pan, 'dancing, dancing, dancing', do so in an almost sinister way, with the cello's pizzicatos taking the place of the tabla. This, while by no means 'frenzy', certainly has a pagan touch, a decade before, for example, Henze's stage picture of Bacchantes in *The Bassarids*.

At the opposite end of the scale Rubbra can be very sustained indeed. The opening of the Cello Sonata's finale is a fine example. The possible connection between extremely slow tempi and the kind of state of mind one calls 'religious' or even 'mystical' was picked up by at least one super-sensitive critic (see pp. 115–16), and came sharply into focus when Rubbra began to use the term 'meditation' for works, movements or sections. Of his eleven symphonies, the first four, the Sixth and the Ninth end loudly, the other post-war ones very quietly.

The first generation of Rubbra experts always pointed out how some interval pervades a work; one almost gets the impression that whichever piece it is consists entirely of fifths, or fourths, or minor thirds. 'How boring', do I hear the reader murmur? Unity is a great thing, but better sensed than analysed, for until the detail of a musical work has impressed itself on one's mind to the point where one at least recognises it on its return, one is unlikely to care over-much where it came from. Rubbra said[14] that his 'dominating intervals' were no arbitrary choice, but were 'sifted out of the initial idea after it had been stated as a single melodic unit', and the only sizeable controversy over his music, as distinct from the problem of its cold-shouldering after 1959 (see pp. 159–61), came when two experts and admirers, Hugh Ottaway and Dr Elsie Payne, contradicted each other in *Musical Opinion* as to whether the Sixth Symphony was 'derived' from the four notes E–F–A–B he had somewhat rashly placed at the head of the score. Ever the diplomat, he settled the conflict by saying they were both right in their different ways, typically withholding the reason why he had chosen the notes (see p. 133). There is a place for analysis (the lecture-room) and a place (the home) for what used to be disparagingly called 'musical appreciation' (even if that was a term Rubbra despised!), and this writer at least would rather not wish on his readers too many 'omnipresent intervals': the traditional Western scale offers a choice from a mere dozen – not many when spread over an output such as Rubbra's.

What Rubbra does with constant transformation of rhythm is as crucial as what he does with intervals. There is no melody without rhythm, and tunes have an intrinsic emotional charge, impressing themselves as mere intervals don't. They are better remembered, and are no rarity in Rubbra's music; he is often at his best when they are about. Just now and then, as in discussing the Eleventh Symphony, which hardly has themes at all but rather (to quote Grover) 'what is known as material', the sceptic must finally come round to those 'omnipresent intervals' he started off so determined to ignore. But Rubbra's order – first melody, then dominating interval – is all-important. For the listener, the audibility of omnipresent intervals is a little like that late-twentieth-century bone of contention, the audibility of serial technique. They are and they aren't ...

Rubbra wrote interestingly about his mid-career 'conversion' to the 'dramatic value of intervals as such', saying of his preparation for writing the Eighth Symphony

> I was afraid that, if I allowed a new work to grow from a knowledge of this, it would lose the instinctiveness that I had always treasured as part of the creative process; that intervals would, as it were, detach

themselves from other aspects of the music and become entities that, in my new awareness of their possibilities, would be liable to cerebral manœuvring. This at all costs I wished to avoid (for the prime excitement of composition is when things click into position without the will being consciously involved).[15]

For the listener, too, the crucial thing is that things 'click into position' without 'cerebral manœuvring', a consideration never lost sight of (I hope) in the course of this study.

Rubbra was reserved about musical colour. In 'The British Composer and the Symphony' he came out strongly against 'the desire for continual contrasts of colour in orchestral music; often, one feels, for the purpose of deflecting attention from the essential poverty of thought'. For him, contrasts of whatever kind were far less important than making contrasted ideas 'different facets of one pervading idea'. This is so general a theme in high-level thought about the nature of art, whether from Goethe, from Webern, or in Hans Keller's 'unity of contrasted themes', that it is scarcely surprising to find Rubbra, too, taking it as part of his credo.

Given his attitude to colour contrasts, it is not surprising that Rubbra was often reproved for a certain monochrome quality in his scoring. His reply was the one with which he defended Brahms against similar criticisms – that the orchestral colours in his symphonies entirely suited the ideas they clothed, and that had he sought any others he would have been falsifying his inspiration. Certain instruments come off well in his major scores, notably the oboe and cor anglais, his predilection for bell-like sounds made him often turn to the harp or the stringed instruments played pizzicato, and though he was very sparing with more outlandish resources – xylophone, celesta, gong, side drum – his use of them was invariably timed to perfection and the more effective for its economy. Certainly there is at times a preponderance of string sound, especially in the earlier symphonies, but that in part reflects his deep understanding of stringed instruments, both to play (however limited his ability) and as husband for a quarter of a century of a highly talented violinist. Like Mozart, he discovered in the course of his career just how much the wind instruments could contribute.

From the Eighth Symphony onward an added element played its part: 'new in the work was a method of composition I hadn't hitherto employed: that is, to compose straight into full score, without the preliminary reduced score which had been my previous practice. So the ideas arose spontaneously clothed in an appropriate colour, and the balancing of these colours was an important element in the overall formal scheme of the symphony.'[16] Orchestration, standby of colouristic composers and theme of countless student classes down the decades,[17] thus ceased to be a 'technique' and became part of a work's deeper structure.

Rubbra was very seldom a composer with 'the common touch', save in a few of his scherzo tunes; it would imply a degree of identification with the actual contemporary world, which some composers have more than others. That could be one reason why a man like William Walton, despite a relative lack of media interest in his later years, retained a measure of deserved popularity even in the waste land of the avant-garde vogue. The idea of Rubbra and 'timelessness' will emerge at a later stage in this study.

CHAPTER 2

The Early Years

Charles Edmund Rubbra was born on 23 May 1901, at 57 Cambridge Road, a simple 'two up, two down' house in a poor area of Northampton. The town would also be the birthplace, four years later, of William Alwyn, and in 1921 of Malcolm Arnold. Those opening years of the new century produced a fine crop of future English composers: Alan Bush was born in 1900, Rubbra's later best friend Gerald Finzi likewise in 1901, William Walton in 1902, Lennox Berkeley in 1903, Alwyn, Constant Lambert, Alan Rawsthorne and Michael Tippett in 1905, with Arnold Cooke, Benjamin Frankel and Elisabeth Lutyens following in 1906. The family soon moved to 2 Balfour Road, near open fields which, in his biographical recollections up to the age of about twenty,[1] he said meant a lot to him, and which he missed after a further move in his early teens.

Rubbra started life with few advantages save his talent, though one must never underrate the influence of parents with 'an untutored love of music', in particular a mother who had a fine singing voice and a lot of energy. As he grew up, he not only learned piano parts in order to accompany her, but wrote out transpositions to suit the compass of her voice. His father, also named Edmund, had been trained as a watch and clock repairer and had a particular skill at mending musical boxes. Around the time his eldest son was born he had to work at Miller's factory, where wooden lasts for boots and shoes were made, Northampton being at that time the centre of footwear manufacture in England, but after a second move he was at last able to open his own shop. Rubbra remembered him as fond of Verdi's operas. His father's elder brother Frederick owned a factory, appearing in the 1901 England and Wales census as a boot-and-shoe manufacturer; the younger brother William was listed as a foreman shoemaker. Edmund junior, who came into the world just too late for the census, attended Kettering Road School,[2] 'reaching the highest stand-ard' and then learning shorthand, which, after a very brief spell in one of the unavoidable boot-and-shoe factories, he used as a clerk for the London and North Western Railway. He was one of the countless poorer people who had to discover the most important things for themselves, and made sure they did so.

Details of his private life would have struck Rubbra as of interest only to his immediate family and (after his 1948 conversion to Roman Catholicism) his confessor, but important exceptions to a policy of extreme reticence about his 'inner world' come in his accounts of two crucial pre-pubertal experiences which he felt had permanently influenced aspects of his music. They throw light on his frequent insistence that a composer's musical world and language are determined early in life. One of them offers a background to his contrapuntist's habit of using themes in inversion (i.e. with their intervals moving in the opposite direction to the one in which they went when first heard), the other has to do with bells.

Inversion had for centuries been a basic constituent of counterpoint, pervading Bach's '48' and especially *Die Kunst der Fuge*; when one knows the latter work well, it becomes ever harder to remember which way up its theme first appeared, so convincing are Bach's many uses of it in inversion. (The same goes, on a far smaller scale, for the 'refrain' tune in Bartók's orchestral *Dance Suite.*) Inversion appears at crucial points in Bruckner, such as the opening of the development section in the first movement of his Seventh Symphony, and in due course, inversion of the entire tone-row would form an essential part of Schönberg's twelve-tone serial technique. Rubbra hardly ever followed Schönberg's further step of turning things backwards to provide two more forms (the inversion being also usable in 'retrograde'), and inversion in Rubbra has, by his own testimony ('An Essay in Autobiography', *ERC*), a biographical background:

> One of my earliest memories, and still vividly with me, is of waking one winter morning (I must have been three or four years old at the time) and finding that the usual position in the room for light and shadow had been completely reversed. The ceiling was bathed in a strong white light instead of being in relative shadow, and the floor, on which the morning sunlight usually lay, was darkened. As I rested wonderingly in bed, with my eyes fixed on that dazzlingly white ceiling, my father came in to see if I was awake, and I asked him why the light of the room was so altered. He told me that there had been a heavy fall of snow in the night, and the light of the morning sun on it was reflected on the ceiling, making the lower part of the room in relative shadow. I suppose I accepted the explanation, but it did not lessen the impact of what I had seen, and its clarity seventy years later is evidence of the deep impression it had made. It is only now, looking back, that I intuitively know that this topsy-turvydom, working subconsciously within me, influenced the way that I look at thematic substance and its related counterpoint in my

music, these being instinctively so shaped as to be capable of inversion without diminishing their effect.

There followed two music examples, one from the slow introduction to the finale of the Fourth Symphony, the other from the second variation in the finale of the Cello Sonata. Rubbra's testimony ended:

> I can now see that these thematic processes, which seemed at the time of writing to evolve naturally through the experience of composing, are linked indissolubly to that unexpected re-distribution of light and shade in the early childhood memory I have described.[3]

The other important recurring memory was:

> An equally vivid experience, and one that nothing since has been able to eradicate, occurred some years later, when I was perhaps nine or ten years of age (chronology seems beside the point in such matters). It was a hot summer Sunday, and my father and I went for a longish walk which took us out of the town and through a wood ... Before entering the wood we rested a little, leaning on a gate that gave us a distant view of the town. Suddenly, through the hazy heat, I heard distant bells, the music of which seemed suspended in the still air. I was held motionless, the scenery vanished, and I was aware only of downward-drifting sounds that seemed isolated from everything else around me. I have no doubt now that this experience, held captive for so long in my inner conscious-ness, gradually became so embedded in my musical thinking as to be the means whereby the disembodied bell-sounds I heard that summer after-noon became transmuted into those downward scales that constantly act as focal points in my textures.

The memoirs of the late-nineteenth-century composer Karl Goldmark (1830–1915), who grew up in the Jewish quarter of a Hungarian town where he and his family were not even allowed to enter the church, so that he never heard music, tell the story of his being alone one Sunday morning on a hillside and catching the sound of a choir faintly in the distance as Mass was celeb-rated. It was an epiphany that aroused the irresistible compulsion to become a musician. Bell-sounds played an important role for the Austrian Joseph Marx (1882–1964), while in the later twentieth century the Estonian Arvo Pärt (b. 1935) revised his entire way of composing to base his music on the idea of 'tintinnabulating triads'. Rubbra pointed out that descending bell-like lines constantly appear in his work, which may be why in their case he omitted to single out any one instance.

There was a not unimportant difference between his two experiences; bells, despite differing emotional associations and connotations for each of us, are something known from everyday life, to which we respond when transmuted into music. Inversion of melodies is less immediately comprehensible and may go unnoticed unless, as in Rubbra's two examples, it maintains the same rhythm, and it is emotionally neutral, its appeal being more to the intellect. Rubbra's examples are, moreover, from passages where a theme is simultaneously heard both ways up, chasing itself ('stretto'), although his actual early experience involved only one way round (the wrong way!) for light and shadow. The parallel between experience and musical manifestation is to that extent more far-fetched, evident even to him only after a great lapse of time, and not something even the most willing listener may be able to share.

Rubbra was emphatic that early experiences, and music absorbed in one's most formative years, are absolutely crucial in deciding what sort of music one writes, with later things far less important or effective. Almost the first words of his reminiscences in *ERC* were 'music does not grow and flourish in a narrowly confined area, but is the product of every force to which one is subjected through the very fact of living an active and expanding life', and near the start of an analysis of his Fifth Symphony he wrote

> I believe everything in life is connected and interdependent so that when one thing in the body politic changes, everything is affected. This is why I am especially interested in Taoist philosophy, for it is concerned with this close interdependence of all aspects of life. The nineteenth-century philosophical systems and the economic changes that took place at that time were more responsible for the changes in the basic compelling concepts of music than any purely technical experiments. A composer begins to use a new harmonic or melodic language because somehow it corresponds better with the time in which he lives.

It is a fascinating paradox to find a supposedly unworldly composer still maintaining at sixty that music's 'basic compelling concepts' are sociologically conditioned. More politically specific composers like his communist colleague Alan Bush viewed the connections as far closer, obliging them to courses of conduct (*BCI* shows Bush approving of the Soviet insistence on a composer's overriding social responsibility), but for Rubbra there was a counterweight in his religious nature and reading.

Early cultural passions were Debussy and Cyril Scott (1879–1970), a man of many talents now even worse forgotten than Rubbra has been since the later decades of the twentieth century. He came across music by both at a music shop run by an uncle on his father's side, Mr Gibson. Piano lessons were given, first by 'a little hunch-backed lady who had a high reputation as a teacher … The piano she used for teaching had, I remember, discoloured ivory keys and a silk and fretwork front'. Through Mr Gibson he earned his first money while his father was out of work, demonstrating a piano – 'in marked contrast, a new upright' – to possible buyers; no sale, no commission, so he had to make the instrument sound as good as possible! He did so at home, with the piano on loan from the shop, and remembered that his 'war-horse' was a Mozart Sonata in C.[4]

Further piano lessons followed with 'a celebrated Northampton organist, Charles J. King'.

> One day, waiting for a lesson, I was idly turning over some music lying on the dusty shelves of his music room when I came across a volume the title of which immediately fascinated me – *4 Rig Veda Hymns by Gustav von Holst* … To my astonishment I found there not the slightest trace of the ornate and highly coloured music which so often passes as 'oriental'. Instead, there was an almost forbidding starkness and directness, but which yet seemed curiously genuine in the invocation of the East. The volume was my companion for weeks, and I can say that by its means Gustav Holst began teaching me years before he actually became my teacher when in 1920 I entered Reading University.[5]

In a BBC Third Programme talk, *Master and Pupil*, in 1978, Rubbra said that once he came across Scott's music, 'from the moment of that discovery all my spare pocket-money went on the purchase of his piano pieces and songs'. At the age of seventeen he organised and took part in a concert of Scott's music given four days before the end of the war (7 November 1918), to aid the Church Soldiers' Comforts Fund; it took place in the grandly named Carnegie Hall that was in fact part of Northampton Public Library. The vicar sent the programme to Scott, who reacted very quickly, to judge by the subsequent review in the local paper, which already described Rubbra as his pupil. The proceeds, the war having meanwhile ended, probably went towards new Sunday School buildings for the local Congregational church. Concert programme and review were reproduced in *ERC*. The anonymous reviewer could make nothing of Rubbra's own still pre-student work, but greatly admired his piano playing and headed his article 'The Genius of Mr. C. Edmund Rubbra'.

Rubbra turned his railway job to advantage, travelling at a quarter the normal fare to London for lessons with Scott, who appears not to have taught anyone else. His first visit to Scott's home made an unforgettable impression, which he evoked more than once later in life; for BBC Radio's *Music Magazine* ('Cyril Scott; A 90th-birthday Tribute', 28 September 1969) he put it as follows:

> Imagine a boy brought up in an ugly working-class area of an industrial Midlands town being ushered into a house where every object was strange: the heavy Gothic furniture, the stained glass, the faint smell of incense, the writing-pad containing an austere quotation from the Indian Song Celestial – 'to work thou hast the right, but not to the fruits thereof' – and the piano with another quotation in large lettering, painted in gold, a quotation that I couldn't complete because the end of it was lost in the curve of the instrument.

A principal subject discussed in Scott's very readable 1917 collection of essays and articles *The Philosophy of Modernism in Relation to Music* was the nature of 'new music', and they would have appealed to Rubbra at an impressionable sixteen. Scott opened up with a blast that Rubbra certainly came to disagree with in the end (see, for example, his remarks about 'content and style' in 'Letter to a Young Composer', p. 11).

> (Scott) The prerequisite to immortality in the world of art is the capacity to create something new, or, in other words, to invent a style.

> (Rubbra) It is not musical style that matters, but the thought behind the style; it is the stature of the thinking that gives music substance.

But other passages tally with Rubbra's later view of the composer's responsibilities:

> (Scott) To admire everything means to select nothing, and probably to imitate all things ... The aggregate of a certain number of admirations, then, is the first step, but the second step is of equal, or even more importance, and that is – a continual self-criticism and mental control, which untiringly rejects from one's creative arena all the obvious and unsuitable and weaker ideas which are continually flowing into it ... (Of the typical minor composer) In short, for, let us say eight bars, he *invented*, and then for ten bars he merely *composed*.

> (Rubbra) The composer has often accepted too much from the abundance and rejected too little: in other words, his inner standards

have been smothered by the possibilities open to him. Too many ideas can be far more difficult to deal with than too few, unless one has that inner capacity rigidly to enforce a veto on those that don't conform to the highest inner tests.

A normal day sees me working for six hours ... a 'sitting' can produce anything from two to twenty bars.

(Scott) The most potent music must be exaltedly emotional before everything else, and although it should contain intellect, yet, at the same time, it should be beyond it as the sky is beyond the clouds which are contained in its blue infinity.

(Rubbra) I do require the players to play everything with intense expression.

That assumption of intense expressiveness from his performers is among the reasons why Rubbra is one of the composers whose scores, in themselves, often convey remarkably little idea of how the music sounds and feels.

Scott saw his composing contemporaries as faced by a choice between 'classicism', which he felt must lead to stagnation and repetition of existing achievements, 'romanticism', which meant striving to create something new and beautiful without destroying whatever of value already existed, and 'futurism', which he equated with 'monsterism', the sense that nobody until oneself had really had any idea how to compose and that beauty was irrelevant. It is worth noting that Scott wrote before the explosion of modernism in the 1920s. His solution of choice was very clearly 'romanticism', and in the waste land of the 1960s Rubbra could well have been reminded of Scott's words on 'monsterism'. To the end of his life he remained faithful to Scott, basing a Prelude and Fugue for piano (Op. 69) on a Scott theme when the great man turned seventy in September 1949, and accompanying Peter Pears at the inaugural concert of the Cyril Scott Society in 1962.

After a year with Scott he was far enough on to win a scholarship to Reading University, where he had composition lessons with Holst and continued to take piano lessons from a good teacher whom Scott had recommended, Evlyn Howard-Jones, also violin lessons with Howard-Jones's wife, the quartet-leader Grace Thynne. Part of Holst's familiarisation process with a new pupil was to go on long walks together and discuss the world, so that in his student years Rubbra was introduced by his teacher not only to Joseph Conrad but also to political thinking and socialist ideas, in books such as Benjamin Kidd's *Social Evolution*.

About the time he discovered Scott he also became fascinated with a book, *Isis Unveiled*, by Elena Blavatsky (1831–91), initiator of the discipline of Theosophy along lines adumbrated a century earlier by the visionary Emmanuel Swedenborg and first 'Corresponding Secretary' of the Theosophical Society, founded in New York in 1875. Her book, published two years later, was subtitled 'A Master-Key to the Mysteries of Ancient and Modern Science and Theology'; running to two volumes (I Science; II Theology) and more than 1,200 pages, it was 'A Plea for the recognition of the Hermetic philosophy and anciently universal Wisdom-Religion, as the only possible Absolute in Science and Theology'. Blavatsky came no closer to music than a couple of subsections on 'Music in nervous disorders' and 'Charming serpents by music', but her comprehensive and polemical invocation of every kind of ancient Oriental wisdom, plus her frequent readability, would have made the book just the kind of brain-fodder for the omnivorous intellectual appetite of an extremely bright teenager. The later Catholic convert may have looked back on it, and especially on its attempt to demolish the validity of the Christian faith in favour of a broader and more universal force and belief, as the heady stuff with which youth intoxicates itself!

Blavatsky's openness to Oriental thought strengthened in Rubbra an interest already aroused by a sermon delivered at the Congregational Church during the visit of a Chinese Christian missionary, Kuanglin Pao. The two subsequently became friends. During the 1920s he came to know a leading authority on Theosophy, R. G. S. Mead, and his first work, *The Secret Hymnody*, set Mead's translation of a Greek text, suitably enough a 'Hymn to Hermes'. In the best Blavatsky tradition, Mead drew on every possible source of spiritual wisdom from ancient civilisations east of the Mediterranean. The most significant reflection of such mystical ideas in music was to be found in the work of Alexander Skryabin (1872–1945); his influence on Rubbra could be estimated at nil, were it not for some surprising consecutive fourths in an idea at the start of the Eighth Symphony (1966–8, see Ex. 46). Rubbra did, however, have a high opinion of Skryabin, which he put on record in a BBC Third Programme talk, *Skryabin and the Piano* around the time of that symphony. In his view, Skryabin's maturest work showed 'a strength of purely musical thought that's far deeper and more satisfying than any allegedly mystical purpose behind the works'. There was 'nothing slipshod' about even Skryabin's wildest and most ecstatic late piano music.

Rubbra's own recollections made no bones about describing himself as working-class and the family as poor. He never (according to a personal communication from his son Benedict) totally overcame a certain awkwardness in dealing with 'the privileged', but the Scott evening showed the extent to which as a youngster he profited from the practical support of Northampton's many musical citizens. A number of them now helped augment a further scholarship he had won, allowing him to continue his studies at the Royal College of Music in London. He said (*ERC*) that he had been endowed with 'enough money to keep me for two or three years', and his diverse talents soon began to augment his income. Between 1922 and 1925 he went on working with Howard-Jones, and with Holst and R. O. Morris, an unequalled connoisseur of counterpoint.

An early exercise of enterprise came when in 1924 he took unapproved leave of absence from the College to tour for three weeks with the Arts League of Service Travelling Theatre. This paved the way for a great deal of similar activity later, during a decade and a half of 'piece-work' from a London base. Rubbra's greatest friendship began in 1926, when Howard-Jones introduced him to Gerald Finzi. They were both pupils of Morris, as of Howard-Jones, but did not know each other until Howard-Jones mentioned to Rubbra that there was a young music student living upstairs at his house who wanted to meet him. He lived first in Wildwood Road, which wound its way round the Hampstead Heath Extension at the more rural end of the newly built Hampstead Garden Suburb. A first marriage to Lillian Duncan, his landlady there, was never consummated, but for a while he added her surname to his own, an act one might now associate with the 1960s rather than the 1930s. Oxford University Press published the 1927 *Phantasy* for two violins and piano, Op. 29 as by 'Edmund Duncan Rubbra'. He then moved even 'a little farther out', but eventually further back in, to Camden Town, where he had 'a quite large flat' and ran a club to introduce new chamber and piano music. He supported himself by school-teaching, by accompanying ballet-dancers and others, and by music-reviewing for both the *Monthly Musical Record* and a BBC weekly, *The Listener*, so that a great deal of new music came his way. The impression he made at the time was recalled thirty years later in an anonymous profile in the *Sunday Times's* 'Portrait Gallery' of 6 October 1957, occasioned by the London première of his Seventh Symphony and first performance of his *Festival Gloria*. The writer recalled him 'beardless and sandalled ... with his mop of blonde hair and open-necked shirt at all London's concert-rooms'.

Photographs from different times in Rubbra's life suggest a progression not unlike that found in the case of Brahms. One taken in the 1920s shows a handsome young man with a sensitive, boyish face but a very clear and lively vitality, an impression confirmed in retrospect by the *Sunday Times* profile. Such young men are immensely attractive to women, and before too long he found a second, far more lasting marital partner in the violinist who became not only his wife but an indispensable muse. In later life his frame filled out, a well-tended beard adding an impression of weight and seriousness.

Between 1933 and 1936 he was pianist and composer for a ballet company and theatre group at Dartington Hall, the pioneering educational centre near Totnes in Devon founded and run by the millionaire Leonard Elmhirst and his wife Dorothy. The inner covers of *ERC* show how hard Rubbra worked for the Dartington Dance-Mime Group (with whom the young Alan Rawsthorne was also associated), but that was also the time when his compositions began to show a truly individual voice.

At all stages in Rubbra's life he was keenly interested in religion and philosophy. For those who write about major composers there is a constant temptation to divagate onto their life outside music and their more purely intellectual pursuits, since those may offer an opportunity for exegesis of the music's intrinsically 'unverbalisable' content. The music itself must be one's guide and corrective, since all musical biography is bedevilled by the fact that while a composer's music can sometimes shed light on his life, his life rarely sheds light on his music. He may set a text because (like, most famously, St Paul's words on Faith, Hope and Charity in the last of Brahms' *Four Serious Songs*) it is about things which fascinate him and which he would wish to have, or because it reflects what he already has.

Rubbra had grown up in the United Congregational Church; early in his career he set many liturgical texts less likely to attract a non-Christian, but such texts are prescribed rather than tailored to any man's own experience. The 'tailoring' begins, sometimes to the dismay of the authorities, when the music is added. There are also two cantatas to translations of mystical poems by St John of the Cross (*The Dark Night of the Soul*, 1935, and *Song of the Soul*, 1953). One does not become a mystic by setting mystical poetry to music, and Rubbra's choice of texts could have arisen from a genuine identification with the experiences enshrined in the poems, or pure fascination with them, or from the fact that St John never went out of fashion after a three-volume translation of his complete works appeared in 1935, as did further versions by a notable poet, Roy Campbell.

Benedict's analysis of his father's early decades is that the vivid and varied experiences of his first thirty-odd years 'threw his mind into discovering the world and possibly how people thought, and hence interest in religion (treated

intellectually). Hence going from low church (childhood) to Catholic (Antoinette) [his wife from 1933 onward] to Buddhism'. (His Buddhist phase was very
short and he remained a devout Catholic.) That could be a useful corrective
to speculation about an intense religious life amounting to mysticism: Rubbra,
like all great composers, lived above all in his music. It might be worth adding
that those with more of an inborn intuitive feeling for how the world is, and for
how people think, are less likely to need an intellectual approach.

A good deal of Rubbra's work between the Royal College of Music and the
1939–45 war was for organisations favouring the broad spectrum of thought
known as 'left-wing', with which Holst had first familiarised him. In the 1930s
awareness of impending war went along with the sense that much in society
needed changing. In addition to Rubbra's stated belief in the sociological con-
ditioning of musical development, a certain pattern of 'progressive' behaviour
can be made out from known details of his life, such as his pacifism, temporary incorporation of his first wife's surname, and vegetarianism. His recording for Grover recalled being 'an ardent vegetarian until the outbreak of war
when I could no longer be one in the army without starving to death, so that
was that!'[6] Like many 1930s people he was certainly a pacifist; he provided the
music for a 1930 anti-war play by an American author named Velona Pilcher,
The Searcher, whose vividness is documented in the notes for the complete
symphony recordings. But as the 1930s unrolled, events in Europe posed an
ever-increasing problem for pacifists. One of Rubbra's jobs was to teach young
German refugees from Nazism, most of them Jewish, at a special school set
up to receive and educate them in South London.[7] He was thus well placed to
learn before most of his compatriots the full awfulness of what had been going
on after Hitler's election as German Reichskanzler in 1933. It became clear to
a small but significant proportion of the British people that his policies, whatever their origins in the punitive Versailles Treaty or the post-war inflation and
depression, were bound to lead to war. That must in some ways have been a
still more depressing prospect than the nuclear holocaust feared by many after
1945, which, while distinctly possible, was by no means a certainty, whereas
to the clear-sighted there appeared absolutely no way to avoid a second world
conflict as from the time when the dictators Mussolini and Hitler intervened
to support the Fascist cause in the 1934–7 Spanish Civil War.

Until the world heard of the brutal contradictions in the conduct of the
Russian-controlled communists during that war, a great deal of hope and ide-
alism were centred on the Soviet Union, with its aspiration to Communism
and Stalin's interim development of 'Socialism in One Country'. It was some

time before the truth became clear, since participants deliberately falsified their accounts of the conflict. Arthur Koestler was one such author, in *Spanish Testament* (1937); a decade later, as a disillusioned ex-Communist contributing to an important symposium entitled *The God That Failed*, he owned up, also giving the world an unforgettable evocation of the Orwellian world of Stalin's great purges in his novel *Darkness At Noon*. The purges went unnoticed or mis-represented,[8] and though with the 1939 Hitler–Stalin pact the scales dropped from many people's eyes, Germany's invasion of Russia two years later made the Soviet Union an ally of the West, with much fund-raising and posters here reading 'Open a Second Front NOW!'

So much for foreign affairs. As to the situation at home, the post-1918 oppor-tunity to change society for the better had been dismally allowed to pass, to the great disappointment of many ex-servicemen who had known wartime camaraderie. The vain hopes of the time were summed up in Arthur Symonds' poem *These Things Shall Be*, set by John Ireland for chorus and orchestra as the BBC's commission to mark George VI's coronation in 1937. Maybe, just maybe, if Britain survived another war it might make a better job of improving things than it had after 1918. The general election of 1945, at which the British people emphatically rejected its wartime leader in order to give Labour a real chance of changing peace-time society, reflected such feelings.

Throughout the twentieth century a variety of esoteric philosophical and religious disciplines had an appeal in Britain. That reliable barometer of the English semi-cultured classes, Anthony Powell's *roman-fleuve A Dance to the Music of Time*, offers the hermetic Dr Trelawney in *The Kindly Ones* ('The Vision of Visions heals the Blindness of Sight'), his spiritualist follower Mrs Erdleigh, based at the Ufford Hotel in Bayswater and appearing in half the cycle's dozen novels, and the alarming Scorpio Murtlock in the final *Hearing Secret Harmonies*, who at last puts paid to the villainous Widmerpool. Theo-sophy and spiritualism coexisted with the arcane doctrines of Gurdjieff and his disciple Ouspensky; there were Taoism, the humane anthroposophy of Rudolf Steiner, and the Theosophy-related ideas of Krishnamurti and his Order of The Star of the East, one of whose camps Rubbra attended in the Netherlands during the 1920s. It was all calculated to engage the intellectual curiosity of a sensitive and enquiring mind. In the fullness of time Rubbra found his way to the things that for him best represented truth, rather than fashion or specula-tion.

It is worth outlining his early production to show the direction from which he eventually arrived at symphonic composition. His earliest music, apart from *The Secret Hymnody*, shows a fairly predictable reverence for the twin Christian stars, Jesus (*Rosa Mundi, Jesukin*) and Mary (*Hymn to the Virgin*). *Rosa Mundi* (Op. 2) was composed in 1921, with accompaniment for two violins. Holst had a few years earlier written a set of four songs for voice and violin after hearing a woman play and sing as she wandered round the church at Thaxted; he liked his pupil's effort and Rubbra was encouraged, feeling that 'I had discovered a lyrical direction for my music that I could happily follow in the knowledge that the root of it was in myself. I think it would be true to say that this little song was the point of departure for my future development'. That 'lyrical direction' led to the *Phantasy, Lyric Movement,* and in due course to the *Sinfonia Concertante.*

Specifically mystical texts enter his work with the cantata *The Dark Night of the Soul,* composed in 1935 to E. Allison Peers' translation of the famous poem with the same title (*Noche Escura del Alma*) by St John of the Cross (Juan de Yepes y Alvarez, 1542–91). The written works of St John, a follower of St Teresa of Avila and almost exact contemporary of El Greco, consist for the most part of lengthy prose pieces grouped into collections with titles such as *Ascent of Mount Carmel, Spiritual Canticle, Living Flame of Love* and *Dark Night of the Soul* (an 'exposition', in two books comprising twenty-three chapters, of the content of the one very famous but quite short poem). It all offers an enormously detailed guide to the mystical life, and the opening of the last-named collection throws light on the poem's title. Though it suggests suffering and deprivation, the 'night' of St John's inner world signifies the death of desire, and is equivalent to the light of heaven. That is not the sense in which it tends to be used when modern generations trot out the cliché 'the dark night of the soul', for the poem *Noche Escura del Alma* is a passionate evocation of the discovery of God's love, couched in the erotic terms familiar since the biblical Song of Songs.

Rubbra would return to St John of the Cross after another twenty years, for the important *Song of the Soul,* but in the later 1930s 'my main reading was the earlier metaphysical poets' (Grover tape, which specifically mentions the *Five Madrigals* (Op. 51, 1940) for mixed voices, to texts by Thomas Campion (1567–1619)). Other vocal works with instruments from a few years earlier were the *Five Motets* for mixed voices (1934, Op. 37) to poems by Herrick, Vaughan, Donne, and Crashaw,[9] and two sets of Spenser sonnets Op. 42 and 43. The motets constitute his first sizeable work for unaccompanied voices; with their rich texture, often involving superimposed triads, they show Rubbra not yet disabused of 'the delights of harmony'. Each of the Spenser sets took as texts five of the eighty-nine poems in the 1595 collection *Amoretti*, whose title should be enough to suggest that a musical work based on it will not be mystical but will belong very much to the world of courtly love. The Spenser collection does in fact contain just a few religious, even penitential, sonnets, and Op. 42 ends with no. 68, 'Most glorious Lord of life', reflecting on the Resurrection and on universal love, whose more mundane forms are treated in the previous four choruses, to Sonnets 2, 4, 6 and 53, and in Op. 43.

Other distinctly secular and full-blooded works from about that time include the *Four Mediaeval Latin Lyrics*, Op. 32. The work was originally for *a cappella* chorus but Rubbra thought it too difficult; a version for baritone and strings was first performed in 1947 and published in 1949. The first three texts are from the collection discovered during the nineteenth century at the monastery of Benediktbeuern in Bavaria and known ever since as the *Carmina Burana*. Rubbra's first text, 'Tempus est iucundum' was one of those Carl Orff would choose five years later for the supremely 'common-touch' cantata which in our time fascinates the many and repels the few; in fact it includes one of the phrases which has helped sear the Orff into the popular memory – 'O, O, totus langueo'. Rubbra took a surprising interest in Orff, commenting with approval on his mid-life change of 'style', which came, he felt, from a genuine rethinking of his musical ethos rather than the following of a trend. Like the later Op. 42 Sonnets, the *Four Mediaeval Latin Lyrics* end with a more reflective and in this case sombre piece, Abelard's translation of David's lament for Jonathan. It is otherwise the most 'pagan' of Rubbra's works.

By the time of Rubbra's 'First'[10] Violin Sonata (Op. 11, 1925) his 'lyrical direction' was an integral part of his nature. Dedicated to Grace Thynne, it marks a distinct step forward, possibly reflecting an interest in the music of John Ireland, who became a Royal College professor in 1923 during Rubbra's time as a student. His very successful Second Violin Sonata from a decade earlier would have been an obvious model for a new essay in the form. At a greater distance one may well sense in the first two movements of Rubbra's 'First' Sonata a kinship with that most expansively lyrical of composers, Gabriel Fauré. In search of a partner for its first performance, Rubbra placed an advertisement in a musical periodical. That could be taken as an early sign of a certain isolation from his peers, with the exception of fellow-composers such as Gerald Finzi and Maurice Jacobson who were also friends – or so it must seem in our time, almost a century later, when the ever-growing idolisation of youth and glamour means that the majority of successful musical partnerships, apart from those lashed up by the companies for which the few 'superstars' are still paid to record, stem from student years. Whether the cause was the 'awkwardness' mentioned by Benedict, or sheer pressure of work brought about by all Rubbra's other musical and literary activities must remain a matter for speculation; thrown into a chamber-music group in the army during the 1940s, he got on well with his partners and found another lifelong friend in the cellist William Pleeth.

His advertisement proved even more productive than he had hoped, for it was answered by a young French violinist, Antoinette Chaplin, a graduate of the Bologna Conservatoire who had gone on to three years' study in Budapest with Jenö Hubay and Jenö Lener, giving a Wigmore Hall recital in 1926. She and Rubbra performed the sonata for the first time at the Grotrian Hall, London, on 21 March 1932, and travelled as far as Milan, where they gave a recital in the Sammartini Hall of the Conservatoire. In 1933, two years after first meeting, they married. Given the First Sonata's date of composition, Antoinette can not have been responsible for any Faurean echoes in it, but she soon became and long remained his muse. A further violin sonata was written for her after that tour. She represented, in Benedict's words, 'a wild new Romantic world' (so much is apparent from the photograph of her in the Milan programme, which was reproduced in *ERC*). 'He entered the world of Dartington at the same time. This must have been dazzling.'

Something more gaunt and a little wilder emerges in the contrapuntal sections of the First Sonata's finale, and here not only Ireland but Rubbra's old idol Cyril Scott have been 'fingered' by Lewis Foreman in his notes for a CD of the violin sonatas. Fauré again seems reflected in the third ('Slow Dance') of the *Four Easy Pieces* for violin and piano (1926), which were tailored to Rubbra's own modest violin technique acquired from Grace Thynne.

Another work featuring the violin – not one, but two – was a *Phantasy* with piano from 1927. A whole period in English music around the turn of the twentieth century was influenced by W. W. Cobbett (1847–1937), second major Englishman of that name and a businessman who despite 'devoting to commerce the little time he could spare from music'[11] acquired great wealth, which was put to good use encouraging generations of composers in the cultivation of chamber music. Cobbett was an amateur violinist, in days when 'a nice little Italian violin' such as his Guadagnini cost a few hundred pounds rather than the current few hundred thousand. He commissioned what became a standard reference book, the *Cyclopaedia of Chamber Music*, engaging only the best commentators from Sir Donald Tovey downward, and endowed a variety of prizes for new chamber works, which had to be in a single movement and carry the title *Phantasy*; Cobbett took the not unviable if (in view of Elgar) slightly outdated view that Purcell, who had spelt the word 'Fantasy' in that way, marked the high point of English music, and that the single-movement form with contrasting sections was by all means to be cultivated. The idea of a 'small form' rather than the imposing, full-scale three-or four-movement sonata was timely, a modest British counterpart to the 'small forms' forced on composers such as Schönberg and Webern by the disappearance of tonality from their world (it somehow hung on elsewhere).

Rubbra's *Phantasy* (Op. 16) dates from after the end of his time at the Royal College of Music, one of the places where Cobbett endowed prizes. It was dedicated to Finzi, by then a close friend. Rather than emulating the concise section-by-section layout of the seventeenth-century 'Fancy' it is a lengthy single movement elaborating some fairly uniform material at more length than it will take, without major changes in mood. The second violin seems there primarily to add a touch of restlessness, an obligatory 'further part': Morris had taught Rubbra the craft of imitative counterpoint all too well. What will later become an integral and original facet of his musical personality is at this stage still a vague itch, a Brahmsian compulsion to add a further part to a texture already well provided. (Important works of his early maturity such as the Second Symphony and Cello Sonata show how such 'overload' was eventually turned to advantage). All the same, the piece had what were to become typical Rubbra features; an unsigned review in the *Monthly Musical Record* said its composer was 'particularly fond of taking a simple phrase and exploiting it throughout the whole of a composition, viewing it from different angles and taking scraps of it for development and transformation'. Nor has it lacked its advocates, for example Ivor Keys, who in an October 1959 article in *Music and Letters* called it a 'tour de force'. A final pentatonic echo of Vaughan Williams's *The Lark Ascending* comes as a relief from the prevailing and somewhat anonymous piano-trio heaviness.

A string quartet from Rubbra's late twenties eventually emerged, with a piano added to the ensemble, as the 1929 *Lyric Movement*, Op. 24. This single-movement piece was more in the Cobbett tradition, but even at the time it struck Rubbra as in need of attention. He further revised it in 1946, and like the *Phantasy* it shows the limitations rather than the possibilities of mono-thematicism, about four-fifths of its ten minutes being taken up by statements and restatements of the opening four-note figure. In the brief interregnum between 'Moderato assai' and 'Primo tempo' there is just time for a glimpse of a more flowing melody and then a rather gawky outline of a scherzo. If any

Rubbra works deserve to engage the loyalty of the 'cow-pat' apologists, these last two do.

Rubbra might have agreed, for in his interview with Murray Schafer three decades later he said his 'first work of value' was not written until he was thirty. Sure enough, in 1931 he started work on another violin sonata, and that piece (Op. 31, completed the following year) must have been what he had in mind. Truscott, in *ERC*, called it 'unique, both original and individual, and the most complete statement of Rubbra's musical personality up to 1932'. In notes for an undated lecture, the composer said 'it occupies a midway position in my output ... it looks both back, to the time when harmonic colour uppermost, and forward – texture out of several strands of melody'. Its purposefulness and economy show him safely emerged from the temporary fog of the *Phantasy* and *Lyric Movement,* and it covers a far greater expressive range than his previous violin sonata. The leading violinist Albert Sammons took it up and recorded it, giving Rubbra his first sizeable public success. The sonata's Spanish-sounding, breathtakingly vigorous finale adds a further name to the roll-of-honour of those briefly influencing him, the Ravel who could wreak comparably lovable havoc in the finale of his own sonata for the same two instruments. Some passages could almost be called Bolero-like, except that a Bolero is in three-time and Rubbra's piece is not. Another possible tug-of-the-forelock in the Second Sonata's finale could be to the Sibelius of the *Lemminkäinen Legends.* In an undated lecture Rubbra commented that its 'stress is strongly upon rhythm of – it has been said – a strongly Spanish caste. Why this should be I have no idea, unless some far-distant Spanish ancestor was having a final fling.' (Or, as will emerge in the course of this book, not quite final.)

In 'A Composer's Problems' Rubbra wrote in some detail about the way he had worked with intervals in the Sonata's second movement:

> the mood ... (a lament) is invoked and sustained by the melodic interval of the augmented second in the phrase B, C, D sharp, C, B. Once this augmented second (C to D sharp) had been stated, and stated so definitely as to become immediately the chief focal point for the movement, my problem was to develop and continue it without becoming nauseatingly pseudo-Oriental.

It is good to find Rubbra for once using a thoroughly subjective adjective in talking about music. He went on to describe the technical procedures by which he had avoided 'nauseating pseudo-Orientality', and his 'development of another facet of the opening idea' in his second subject.

Four years after finally redesignating the abortive quartet, Rubbra composed its successor, which he must surely have regarded as another 'work of value'. In a 1969 broadcast talk he spoke of 'an inner desire to sum up my progress periodically in the purest and most lucid texture available to a composer'; his four quartets are indeed very regularly spaced over his career (fifteen years from 1934 until 1949, fourteen until 1963, and a further fourteen till the 1977 Fourth Quartet). From student years onward, his relationship with Vaughan Williams was excellent, and the score of his First String Quartet (Op. 35, originally composed in 1933–4) bears the dedication 'To R.V.W., whose persistent interest in the original material of this work has led me to the present revisions and additions'; yet the quartet as it now stands has expunged virtually all reflections of Vaughan Williams. It opens in a way that seems to pay tribute, both texturally and melodically, to Ravel's quartet. Who knows how it originally stood? – for after the war he revised the first two movements out of a feeling that there the influence of Vaughan Williams had been too strong, also writing a completely new finale to replace the original, which he had come to find too wild. The first movement's unity of character is supplemented by appearances of a more forceful idea hinting at a homeland somewhere between Spain and North Africa; this touch of the 'far-distant Spanish ancestor' comes twice, at points where the second subject would be in a sonata-form movement, and gets up a fair head of steam. If that original finale was really so frenetic, then the climaxes of the first movement could have offered a link to it. Given the work's Ravelian quality, a tendency for its melodies to use the scales other than the modern major and minor need not necessarily mean that Rubbra shared his contemporaries' enthusiasm for the old church modes, which for the most part avoided the crucial 'leading-note' effect of having a semitone as the topmost interval before the recurrence of the 'tonic' (for example, B to C in C major). The effect, to late-nineteenth and twentieth-century ears, was otherworldly and 'folksy', so that our music in particular used the modes to great advantage. Rubbra's occasional 'modalities' could, however, put one in mind of late-nineteenth-century French composers' essays connected with spiritual phenomena such as Rosicrucianism, rather than the more severely modal Vaughan Williams or Holst (who were still there in the background of the *Lyric Movement*).

After a ruminative slow movement the finale, according to Jacobson, was barbaric;[12] the few bars quoted by him are all that remains of it. Rubbra eventually cocked a snook at any idea that it could be difficult to link up with a work composed more than a decade earlier, opening the new finale with a fugal exposition of the figure that had closed the slow movement all those years before. For someone whose organised mind had already incorporated an existing 'finale' into his First Symphony, and would do something similar in his Sixth a few years later, it might have been harder to avoid connecting with his younger self. In the new finale any 'pagan frenzy' is replaced by a fleetness of foot that admirably complements the quietude of much that has gone before. Quick textures in late Beethoven quartets spring irresistibly to mind, a high passage for all the instruments very near the end recalling one late in the scherzo of Beethoven's C♯ minor quartet Op. 131; the ten-year break has replaced the shade of Ravel with that of Beethoven, which will persist in Rubbra's remaining music for string quartet. This very concise movement stands alongside the scherzo of the 1946 Cello Sonata in documenting a new lightness of touch and a fresh, new world that will be immortalised in his Fifth and Sixth symphonies. Because of Rubbra's reservations the work was not heard in public until the Blech Quartet gave the première of the revised version at the Wigmore Hall on 13 November 1946.

Like the quartet, a *Sinfonia Concertante* for piano and orchestra (Op. 38) composed in 1933–4 was later revised. Rubbra was the soloist in the first performance, at a 1943 Promenade concert conducted by Boult. The idea of the valiant soloist matching himself against the full might of a symphony orchestra, armed only with a nine-foot concert-grand, was something to appeal to the pianist in Rubbra, but it needs heartfelt aggressiveness and euphoria to back it up. Here the piano part goes through some of the heroic motions but is rarely carried away into truly dominant virtuosity. (Arthur Bliss's 1938 concerto would bring that off with striking success, as presented by the great pianist Solomon at the 1940 New York World's Fair.) The title, already given by William Walton to a similar work ten years earlier, hints at doubts and reservations, for a *Sinfonia Concertante* is and isn't a concerto. There, indeed, lies the fascination of Rubbra's piece, for it is the first music in which he openly confessed to the wish to master symphonic proportions and thinking.

The monothematic tendency of the *Phantasy* and *Lyric Movement* from several years earlier seems to have returned as he moves into this new territory. (A first attempt from around 1930 was given the title 'Concerto' and the opus number 30, but remained in manuscript, whereas its successor was allowed to become part of the canon.) The *Sinfonia Concertante* is one of his most prevailingly sombre works, for a good personal reason; taken simply as music, much of it seems by turns obsessive and brutal. The opening movement, *Fantasy*, has a darkly cumulative introduction with the piano, over a deep pedal C, dwelling on an arpeggiated seventh-chord, which at one touching moment is also spelled out by the principal cello; the arpeggio will return a couple of times, eventually rounding off the movement. (That A–B–A′–B′–A″ pattern is found again in the immediately post-war Cello Sonata's first movement.) Against the piano, the high strings have a sustained conjunct[13] line, source of various melodic ideas later on. An ingenious analyst could here detect the workings of the 'lyrical direction' that had guided Rubbra ever since *Rosa Mundi*.

Things change abruptly some two and a half minutes in: that was to become the normal length for a Rubbra 'introduction'. The second, quicker section is like a set of variations on an orchestral idea with a prominent rising figure. The piano is used with great power, and turmoil gradually develops, bordering perhaps on the 'pagan frenzy' of the String Quartet finale. But more thoughtful ideas are also in the air, so there is not only the conflict of soloist and orchestra expected in a concerto but also the contrast of material associated with the symphony: this is, after all, a 'sinfonia concertante'. The opening's dark thoughts and arpeggiated chord eventually return, if only for the briefest of calmer interludes. From nine minutes in, until the second reprise of the opening, which rounds off the movement, the music is like a slow, grim procession, in a three-time punctuated by side-drum rolls and timpani beats, as if saying 'All flesh is grass'. Rubbra would soon return to that mood in the First Symphony.

The scherzo-like middle movement is entitled 'Saltarella'; according to *New Grove*, Saltarello is a 'generic term for moderately rapid Italian dances, usually in triple metre and involving jumping movements'. Why Rubbra should have used the feminine is a mystery; maybe he was simply misled by the related 'Tarantella'. The music promises to offer real relief and variety, but its theme is all too soon challenged by competing and very aggressive ideas. From being a dance, it turns into a taxing essay in counterpoint with more than a hint of a 'dance of death' – another plan Rubbra would return to, in the First Symphony's scherzo. In fact composition of the two works overlapped in 1936; with the earlier one ending in a fugue, and the eventual finale of the other, with its fugal final section, written before the rest of the First Symphony, the two 'concluding' fugues could have been written quite close together and indeed in either order. In their notes for a recording of the *Sinfonia Concertante*, Saxton and Yardley detect in the 'Saltarella' echoes of Stravinsky's *Petrushka* with its obbligato orchestral piano; the similarities are only slightly greater than those to passages in Holst's comic opera *The Perfect Fool*, and there are even more passages where (and this is very rare in his music) Rubbra takes on the macho, aggressive quality found in a work such as Hamilton Harty's 1922 Piano Concerto, which thanks to its composer's dual brilliance as pianist and conductor had a good run in the inter-war years. One way and another, this is a powerful movement; its oddest feature is the sudden forty-second eight-bar stillness, with a sustained oboe line, that comes and goes, as from nowhere and as if back to nowhere, four minutes in. The Saltarella ends, however, 'with a bang not a whimper'.

Rubbra named this movement as one of those in which his early 'nervous rhythmic energy' had yet to be mastered, something he said happened as 'the infusion of counterpoint gradually tamed the obsessive rhythms, so that they became more acclimatised to the developing style. It was an extrovert element which is now thoroughly out of my system'. Other movements with it still 'in his system' included the First Quartet's original finale, parts of his Oriental opera *Bee-bee-bei* (later retitled *The Shadow*), and the scherzos of the first two symphonies. It was a feature likely to appeal to the bolder listener, and a 1947 review of the *Sinfonia Concertante* by the faithful Ivor Keys in *Music and Letters* referred to 'the barbaric splendour of some of the climaxes'.

Rubbra's most original thought in this hybrid work was to make its finale a Prelude and Fugue, during whose course the piano soloist recedes further and further into obscurity. Around the time of the *Sinfonia Concertante*'s composition Rubbra made an orchestration (Op. 40) of the famous G minor Prelude by Rachmaninov, fifth in his set Op. 23, but though the movement sets out as if to carry the Rachmaninov torch into new territory, it and the work end in the meekest possible manner. This tells us something about Rubbra, and would sit well in the Sermon on the Mount; it could be taken as a hint of his 'man is not unaided', and of what Pascal conversely called 'misère de l'homme sans Dieu'. Or at least 'the sadness of a man without a great friend and teacher' – for the finale's full title is 'Prelude and Fugue ♩ = 56 in memoriam Gustav Holst 1874–1934', a possibly unique case of a composer's including a metronome marking in the title of a movement. It reveals the personal feelings behind the work and helps explain the curiously mixed impression it leaves behind; over and above its twin musical aims as concerto and symphony, it wants on the one hand to impress as a concerto should, and on the other to release a private grief in solemn and dignified tones.

The Prelude is another impressive build-up, more intense than the introduction to the first movement, and the triple-time slow-march feeling of the music just before the end of that movement reappears. In the fugue the initial exposition of the 'subject' and its counter-subjects is left to the orchestra, the

first entry being on an instrument for which Rubbra was to show a lifelong preference, the cor anglais. The fugue subject, with its chromatic descent followed
by a sudden wide leap, has something in common with an idea, seemingly
derived from Wagner, which will be prominent in music of the middle 1950s,
the Seventh Symphony (see pp. 147–9). It is a sad, lamenting figure in both
composers' work. This orchestral section is long, but finally the piano makes
its entry, once more accompanied by a solo cello, which will also return several
minutes later to 'see it out'. For a while the piano adds a series of thoughtful ideas to the symphonic texture, without ever quite regaining its position
as soloist. In later works, such as the fugue that ends the 1946 Cello Sonata,
Rubbra would find ways to make his cumulative point less repetitiously than
either here or in the corresponding final section of the First Symphony; but
the peaceful close with the piano quietly stating the chord of C major is touching, and the very final high sounds on the strings can send a shiver down the
spine.

Once one has a bird's-eye view of Rubbra's creative work, this early example
of extended composition taking just over half an hour to perform seems prophetic, moving as it does from the tumultuous thoughts of a brilliant young
man in bad times to something that could suggest the quiet of an old composer
finding peace as he completes a life's work. When he embarked in earnest on
his symphonic cycle, Rubbra would repeat the idea of a final fugue but end
very differently.

In 1934 he acquired a home, Valley Cottage, at Highwood Bottom near Speen
in the Chilterns, some thirty miles northwest-by-west of London, where he
and Antoinette lived for almost a quarter of a century. Two sons, Francis, and
Benedict, were born in 1935 and 1938. By the late 1930s Rubbra had been composing for almost two decades, with four symphonies and much music in more
or less every genre. He would remain prolific, producing a constant stream
of music – 164 completed works, which were given opus numbers so soon as
written, or even when he began to write them, as is shown by the few bars of
sketches for a twelfth symphony 'Op. 165'. That was a departure from the tradition that an opus number was given by the publisher when a work appeared in
print. A third of Rubbra's first forty-three works were still in manuscript at the
time Grover produced his book, but almost all the ensuing hundred and ten
had by then (1993) been published.

An enduringly curious feature of human chronology is that despite an ever-
increasing expectation-of-life the early and middle thirties remain as crucial
as they were when Dante opened his *Divine Comedy* 'lost in a dark wood in

the middle of life's journey'. Comparing four significant Rubbra pieces from 1934–6, one finds his mind at some inner Rubicon: the *Five Motets* are unmistakably dominated by a Holstian emphasis on chordal harmony, the *Sinfonia Concertante*, for all its memorial tribute to Holst, is often in a rather heavy tradition of the heroic piano concerto; the First String Quartet balances harmony and counterpoint as a major work for four stringed instruments should, while the orchestral score that became the finale of the First Symphony finally reflects his already-quoted words about the pendulum's swing in the direction of counterpoint, with emotional force redirected from harmony to significant melodic lines.

Maturity had been attained with his Second Violin Sonata and first two movements of the First String Quartet, the *Sinfonia Concertante* got something uncharacteristic but powerful out of his system, and in 1935 Rubbra began work on a major purely orchestral score. It was to have momentous consequences for his creative career.

CHAPTER 3

The First Four Symphonies

The first of Rubbra's eleven symphonies occupied him from 1935 until 1937. It was well received, and he soon composed three more, with little other composition intervening. War-service followed, first as an army clerk and later as a pianist helping to keep the forces entertained. Had Rubbra been even a little older he could have been involved in the 1914–18 conflict, and his first four symphonies often seem to show a mind dominated by the apprehension of war so general among sensitive people during the run-up to 1939. The music is, admittedly, quite far removed from the 'Why, this is Hell, Nor am I out of it'[1] feeling in the German composer Karl Amadeus Hartmann's 1939 *Concerto Funèbre* for violin and strings, written 'at the scene of the crime', but the mood is still striking. In 'Edmund Rubbra, Now 70, Looks at his Eight Symphonies' (*The Listener*, 27 May 1971) he wrote, apropos his First Symphony and its immediate predecessors, the successful and quite disturbing Fourth by Vaughan Williams and Walton's First, 'If there are aggressive factors in all three symphonies it is probably because they all reflect a prevailing atmosphere, for I certainly did not set out to make an aggressive statement.'

Rubbra, along with most other fine traditionalist composers, had without renouncing the forms of the past found ways in which they could serve current needs. As he said in *BCI*, 'the forms that have developed in the history of Western music, although few in number, have no fixed shapes that can be measured and made available, like moulds for a jelly. Rather are they like variants of archetypal ideas which are inexhaustible in potential, yet which always remain the same. This the paradox of form.' The same *Listener* piece went into that in great detail apropos the Second Symphony, treating in particular the bulwark of traditional symphonic composition, sonata form:

> It can no longer be inferred from the word 'Symphony' at the head of an orchestral work that the music is divisible into fairly clearly defined sections, such as, in the first movement, exposition, development and recapitulation. There are of course, and must be, contrasts in subject-matter, but these contrasts need not be in the places assigned to them by the text-book. Nor need the argument (or development) wait for a double-bar, or the recapitulation be anything like a full repetition of the material of the exposition. This does not by any means imply a loosening

of formal principles, only that the modern composer, in using material – as is mostly the case – that is not strongly anchored to a key-centre, must find other means of making the structure cohere in a logical manner.

Now, the nature of the themes of a Symphony determine the nature of the form. If the latter is unsatisfactory, it is usually because the composer has, owing to pre-conceived formal ideas, interfered with the evolution of the melodic thought, instead of allowing it to unfold naturally. It may be thought that if the latter course is taken the music, by continuous suggestion, would move too far afield, and thus lose touch with the initial impulse. This is true, however, only if the composer has no grasp of the formal implications of the idea. Provided he has this grasp, the idea is like a circle which, however much it expands, always has the same centre. When the expansion is at its fullest, then the contrasting idea has every right to appear. This, in turn, will expand and evolve.

Such an ability to expand and control his ideas is part and parcel of the marvellous sense of free improvisation found in Rubbra's best music, with the 'evolution of the melodic thought' natural rather than forced to conform to preconceived notions or even to his own plan laid down in advance ('I never graph out climaxes'). But when form eventuates in this way it is all the more vital to make the correct choice of a starting-point, which is to say of basic material; 'the composer's first task is ... to clarify the idea, or to shed what is not congruous, until there remains not the slightest doubt that it is shaped and stated as perfectly as possible, and accords aurally with a standard that is ever in the individual composer's mind' ('A Composer's Problems'). From there on, the music's unfolding is natural, organic. ('Goethe's primeval plant; the root is in fact no different from the stalk, the stalk no different from the leaf, and the leaf no different from the flower; variations of the same idea' – Webern, *The Path to Twelve-Note Composition.*)

Rubbra summed up his attitude to form in *BCI*: 'I use classical forms in my music, but each time I do I think I am able to give them a new personality. I use them instinctively, never as patterns to which I must shape my thought. Frankly, I don't give form much thought at all.' That was followed by the celebrated 'I never know where a piece is going to go next.'

Rubbra regarded his first four symphonies, composed between 1935 and 1942, as a set: 'when symphonies are written in quick succession the characteristics of each are usually the result of a *reaction* away from its predecessor; in other words, although they are independent works they are somehow different facets of one thought, and a knowledge of all is necessary to a *complete* understanding of one' ('An analysis by the composer of his Fifth Symphony', *The Music Review*, February 1949). For that, one can but take their composer's word, though it suggests that to understand one of the symphonies 'completely', one must not only follow in detail what happens in it, but also give thought to what doesn't – an unusual mode of listening which not every music-lover will find sympathetic or indeed practical.

Completion of a first symphony was followed immediately by work on another ('more austere and contrapuntal'), which he completed in 1937, the year No. 1 was first performed; No. 3 ('more lyrical') came two years later, and No. 4 ('more chordal') was written during 1940 and 1941. The four years between the completion of the First and Fourth show relatively little non-symphonic composition, with the principal works a set of *Improvisations on Virginal Pieces of Giles Farnaby* for orchestra and seven madrigals, plus an orchestration of Brahms's *Variations on a Theme of Handel* commissioned by his publisher.

By the middle 1930s Rubbra's music was familiar to influential figures in English musical life such as Owen Mase, who for a while headed the BBC's music department. After the First Symphony's successful première he introduced Rubbra to the leading music publisher Alfred Kalmus. His Vienna-based firm Universal Edition helped to make Bartók and the Second Viennese School known. Kalmus took his time studying either the score or the favourable press notices, then accepted the work for engraving in Vienna; by the end of the year it appeared impressively under the UE imprint. Universal acquired the rights to all four early Rubbra symphonies, and also had the score of No. 3 engraved. Always an astute businessman, Kalmus indicated to Rubbra that The Firm would in return be glad of something more 'exploitable',[2] hence the 1938 orchestration of the Brahms Variations and the composition a year later of the Farnaby *Improvisations* (Op. 50). The Brahms orchestration caught on, being recorded by the NBC Symphony under Toscanini. Heartened by Kalmus's encouragement, Rubbra worked all the more enthusiastically on the next three symphonies, but in any case he was totally fascinated by the problems and opportunities symphonic form presented. Looking back after thirty-five years, he wrote 'when ... my 1st Symphony took me, as it were, by surprise, I was so excited by the discovery that I could write such a large-scale work that by 1942, only seven years later, I had completed four' ('Symphony No. 7', BBC Music Programme's *Music Magazine*, 3 January 1971). Mase's reward for his help was the dedication of the First Symphony ('to Georgina and Owen Mase'.)

When after the March 1938 *Anschluss* the Vienna headquarters of Universal Edition passed into Nazi administration Rubbra had to find a new publisher. The *Amoretti*, which in a programme-note he described as trying 'to view 16th century devices through 20th century eyes', and one set of Spenser sonnets were accepted by the firm of Joseph Williams. The Second and Fourth symphonies remained unpublished until 1950, by which time Rubbra had revised No. 2. No. 3 appeared in 1949.

Within the 'set' the works pair off, each member of a pair complementing the other. Nos. 1 and 2, as recorded under Richard Hickox, come out amazingly close in length (34' 36", 34' 06", the quick second movements differing by only a single second!), and both, subject to a reservation to be considered shortly, could be considered vintage 'pre-war-Angst' music. (The novelist narrator of Graham Greene's *The End of the Affair* told how 'in those years the sense of happiness had been a long while dying under the coming storm'.) They differ, however, in layout. No. 1 goes quick–quick–slow, no. 2 slow–quick–slow–quick. No. 1 opens with an amazingly twitchy movement that only very gradually subsides, No. 2 with a sustained line for unison strings that gradually bestirs itself.

The First Symphony (Op. 44), composed between 1935 and 1937, was first played on 30 April of the latter year by the BBC Symphony Orchestra under Adrian Boult at a 'contemporary music concert' which also included the première of Britten's *Our Hunting Fathers*. It started life as an independent slow orchestral piece which Rubbra did not then see as part of a symphony; that became the work's finale. At the outset of the eventual first movement (Allegro moderato tempestoso, 3/4, B minor) it as if one were sitting in, and being thrown about by, a train travelling fast over a rough, irregular, endless series of points; in 'Edmund Rubbra, Now 70, Looks at his Eight Symphonies' he said the work opened 'in medias res', and we certainly seem caught up in an argument or struggle that could have been going on for some time. The nearest parallel would be the storm-swept opening to the finale of Shostakovich's Eleventh Symphony ('The Year 1905'), from twenty years later (1957); a roughly contemporary work that also begins as if one had just turned up the volume and joined in is Roberto Gerhard's Violin Concerto of 1942–3. A tight-lipped melody for the entire brass section is jostled and elbowed out of the way by hacking high-string counterpoints, never to be heard again, while the bass lurches about as it tries to copy the rhythms of the 'main line'. The constantly repeated rhythm in the violins (Ex. 1) obscures the underlying 3/4

time-signature. It all suggests an over-full, anxious mind hardly knowing what
to do first.

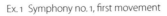

Ex. 1 Symphony no. 1, first movement

Having said which, one should note a statement of principle made by Rubbra in his broadcast introduction to the Fourth Symphony's 1942 première. He
left the listener free

> if he wishes, [to] translate the images of this symphonic world into
> those of the world of his everyday experience, and say, 'here the music is
> triumphant, there it is apprehensive, somewhere else it is carefree', but
> to do so is, as it were, to bypass the centre of the music. The symphony
> is in the philosophical sense of the word a musical 'essence' – rounded,
> complete and independent. In other words, it forms its own world, it is
> subject to its own laws and volition, and not in any sense illustrative of,
> or a commentary upon, the phenomena of everyday life.

That explicit caution can be softened only by Rubbra's having said a few
seconds earlier that the symphony 'does not *consciously* illustrate subjective
states, or seek to convey to the listener anything appertaining to the surrounding *objective* world'. The emphases audible in a recording of his spoken
introduction leave open the possibility that it might *unconsciously* illustrate
this, that or the other, or at least (as he half-admitted apropos the First Symphony) reflect an irresistible and current world-atmosphere that impinged
on the composer's *subjective* sensory processes. Rubbra's remarks in *BCI* on
the sociological background of any current musical idiom show that, however
'abstract' the statements found in symphonies, he did not regard music as her-
metically sealed off from life. To that extent a commentator, too, may likewise
invoke an 'atmosphere' if it helps throw light on the music for those listening
to it. That is the dialectical frame for the countless attributions of mood and
'content' throughout this book. Rubbra's views, if any, on the discipline known
as hermeneutics[3] are not recorded, and most composers might well find it an

intrusion on their privacy – but in this study it will be to some slight extent in evidence, having until now been absent from the Rubbra literature.

As a most unconventional 'statement of intent' at the start of a long symphonic career, the First Symphony's opening ranks alongside the unconventional chord – an unprepared dominant seventh – which began Beethoven's first essay in the form. During its ten minutes the 'train' draws by almost unnoticeable stages to a halt; the skill with which Rubbra gradually filters out his initial frantic restlessness already shows the 'breath of a symphonist'. It is less a matter of 'themes', of separate melodic entities, than of process. As early as 1943 Wilfrid Mellers, apropos the Fourth Symphony, maintained that 'the symphonic problem, as Rubbra conceives it, is probably the central problem of musical evolution today', and reached back to Sir Donald Tovey for a formulation of the basic contrast between 'texture' and 'shape' as guiding principles. He found that Rubbra had by then achieved 'a perfect reconciliation' of the two principles, and Rubbra had his own thoughts on the matter:

> I always like to think of the first movement of a Sonata or Symphony as being in the nature, formally, of a spread-out fugue; i.e. instead of subject and countersubject appearing together they become parted as first and second subjects, and being separated they of course need harmonic support; but just because they are parted in time there is no reason why they should be parted in spirit: indeed, there's every reason for making the linkages more apparent to the listener. If we then find that music so texturally different as a Bach Fugue and say the first movement of a Mozart symphony have a similar basic shape, we shall see that the fundamental problems of music are related to texture rather than to form, which is prevailingly simple and relatively unchanging.[4]

This movement carries one along by its sheer energy, with enough repeated to register in the mind as a 'theme' – notably the opening string figure, present in one form and another throughout the first two-thirds of the movement, and a more melodious line first clearly heard (but already strenuously hinted at on the woodwind) a minute in (Ex. 2). Rubbra offers a whole series of what one is 'free if one wishes' to call restless, noble or wistful contrasting melodies making up the movement's manifest content, while the unruly accompaniment gives it momentum. That more melodious though resolute 'song theme' comes rather too near the start to be plausibly accounted a 'second subject', but can be usefully characterised by appropriating the German term for such a theme (*Gesangsthema*), which usefully suggests the contrast to be expected in the

Ex. 2 Symphony no. 1, first movement

subordinate idea or ideas of a symphonic work. It finally clarifies the movement's triple-time. Two things provide backbone – the way the repetition of
basic figures amounts to ostinato, and a whole series of sustained notes, mostly
in the bass (in musical terminology, 'pedal points' or 'pedal notes'). One can
become aware of them in the course of repeated listening, the one at the start
(on the note B) going on for at least fourteen bars. Later ones on B♭ (first in
an inner part and then high up as a violin trill), F, C (this one also in a middle
part), E and finally C♯ last for anything from nine to nineteen bars, and give a
measure of stability to what Rubbra called 'an intense movement, even in its
quieter moments'.

The churning accompaniment keeps going at anything from a fast boil
down to a steady simmer; a distinct difference can be felt as early as two
and a half minutes in, but such brief remissions tend not to last, and it all
amounts to a roller-coaster ride before the music winds right down to virtual
stillness. The 'song theme' is worked very hard, in a variety of different versions, including a most mysterious one for a solo trumpet around 4′00″. A
minute earlier, connoisseurs of the mid-twentieth-century English symphony
may have noted a curious coincidental resemblance to music in the scherzo
of Vaughan Williams's Sixth Symphony, written a decade later. After a further
surge, there is another hint of rest six minutes in, but a faint drum-beat still
disturbs the principal melody's most elegiac appearance so far; a variant of
its crucial phrase (* in Ex. 2) appears no fewer than twelve times, overlapping
itself in another of Rubbra's ostinatos. This finally stops the incessant low-level
tremolo that has run through the music for a minute or two. Given Rubbra's
affection for Schubert, it is interesting that so much of his first major symphonic essay should, in effect, use the shuddering tremolo often characteristic
of the earlier composer's chamber music – not just the G major quartet, but
the C minor *Quartettsatz* and much of the D minor ('Death and the Maiden')
quartet. As from this point, the restless Ex. 1, which has already become more
sporadic, is not heard again; it is replaced by a constant triple beat, as if the
brief rest between the second and third notes of Ex. 1's main figure had disap-
peared and the notes now ran evenly in groups of three.

Solo strings briefly make their voices heard around 7′00″, as they will from time to time throughout the symphonies; at a very similar point in the first movement of his very last major work, the 1982 *Sinfonietta*, Rubbra would use them again, in that case as a quartet. But it is, once again, a very brief moment of peace, rather as at the start of the recapitulation in the first movement of Schubert's G major string quartet, when the all-pervading fever of tremolo finally remits for a short while. As it all starts building to another climax, the onward three-time of the chords that accompany a further version of the 'song-subject' (8' 50"), plus the drum-like beat of double basses playing in octaves, could put one in mind of 'And all flesh is as grass' in the second movement of Brahms's *German Requiem*. Here Rubbra takes the next step onward from the grim march at the end of the *Sinfonia Concertante*'s first movement. The final and biggest climax ('*fff* possibile') retrospectively establishes the 'song theme' figure as the dominating feature of the movement, but leads into a fade-out with the almost Verdian marking 'morendo, *pppp*'. Here is the first example of something constantly found at the close of Rubbra's symphonic movements, an ending that is no ending at all, but rather a staging post. The feeling is provisional; one is made to wonder, 'what comes next?' (Grover noted that the first movements of all Rubbra's first eight symphonies, which is to say all those that have a true 'first movement', end quietly.)

With the possible exception of parts of the Eighth Symphony's opening movement, this is in places the most chaotic-sounding music Rubbra ever wrote; no wonder it appealed to a publisher closely associated with the avant-garde of the day, even though there was never any question of Rubbra's abandoning the key system. (He was willing to try anything once; a single piece, the 1935 *O Unwithered Eagle Void* for mixed voices and orchestra Op. 41 no. 2, to a text by his neighbour the painter Cecil Collins, was an experiment in 'composition with twelve notes related only to each other', as pioneered by Schönberg a decade earlier in works from the last of his *Five Piano Pieces*, Op. 23, onward. Rubbra later looked on it with some amusement.) At various stages one may be reminded of the more straightforward excitability found in William Walton's very successful First Symphony from a couple of years earlier. But Walton's was a wonderfully lyrical talent, whereas Rubbra had in him something of the tragedian, with all the complexity and soul-searching that brings with it. 'Motoric' was a catchword for a whole inter-war musical movement; most of the music it 'caught' was pretty crude, but Rubbra dignified the genre through the invariable cogency of his contrapuntal thinking. Kalmus's enthusiasm and catalogue notwithstanding, the closest Continental parallel to this music is probably to be found in the Hindemith of the years just before and after the

Second World War, where one may likewise be reminded at times of a heavy train forging relentlessly onward.

On the other hand, the opening movement of the First Symphony already shows Rubbra in command of a long-drawn-out form to which he could give a convincing shape. In an otherwise unidentified publication, *The World of Music*, he wrote that

> All my works, symphonic or otherwise, stem from a single root idea (usually melodic and vocal in conception). There is no formal division into 1st and 2nd subjects, etc. If these occur they are the result of the natural proliferation of the material. Each movement, then, is conceived as a single arc of sound, which implies a long growth towards a climax and then a relaxation of tension.

That formulation will be reproduced in this book's account of one Rubbra movement after another.

What comes next could hardly seem a bigger surprise and contrast, for the second movement (Allegro bucolico e giocoso, A♭ major, 6/8) is based on, or sets out from, a cheery French dance, 'Périgourdine'. It had no personal connotation for Rubbra; he found it in *Grove's Dictionary of Music and Musicians*, where it was taken from a 1780 'Essay sur la musique' by De la Borde and Roussier to illustrate the entry for the French district of Périgord (Dordogne). In 'Edmund Rubbra, Now 70, Looks at his Eight Symphonies' he said it appeared in this one because the work needed 'the relief afforded by the ubiquitous French dance' (no comparable explanation is to hand for the 'Saltarella' in the *Sinfonia Concertante*). He also wrote of this movement that 'in place of a conventional scherzo a theme was recruited for a movement in free variation form'. After so sombre and mysterious an end to the previous movement, its effect is bizarrely out of keeping, and one has to search for any kind of connection. The cheeky tune will pay for daring to show its face; the movement's 'free variations' are an early example of the pattern whereby Rubbra relieves tension with a catchy melody, then proceeds to do what modern theory calls 'de-construct' it. The *Sinfonia Concertante* had done something similar, with the lively Saltarella tune relentlessly challenged by its neighbours. Even at the start the cheery French tune is already 'with reservations', for it makes its way over a pedal point which is not the tonic and which makes it almost sound as if it were in the minor, despite being in the major. It is hardly ever out of earshot, so that one often has the impression of a round, but ever-more-menacing counter-subjects, alternative melodies and indeed alternative, less friendly versions of the tune itself challenge the opening mood. The innocence of a movement like the Dargason from Holst's *St Paul's Suite* is clearly a thing of the past, though a conductor introducing the symphony on Radio 3 in 2006 did detect a touch of 'Ravel in *Tombeau de Couperin* mood'. By the end (F minor) there is mayhem, and the dance has little chance of survival: such is life.

The First Symphony ends with an enormous slow movement (Lento, 3/2, key-signature blank, i.e. C major). When Rubbra began to write it his mind was only just beginning to turn to orchestral composition; once completed, the piece proved so massive and 'conclusive' that it clearly had to be a symphonic finale, so he then had the problem of writing earlier movements to lead up to it. That was his explanation[5] for the tempestuous first movement; 'Having decided that this *was* the Finale and not the first movement, I was forced into making the kind of dramatic statement in the first that would find its resolution in the relatively calm atmosphere of the ending', but clearly such music was in him, just waiting to find a way out. As he said elsewhere, 'my music seems to me to be complete within me from the moment I begin; composing is the conscious act of revealing it'. In doing so, according to his 1971 *Listener* article, he came up with a technical solution that involved the reversal of the direction in which the main intervals moved.

Slow finales had never been more than the rarest exception in full-scale orchestral works; the one in Haydn's 'Farewell' Symphony is probably the most famous example, along with those in Mahler's Third and Ninth Symphonies. There were a few in chamber music, where the line likewise goes back to Haydn and a masterly slow–quick–slow movement like the finale of the C major String Quartet, Op. 54 No. 1, from which Schubert learned a thing or two. It takes in, particularly, Bartók's second string quartet with its Adagio finale. (Bartók, though not named as such in the Schafer interview, figured among Rubbra's favourite composers. One of his BBC talks, on 16 April 1961 for the Third Programme, was on the Bartók string quartets, which he saw as summing up the best of the composer. Bartók's Sixth Quartet, composed in 1939, two years after the completion of this Rubbra symphony, would revert to the idea of a slow finale, a last and fullest development of the 'motto theme' heard ever since the opening.) Rubbra's finale lasts as long as will the two closing movements of No. 2, and he never wrote a longer movement within a symphony. (No. 9, the *Sinfonia Sacra*, is a special case, its ten sections running continuously to make up what other composers might rather have called a cantata.) It sets out like a cortège and reverts at various points to the same sad stately feeling, while developing in three waves the impetus required to carry off a vigorous close.

They to some small extent take in the four sections found in mature sonata form, where the concluding coda is an important entity rounding off the entire piece. Rubbra said this movement was in sonata form, but (as we have already seen) that did not mean it had to break down neatly into sections; it was, to take Hans Sachs's pragmatic line, 'sonata form as understood by the cobbler burning to get on with his work'. To take the most obvious problematic place, the third wave, which one might expect to correspond to 'the recapitulation', was marked by Rubbra 'Fuga. Coda', but as it begins a recapitulation may or may not be already under way, and this new section in one important sense continues it, since it is based on a theme not so far 'recapitulated' (for the sufficient reason that it has dominated the later stages of the 'development').[6]

The first two 'waves' take their time developing. At the start a melody heard on a higher-register solo cello is followed in canon an octave lower by a solo viola (Ex. 3), and dwelt on at some length, with ineluctable drum-beats marking its progress. After a minute its rhythm moves down into a continuous bass line, with wind chords commenting dryly. That dotted rhythm will be the principal propulsive element in one build-up after another, constantly urging the music on, so that the whole thing picks up a good deal of speed, with Ex. 3 developed in a variety of ways. Around the time that process reaches its peak (5′00″), the brass seize on an expressive phrase that has been hinted at for some time and expanded into a genuine and newish theme (Ex. 4; the similarity between its third and fourth bars and the fragment of melody bracketed in Ex. 2 is perhaps more for the eye than the ear, but Rubbra is at all times a master at transforming his basic ideas). The tailpiece (bar 5 of Ex. 4) reverts to the opening's dotted rhythm. This theme is blared out like a call to action. By now the music is all vigour, with a climax six minutes in dominated by a half-speed version of the new melody and by now-quite-thunderous drum-beats. After a brief dignified codetta, with a slightly hymn-tune-like, the first wave has run its course.

Ex. 3 Symphony no. 1, third movement

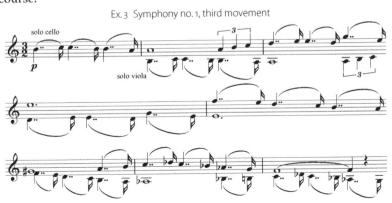

Ex. 4 Symphony no. 1, third movement

In the elegiac transition that follows Ex. 3 shows its friendlier side; the cortège resumes, with solo stringed instruments again to the fore, also the first oboe. Menace re-enters the music with an insistent trumpet and the ever-present drums, and another wave begins to build, again based on the dotted rhythm (9′ 20″). At 10′ 30″ we realise where the first movement took its 'Brahms Requiem' mood from (though both passages look back to the firm, grim tread of sections in the *Sinfonia Concertante*), and this is the point at which Grover detected the start of a typically non-identical Rubbra recapitulation. Certainly the opening cello melody (upper line in Ex. 3) is there struggling to make itself heard in the middle of the uproar. But these seventy-odd bars, at three times the original tempo, take up a mere quarter of the time spent on the 'exposition', and concentrate on further developing that initial idea – so it is probably pointless to look here for the kind of 'recapitulation' found in a traditional sonata form. By 11′ 00″, indeed, there is almost the feeling of a fast dance. This time the speeding-up is stemmed for a while, the cortège reverting (11′ 50″) to a more decorous or sombre pace. The 'dust and ashes' drum-beats set in again, and are to the fore once this second wave has begun to ebb. It has been even more intense than the first; at times the to-and-fro of the high strings gives something of the feeling of Sibelius's Lemminkäinen riding out on his journeys of superhuman achievement, but the closing minute or so has a majesty that makes it a counterpart to the codetta at the end of the first 'wave'.

It all takes a while to die away entirely. Yet another slowly cumulative wave bred out of Rubbra's endless capacity for improvisation might have been too repetitive a solution to the problem of ending so massive a piece. Instead, the closing minutes (from 14′ 15″) are a slow fugue based on the decisive melody from near the end of the initial wave (Ex. 4), which was not heard during the final recapitulatory subsection of the second wave; this is the section marked 'Fuga. Coda'. When first heard, the theme soon became boldly assertive, and here it begins quietly but works up to a blazing finish. Rubbra keeps the music driving ever onward in one long composed accelerando, until its final grandiose slowing-up. He finds an appropriate ending, like some great rallying-cry, to a most ambitious first symphonic essay, and has put down his problems by main force, even if they have not gone away. This could hardly be more different from the meditative ending to the *Sinfonia Concertante*'s fugue. Much later Rubbra modestly called his finale 'a long essay in the kind of inward lyricism that is common in my later works'. If some of this music is inwardly lyrical, one can but wait expectantly for its composer to offer something overtly epic or dramatic! Nor will one be disappointed.

Rubbra's loyal admirer and fellow-symphonist Robert Simpson summed up the effect made by the First Symphony, also commenting with foresight on the composer's subsequent fortunes, in his spoken comments after the work had been heard in his BBC Third Programme series *The Innocent Ear*, which identified its constituent works only after they had been heard, so freeing the listener's mind of preconceptions:

> Its dogged power is not meant to endear itself to the listener; and I'm sure it didn't. On the other hand I hope you found its lapidary consistency as impressive as I do. When it first appeared it created a considerable impact. As so often in this country, such events are easily supplanted by other not necessarily more important ones. I don't think it's the public that's the culprit; more likely the professional opinionists and the official bodies who take too much notice of them ... You will probably agree that it's a severe, even astringent piece. It's rather curious that Britain in the 1930s produced three somewhat fierce symphonies; this one, Walton's First, and Vaughan Williams' Fourth. Some mystics think it was the war coming, though I don't see why three British composers needed some clairvoyant excuse for feeling a bit rough at that time.

There spoke a fellow-composer who had grown up before the days when 'cowpat music' was found an acceptable expression.

Rubbra wrote philosophically about his experiences with the first four symphonies. In his lecture 'A Symphonic Credo' he said that 'the notices for the First weren't discouraging, but [how?] thankful I am now at this stage that little notice was taken of me, for it left me free to pursue a path of my own making ... If it had had a rousing and sensational success I should have been sorely tempted to use the same ingredients for my next effort. Whereas I was left quietly alone to find my way.' As for the Second Symphony, 'it had to wait ten years for a second performance, so that again I was free of any outside pressure to continue or not along the path I had chosen, not by any conscious thought, but by a natural bias of mind'.

Rather than being gradually filtered out as it was in the opening movement of the First Symphony, restlessness slowly creeps into the Second (Op. 45). This is the Rubbra symphony where any marginal influence of Vaughan Williams is clearest (notwithstanding a review of the 1938 première, reprinted inside the front cover of *ERC*, which made play with the heading 'SIBELIUS' 8TH SYMPHONY PERFORMED!' and wrote off Rubbra's work as having the master's mannerisms but not his inspiration). Rubbra's Second was a favourite with its dedicatee, Sir Adrian Boult, who conducted the première in 1938, as he had that of the First a year earlier. The performance was part of a concert at the BBC's studios on 16 December. Decades later Boult went so far as to name the symphony, which had by then been recorded, as one of the eight works he would want to have as and when the BBC parked him on a desert island. Rubbra revised it after the war, making a cut in the first movement, rewriting the end of the finale so that it closed in D major (it begins in E♭ minor), and reducing the woodwind from triple to double. That is the version published, recorded, and discussed here; it was first heard at the 1946 Cheltenham Festival, when Rubbra conducted the London Philharmonic Orchestra.

The symphony opens (Lento – Rubato, 4/4, no key signature) with a leisurely theme played in unison by the strings (Ex. 5). Though striking, it is sufficiently neutral in character to let its composer turn it to varied account in the course of the movement. It could be in the minor-mode version of the D that appears in Rubbra's heading for the work, but could just as well be in C major, F major or A minor; in any case, as early as the fifth bar it wanders momentarily off key. Its fourth, fifth and sixth notes (Ex. 5*) make up an important motive.

Ex. 5 Symphony no. 2, first movement

Ex. 6a and b show just a few of the forms in which Rubbra makes his initial idea appear in the course of the movement; 6a also shows his contrapuntist's mind combining the melody's opening with a different idea from it in lower parts. (To avoid over-complicating the example, I have not shown the further counterpoint played by the cellos and bass trombone.) The movement acquires truly impressive momentum; Rubbra's attempt 'to discover how far the interplay of melodic lines could be made to realise the dramatic tension

Ex. 6 Symphony no. 2, first movement: (a) bar 34; (b) bar 180

necessary in such a work … [and] without the adventitious aid of pattern and colour carry the weight of a large symphonic movement' must be accounted brilliantly successful.

Rubbra looked back on this symphony as the 'more contrapuntal' member of his early quartet. The 1920s saw a wealth of trendy speculation about something called 'linear counterpoint'; the term originated in a treatise by the Austrian musicologist Ernst Kurth, *Grundlagen des linearen Kontrapunkts*, published in 1917. It often went hand-in-glove with something else called 'the toccata style'. Counterpoint is by definition linear, but the premise was that composers could spin simultaneous lines without thought for the harmony their combination produced, despite which all would still by some minor miracle be well. Hindemith and Krenek were among the better composers who touched their cap to the idea, the related 'toccata style' particularly appealing to the ever-restless, bustling Hindemith, whereas Schönberg commented sharply on 'linear counterpoint' as a nonsense.[7] Rubbra's mind was far too acute to fall for such theorising, which was in any case less prevalent in pragmatic England, but what his intuitions told him at the time made him pen some of his wildest and most hair-raising pages. In a note on his Fourth Symphony he wrote the revealing words 'Flexibility of conception is the one prime necessity – my music is nothing if not impulsive – because it is linear there is a feeling it must be *rigid!*'

Near the start of the Second Symphony he is in no hurry to leave his first sustained melody, which is restated with a variety of counterpointing parts against it, in an 'exposition' of Schubertian leisureliness. The term 'exposition' has two different meanings, depending whether the context is fugue or sonata form. There would be little point in looking here for the outlines of a sonata-form section; in 'The Symphonic Credo', Rubbra said this symphony 'starts with a slow quasi-fugal texture of increasing complexity', and it would be stretching a point only slightly to speak of a series of semi-fugal expositions, each of which rests firmly on a pedal-note, stated or implicit, developing great momentum like that of the waves in the finale of the preceding symphony.

Eventually (2′15″) a storm-wind begins to blow ('poco a poco stringendo'): the 'interplay of melodic lines' is undoubtedly 'realising dramatic tension', and whatever apprehensive thoughts were to the fore as the First Symphony lurched into its opening bars are surely back in it at this point. Over the next half minute, the prevailing note-value halves from quaver to semiquaver and the speed at which the beats move has more than doubled, eventually reaching ♩=92 (from an initial ♩=40 circa), so that things feel four times as fast. Ex. 5 returns at twice its original speed, creating for the first of many times in Rubbra's symphonies the impression that a slow opening has moved imperceptibly but irrevocably into something quicker, which if the proportions were different one would be tempted to call the 'main section'. (Schubert's 'Great' C Major Symphony offers perhaps the classic example of that.) But with so much having already happened, and given so imperceptible a transition, what happens here is just a hint, a work-point to be returned to in the future.

For a while the bass line tries to batten down the hatches with a long-drawn-out pedal on the work's key centre, D, but as the wave breaks on the shore the music is stranded a semitone higher than it started, on E♭, and in the minor. There (3′30″) the woodwind start a new tune, which not only appears in its own right but also accompanies itself at half the speed, a classic contrapuntist's device. This 'augmentation' follows nicely on the diminution of the opening idea, but lasts no time at all, leading on to what seems a new melody for the violins in octaves (Ex. 7), one that does however share the first idea's way of undulating to either side of a central note. It could be felt as a new derivative or variant of the main melody.

Ex. 7 Symphony no. 2, first movement, bar 64

Things have briefly quietened down (♩=86) as the new violin theme seems to feel its way with the preceding short-lived idea in tow, but it in turn begins to work up a head of steam, and is succeeded at five minutes in by something more resolute, in a new metre (3/4, at ♩=112 and still tending to speed up, 'poco stringendo'); it has the same way of dodging back to a lowest note (here D♯) that the opening theme showed in constant returns to a low B, but the atmosphere has changed totally. The central part of the section runs at ♩=126. Despite manifest relationships with what has gone before, the music in this part of the movement provides a genuine sense of contrast and release; Rubbra was well aware of the possible comment, 'How boring', if he had stuck relentlessly to his basic melody and its derivatives.

With no detectable transition save a 'rallentando' (immediately contradicted by an 'accelerando'), the music a further minute on is suddenly back with the opening tune, though now in the triple time that has established itself; it wants to be in its native D minor (or, as it might be, C major/A minor), the accompaniment would rather go on in F minor, and to break the deadlock Rubbra's hat delivers a rabbit – a quiet transition with an expressive oboe line, a solo violin and some expressive woodwind figures, pulling the music down to the lowest note on which it has rested, D♭. But nothing can stop it from welling up again, with the 'feeling its way' second idea now very sure where it has got to and not reluctant to tell us – namely B minor, which is but a step away from the work's initial D, major or minor. It all adds up to a very simple scheme, but one that absolutely fulfils Rubbra's wish to let sheer counterpoint, 'the interplay of melodic lines', do the trick.

This further and longer wave culminates in a final most determined assertion of the main theme on violins, violas and cellos spread over three octaves, which gradually hammers the competing tunes into submission and re-establishes the D tonality of the opening. Ex. 5* is here at its most threatening, while the array of clashing figures, both from the original melody and from later, makes for a truly competitive and strident climax. To lead on to the next movement, Rubbra gives us a final wistful echo of the big tune on the oboe (Ex. 6b); the end is in neither the minor nor the major, since the third of the tonic chord is omitted. In a note written for the Hickox recording of the symphony the composer Robert Saxton, who became Rubbra's successor as Oxford University music lecturer based at Worcester College, spotted that this matches the point we have reached in the work's long journey from the one mode to the other.

The stage is now set for the scherzo (Vivace assai, at the fast and furious metronome marking ♩. = 176, 9/8), which follows 'attacca'.[8] It is a rather different matter from the one in the First Symphony with the jolly French dance-tune, but it, too, ends in uproar. Taking its time before it settles down on C minor, it seems at first to nod more than casually to the music from Vaughan Williams's turbulent 1930s; Saxton's note detects 'a Holst-like rhythmic sense', which is undoubtedly also true and goes for a good deal of the quick music in early Rubbra. But here his seething mind turns a genre upside down; this scherzo, so far from being a 'game' or 'joke', is truly wild, a whirlpool of competing ideas and melodies dominated by the complex sentence heard at the outset (Ex. 8). When Elisabeth von Herzogenberg first heard the opening movement of Brahms's Fourth Symphony, played on two pianos, she said it put her in mind of two learned gentlemen belabouring each other, but here we should have to identify a whole squad of monks unleashing a hail of Shaolin manœuvres. Naturally there is method in the madness, and even a recollection of things past, as when the first really contrasting idea, just over half a minute in, offers us a new version of that 'feeling-its-way' motive from the first movement. Things become particularly rowdy when the tenor trombone weighs in with yet one more tune around 1′15″; the trumpets play the same trick again near the end, with a repeated phrase whose five-beat period runs counter to anything in the rhythm of the surrounding music, amounting to two and a half bars of 2/4. The feeling of 'a tune too far' was another sign of Rubbra's 'inner dynamic demon' and would persist into the 1946 Cello Sonata's scherzo, though by then it had mellowed and shed the pre-war feeling of near-anarchy.

Ex. 8 Symphony no. 2, second movement

There are episodes in 15/8 (i.e. five beats to a bar), beginning at 0′50″, and in 2/4 (2′15″), each with its own new melodic idea, against which the basic one from the outset protests forcefully. In fact the duple metre persists until the end, but rather than having ousted the initial three-time it has 'gone native', since within the new rhythmic frame the old ideas become more and more dominant again. As Saxton says, the movement's 'energy arises from the interplay between accent and metre'. The budding chaos is held in check by a tight rhythmic sense, with constant if varied repetition of the initial pattern; ostinato is at least in the background lest things get totally out of hand, and the latter part of the movement is over a steadying series of bass passages that without actually sustaining one note do all the same make the music rest above an audibly unchanging pitch for many bars on end. The riotous conclusion still lets one know that there is order there, of a kind! The music has in the course of the movement moved off its initial C minor, to a close a semitone higher, in C♯ minor.

Hearing this music, one at times recalls Dittersdorf's complaint about Mozart. Only here it is far worse, or better, since the bewildering plethora of ideas is not successive but simultaneous. (Mozart was, of course, up to that too

– one need only recall his combination of six salient motives in the finale of the 'Jupiter' symphony.) Such contrapuntal overkill conflicts with what Rubbra later said about following more than three real parts, and in 'Rubbra, at 70 …' he pointed specifically to the fact that at this movement's climax four different themes are all there at once; so 'Do as I do, not as I say' – he meant what he wrote, as and when he wrote it, and the result, though something of an aural conundrum, is intimidatingly impressive. No wonder Boult, master of the intricacies of *Wozzeck*, took to it so.

The Adagio tranquillo (♩ = 42, 4/4), despite its blank key signature, opens back up in D major again; the tranquillity proves quite intermittent, not surprisingly given a man with an inner dynamic demon at a time of approaching war. But at the start, at least, the contrast with what has just ended could scarcely be stronger. The opening paragraph consists of a slightly Elgarian, wistful tune for the strings, answered by a more biting, Sibelian thought for paired wind instruments that takes up the falling figure heard so much ever since the start of the symphony (Ex. 9). When the paragraph is restated its mood is already darkened by a brooding pedal-note (timpani and basses) beneath the opening melody, but the first precious seconds of serenity are a sign of the Rubbra to come – his 'essence', one might say. Here was a further side of its composer, and one likely to appeal to the Elgarian in Boult.

Ex. 9 Symphony no. 2, third movement

At the repetition the opening figure's second four bars are less upwardly aspiring, for the oboe sits patiently on four statements of the same simple interval; the second figure, on the other hand, is developed at length, with an eloquent counter-melody for the principal cello near the end. That is restated and carried further by the first violins, by which time the initial lyricism, always under pressure, has been totally dispelled – we are into a middle section with a feature already met more than once, and to be met over and over again in Rubbra's symphonies, a sustained drum-beat that has already cast a faint shadow over the repetition of the opening paragraph. So the tension steadily rises. After a strategically placed 'general pause' a new development of the melodious opening figure takes over, followed in canon at one beat's distance in the bass, and another endless series of drum-beats runs beneath the still more massive build-up that follows. This penultimate section of the movement is organised around what amounts to an extended ostinato, similar music returning many times in a static but tension-building way. It all reaches its climax with a return of the opening idea's second thought, in a quite different and urgent dynamic and mood – it could scarcely have become more minatory. After one last regretful backward glance at the opening tranquillity, the ending in B major is purely provisional and meant to create expectation of the ensuing finale.

The two mighty waves that develop in the course of this slow movement recall the three-fold structure of the First Symphony's finale, or the waves in this symphony's own first movement, but it takes only half the time needed for that finale, and rarely can ten minutes of music have seemed so short and economical. The ideas impress themselves more firmly on the listener's mind than those in the preceding symphonic finale, and its build-up shows again Rubbra's command of sustained, cumulative thought independent of preset formal patterns.

The finale, however, he explicitly called a Rondo (tempo and character-marking Allegretto amabile, ♩. = 66, 6/8, opening in E♭ minor, mediant of the B major where the slow movement ended: D♯, the third in the one key, is equivalent to E♭, the tonic of the one that follows). A coda is marked Presto, though to keep things simple the composer omitted to mention that the final minute or so is not 'presto' at all, but in a measured, severe triple time (Maestoso, the speed of the beat decreasing to a third of what it was immediately before). That helps bring about an impressive and dignified conclusion.

In a traditional Rondo, recurrences of a first idea, rondo theme or 'ritornello'[9] are separated by episodes, which may or may not overlap in content. The ritornello (Ex. 10), first heard on a flute and bassoon two octaves apart, makes play with the possibility that 6/8 is interchangeable with 3/4 (in the example this is pointed out by means of square brackets), rather as does the finale of Dvořák's Violin Concerto. The ambiguity – 2 × ♩. = 3 × ♩ – is given what one might call the composer's official sanction when after three bars in his basic 6/8 the tune tacks on an unamiably bald fourth one in 2/4 (Ex. 10*). So far from being a

Ex. 10   Symphony no. 2, fourth movement

mere interjection, that turns out to be part of the basic eleven-bar phrase. So the stage is set for a recurrent clash of triple and duple time. Only from bar sixteen onward does a more regular, swaying, perhaps-still-just-amiable tune for the strings in all their various octaves (Ex. 11) confirm the 6/8 (which is to say two-in-a-bar or duple) time-signature. It offers the most Vaughan-Williams-like music in the movement.

Ex. 11   Symphony no. 2, fourth movement, bar 16 (fig. 63+1)

Anyone who has begun to gather the first thing about Rubbra's ways is likely to wonder how long he will be able to keep up the 'amiability': the answer is that in the most recent recording, under Richard Hickox, the movement lasts eight and a quarter minutes, of which perhaps the first few seconds, and then Ex. 11, could prompt the uninformed listener to presume on the composer's own rashness in attaching a mood-word to something as ambiguous as music, and think of it as 'amiable'. Rubbra's greatest friend Finzi more than once detected in his work a 'ruthless' quality (see pp. 65, 80), and if there is amiability here, it is the relative amiability of a very strong man who would never think of presuming on his strength. As Isabella says in *Measure for Measure*, 'Oh, it is noble/To have a giant's strength, but it is tyrannous/To use it like a giant.'

Were we dealing with a traditional rondo we should regard Ex. 11 as the 'first episode', but the way it is treated in the course of the movement makes it into something more like a further component of an opening paragraph. That is felt all the more because of its close relationship to the tune that opened the movement not so many seconds earlier. Against it, the wind develop a typical Rubbra cat's-cradle of counterpoint based on the opening 6/8 rhythm, and before long the opening melody and swaying tune are working happily together. Some of Rubbra's polymetric combinations of themes in the course of this movement could put one in mind of similar ingenuities in roughly contemporary music by Hindemith.

These ideas are given a forty-seven-bar exposition lasting about a minute and a quarter, after which that 2/4 fourth bar sees its chance to hijack the music and we are into the first true 'episode' (2/4, ♩ = preceding ♩., no new tempo marking, notated as if in D major but in fact in A major with a touch of the church modes in the form of a recurrent flattened seventh, G).

The main new idea is another Vaughan-Williams-like tune (Ex. 12), which strides out manfully rather than amiably, in 2/4 where the first one swayed along in 6/8. The first movement's succession of less- and more-resolute secondary themes is thus repeated. The new theme duly becomes the centre of a contrapuntal web with an interesting texture; having been heard straight through, it is heard a second time, blasted out manfully by the trombones and horns, the trumpets following in canon, while the rest of the orchestra has a similarly imitative paired accompaniment. Throw in a bass line and you have five real parts, two more than Rubbra's ideal quorum. The regularity of the imitation, plus the play of different tone-colours, makes it easier to follow than it otherwise might have been: Bach did more or less the same in the 'Domine Deus' of his B Minor Mass, with two imitative vocal soloists plus flute and violin in imitation over a bass line.

Ex. 12 Symphony no. 2, fourth movement, bar 48 (fig. 66+3)

A darkening of the mood takes us back to the 'ritornello', and the repeat manages to stay literal for as long as fifteen bars, which is normally not bad going for Rubbra, before wandering off into an expansive development of the ritornello and swaying tune. One feature, possibly involuntary on Rubbra's part, is the hint of a Spanish atmosphere, perhaps as translated into music by a Chabrier or a Rimsky-Korsakov. That takes up all of fifty bars, and covers a range of fairly sombre moods. The woodwind playing in thirds are also prominent, as in the slow movement's answering figure. There is a rather complicated canonic ostinato accompaniment in the bass: the section (ending about four and a half minutes in) is long enough for tune and ostinato accompaniment to swap places and for their original layout to return.

And so we reach the closing section or recapitulation (not that such things exist in a pure rondo, though in the hybrid form known as a sonata rondo they do, and by now enough has happened to show that we are dealing with some quite original Rubbra mixture of the two). Here he proves much readier than usual to repeat literally. No fewer than sixty bars recur more or less as they were, with ritornello and swaying tune. Indeed, the striding tune (Ex. 12) also reappears, as a true 'episode' might or might not do; a 'second episode' would be less likely to than a 'first'. It is now in D rather than A, matching the key scheme for a sonata-form recapitulation or sonata-rondo, though what either has to do with the movement's initial E♭ minor is another matter! As ever, Rubbra is 'thinking on', to his anticipated ending in D. The dynamics and scoring, however, are basically altered, the initial quiet being replaced by *fortissimo* markings for far more instruments, with the kettledrum banging away; only at the swaying tune does the original *piano sempre* return. Rubbra simplifies the music that followed the first hearing of the striding tune, with the five-part imitation replaced by a straightforward and forceful further hearing of the same melody.

And that, you might think, is that, as it might well have been with a naïve composer, but this one has more doubts and scruples to overcome before he can bring himself to end on a flourish. In fact it takes him a whole section, marked initially 'Coda, Presto' (♩. = 84, by some way the quickest metronome marking in the entire movement) to settle the issue. For the first time in Rubbra's symphonic output, but not the last, we meet a curious high-pitched skirling that feels slightly exotic or North African – a memory, perhaps, of Holst's Algerian piece *Beni Mora* (a 1908 work remarkably forward-looking for its time, with its dancing ostinato all of twenty years before Ravel composed the *Bolero*), and more immediately of Rubbra's own Second Violin Sonata and First String Quartet. This speeds up even more, debouching into the Maestoso final section: here the metronome marking is still 84, but since that now governs a single beat out of six, within a 3/2 tempo, the speed has effectively halved. The relationship between pulse and tempo in music is always fascinating. The change is in keeping with a stately minor–major melody in the home key, D. It opens with the relative of Ex. 5* also found at the outset of the rondo's first theme (a typical Rubbra inversion in fact), then descends rather as that theme did, though with different intervals and producing a totally different feeling. Here already we have the combination of semitone and fifth that will be a characteristic recurring feature of various Rubbra symphonies. From the listener's point of view, as distinct from the analyst's, this 'new' theme is audibly unlike anything before. Rubbra's way of building in some new final idea will be met time after time in this account of his symphonies; at the end of a first, second or third movement it is meant to lead on somewhere new, but coming at the end of a finale it needs to sound like a crowning and summation of the whole, if it is not to remain a bewildering anomaly. To this writer's ears it just about makes it.

By the same token, Saxton's note on the symphony says the finale ends in a 'life-asserting D major'; no possible quibble about the key, but as a comment on a composer who can never be accused of being 'anti-life' (an accusation Robert Simpson was given to hurling at the Second Viennese School), the adjective is as inadequate as most others applied to music. Determination should not be confused with achievement, and one would be wise, after all that has happened, not to set too much store by the final moments. Here it is hard to distinguish minor from major, so inevitably does the one displace the other (the same often happens in Schubert), and a different possible summing-up of Rubbra's impressive triple-time Maestoso exordium, with its relentless drum-beats, would be that a basic minor is shot through with flecks of major until the very last few moments. Those might seem the merest *tierce de Picardie*,[10] or perhaps the major mode is expected after such a great deal of effort and striving?

Despite the ironic newspaper tribute after the première of No. 2, Rubbra's Third and Fourth symphonies are the ones most noticeably influenced by Sibelius; they suggest at times a strong national pride not unlike that shown by the older composer as Finland's sense of nationhood grew. Something of the sort emerges overtly in the resolute final movement of the Fourth. The climate of thought in the 1930s must be borne in mind when one comments on echoes of Sibelius in a youngish English composer: a slightly younger ex-College student from Rubbra's time there, Constant Lambert, had been the dedicatee of the *Triple Fugue*, Op. 25, for orchestra, and his witty, provocative book *Music Ho! A Study of Music in Decline* (1934), set up Stravinsky and Schönberg as complementary anti-Christ figures, one with his 'time-travelling', the other with his 'Black Mass' feeling. Lambert needed a Messiah to counter the 'decline', and at least he lit on the greatest composer recently active in the symphonic field; Sibelius's Eighth Symphony was one of the great chimaeras of the day, a Godot eagerly awaited and never arriving. Lambert was no superficial journalist but one of the finest musicians and best-regarded composers of the decade, so his mental picture of 1930s music needs examining with respect; no matter that over the ensuing seventy years a consensus of media-men, scholars convinced of 'historical necessity' and composers, one or two of them at least as good as Lambert if not better, has decreed it to have been archaic, narrow-minded, parochial (for Lambert had his own music to write) and inexcusably negative. Other leading British musicians were more open to the full range of contemporary music, particularly Adrian Boult, whose radio performance of

Wozzeck prompted Alban Berg to write him a cordial and appreciative letter. Edward Clark invited Webern over from Vienna to conduct his music for the BBC, though there was also a 1938 London concert with an attempt to perform his String Trio, at which the cellist James Whitehead stopped, said 'I can't play this thing', and walked off the platform. Rubbra was very active as journalist and reviewer during those years, and little of it would have escaped his notice.

Despite the constant anti-climax over an eighth Sibelius symphony, Finland's national hero was very much in people's minds. Rubbra was a fairly new composer at the time, but followers of the English musical scene already regarded him as being in the mainstream of which Sibelius formed an essential part (Bruckner and Mahler being still thought obscure central-European aberrations), whereas the fascinating or rebarbative products of Herr Schönberg, Herr Berg and 'Herr von Webern' were on the outer rim and might or might not lead to anything; the consensus, then and for a long time after, was that they hadn't and wouldn't.

Rubbra's Third Symphony (Op. 49) was composed in 1938 and 1939; on 15 December 1940 Sir Malcolm Sargent conducted the Hallé Orchestra at its première in the Odeon Theatre, Manchester, a planned London première in September having had to be cancelled as the Blitz got under way. The Third carries a dedication, to Arthur Hutchings, a critic who had written about the Second Symphony in a 1939 issue of *Music and Letters*. His *Master Musicians* volume on a favourite composer of Rubbra's, Schubert, would appear in 1945.

This is the symphony Rubbra himself called 'more lyrical', in reaction to the Second; Gerald Finzi called it 'the most properly realised work that he has done so far … characteristic Rubbra in its hardness, its grinding, ruthless quality and superb technique'.[11] It is described in Saxton and Yardley's notes for the complete recordings as one of his two 'most classically modelled', along with the Seventh, and its first movement as 'nearer classical sonata form than any of his previous or subsequent symphonic works'. From start to finish it eddies between E major and C♯ minor and as recorded under Hickox it yet again lasts thirty-four minutes. In that context the opening movement, at nine minutes, is not of dominating proportions. Its opening is the brightest so far (6/4, Moderato), with a friendly theme whose oboe sonority and constantly moving pizzicato bass are particularly Sibelian (though one of Rubbra's favourite composers, Schubert, was also given to such placidly positive, 'walking' moods, and for him E major was a key often associated, especially in his early output, with brightness). This relatively complex opening is shown in some detail in Ex. 13, which in order to make it more legible is here written out with an E major key signature not actually in Rubbra's score, and in a rather skeletal form so that the salient ideas such as the answering figure at * stand out. That figure expands into something more aspiring, more of a theme in its own right (continuation from bar 8 onward). Though not specifically 'developed' in the course of the movement, merely surfacing again in the recapitulation later than one might have expected, it gives rise to other conjunct melodic figures heard as the music proceeds.

Ex. 13 Symphony no. 3, first movement: schematic presentation of opening

Since this movement offers the clearest manifestation of sonata form in Rubbra's symphonies to date, it is worth listing what each of its sections offers. In the quite concise exposition there is, first, that initial complex (Ex. 13) with its smooth oboe theme, 'walking' accompaniment, and singing cello line – they are nicely contrasted but certainly merit Rubbra's description, 'lyrical'. 'Development', however, begins straight away, the only really contrasted idea being the codetta figure (Ex. 14), like a mild 'Watch it!' echoed low down by the strings' 'I told you so!'; its pronounced upbeats will be a feature of much of the remaining movement, while the first three notes of its complete bar are fundamental to the entire symphony. This exposition shows an admirably clear-cut succession of concise ideas, and if one looks back to the rumpus at the start of the First Symphony or the stiff-lipped unison line in the Second, one sees Rubbra's point about reciprocal reaction among his first four symphonies.

Ex. 14 Symphony no. 3, first movement, bar 26

The 'development section', being twice as long and pretty eventful, is harder to sum up briefly. The lead into it is the 'I told you so!' figure; a peremptory call on the brass (2′00″) seems to bring a new idea, but in fact it has grown out of that middle line in Ex. 13, and it also turns to good account a dotted rhythm from the first subject, in a very different and more assertive mood. It was always the function of the development section to 'stir things up', and Rubbra the symphonist certainly does so here; his new symphony may be 'more lyrical', but, as he said, the form itself was dramatic, and it might have been more accurate to call it 'lyrical and mercurial'. The other main elements are another variant of the *cantabile* line, a little easier-going, which is dominant around 2′30″ and 5′00″, and another, even more commanding brass idea about three minutes in, which with its scoring for the entire brass choir could almost come from some Baroque ceremonial piece. At this point we meet something that was very important in Rubbra's eyes, a long series of drum-beats dominating the improvisatory second part of the section (they are first clearly noticeable around 3′30″).

He went so far as to say (in *BCI*) that a pattern of four short notes and three longer ones was the 'underlying rhythm' of the entire first movement – its basic form is shown in Ex. 15, though its two elements have already appeared in groups separated by other music. In Rubbra's mind they made up an entity, which would come to occupy the foreground with the main tune of the second movement, and already in this development section it is a reminder that such a group of quick repeated notes can easily become menacing.

Ex. 15 Symphony no. 3, first movement

As for the 'recapitulation', the processes of development proceed unabated. The opening returns at a higher level of intensity, as if the composer were testing whether his theme still worked under changed circumstances. This is very clearly the start of the, or a, recapitulation; Beethoven had done something of the sort, more drastic by far, at the start of the corresponding section in the first movement of the 'Choral' symphony, but the effect here is distinctly abrupt.

The first idea, once recapitulated, proves the merest marker amid a continuing flux of development, with almost every detail altered to sound more threatening, and changes to the order in which things occur. This recapitulation reduces the exposition's thirty-four bars to thirty, yet the further development of the main ideas leaves the impression that it has actually been longer. Mature sonata form could be a paradigm for the entirety of a life, and here it is as if Rubbra, having lived more since the exposition, has learned and found new things to say on subjects of continuing interest. Grover's account of this symphony quoted remarks from a book by two other American scholars, to do with the ideal difference between exposition and recapitulation:

> If, in the last chapter of a novel, the major characters appear exactly as they were in the first chapter, one would seriously question the meaning and the value, either to the characters or to the reader, of the cycle of experience to which they have been subjected in the course of the intervening pages. A literal recapitulation implies that nothing has really happened to alter one's perspective with respect to the original presentation.[12]

The great composers who left us hundreds of literal recapitulations might have raised an eyebrow at that, but times change, and for the twentieth century it was a cogent observation. Like 'repeats' in classical music, the difference in recapitulations must often be a matter rather for performers, who have been known to show a blissful disregard for such niceties.

Mature sonata form included a coda, originally brief but expanding in Beethoven's symphonies from the 'Eroica' onward to become a second development section. Rubbra's coda (a minute and a half of music, which is to say a sixth of the movement) brings a wonderful change of mood; despite its relative length it is no 'second development' but definitely a coda, literally a 'tail-piece'. The music falls into something one could well call melancholy, unfamiliar in so committed but positive a composer; the third movement will bring a cognate but far deeper mood, and a decade later, the first movement of the Cello Sonata will likewise end with a surprising admission of something that seems like a private grief. After quite a little unfamiliar music, the opening tune's final appearance rounds off the slower-tempo coda like a beautiful memory – a fine example of Rubbra's way of setting up the next movement.

The intermezzo-like piece that follows (Allegro, A♭ major, 6/8) is another classic case of Rubbra setting out cheerfully but soon darkening the mood. There is a legend that King George VI commiserated with the painter John

Piper on 'always getting such bad weather' for his pictures;[13] other things being equal, he might have said to Rubbra, 'What a shame the sun always seems to go in just as you're on your way' – to which the composer would either have smiled respectfully and replied 'It's the human condition, your Majesty', or declared, like Ralph Rackstraw in *H.M.S. Pinafore*, 'I am an Englishman!'

This movement's engaging main tune, with four upbeat repeated notes (Ex. 16), was what first made me suspect that Rubbra's symphonies might have something for me when I heard it as a boy, about the time the Second World War ended. At that age I was not up to noticing that its repeated notes had already dominated the first movement – for the all-pervading four-note upbeat and three ensuing longer notes look back, as Rubbra pointed out, to the preceding movement's 'underlying rhythm' (Exx. 16, 15). Nor, of course, did the grown man later remember what a formidable piece arises out of this amiable beginning. Given what has happened so far, the four-note rhythm here seems to be saying 'You see, I can be friendly too.' But the music soon loses its neutral quality, moving back within half a minute towards the unease found in much of the first movement. The initial tune never gives up, even in passages where the limelight is usurped by a contrasting melody (in fact an augmentation of one of its main figures, Ex. 17). Rubbra's easy way with counterpoint makes that feel simple and inevitable, but what he has to say is complex; he is torn between the ever-increasing unrest that took over the initially innocuous first movement, and a turning-in on himself that is a distant relative of Elgar's inimitably moving moments of introspection.

In this kind of middle movement one might expect a clearly demarcated middle section or 'trio', but here there is non-stop alternation between the main idea and its augmentation (Exx. 16, 17), with Ex. 16 constantly heckling even when it briefly has to give way. A more sustained line for the strings tries

Ex. 16 Symphony no. 3, second movement, schematic presentation of opening

Ex. 17 Symphony no. 3, second movement, bar 27 (fig. 21+1): augmentation of main idea

its luck a couple of times, but eventually the original layout and melody recur, marking the start of a second section, exactly as long as the first. Some landmarks are revisited and the end brings a series of augmentations very like the one that concluded the first half – and yet hardly more than a couple of bars are repeated literally. Rubbra's improvisatory skill and constructive intellect are equally to the fore, with character decided by a passage's function within the whole – and, bearing in mind where he is finally going, that makes it natural for the second half to be for the most part more sombre than the first. More than one seemingly endless background of drum-beats casts its shadow, which is all part of the movement's growth from 'intermezzo' into something a good deal more substantial. There is the danger in such a piece of leaving the listener feeling 'I've been here before, he's going on too long', and this could be one of the movements Grover had in mind when he commented (see p. 88), apropos the Fifth Symphony, that in earlier fast music the notes had not always done Rubbra's bidding: a composer may find his ideas leading him by the nose, and go a longer way round than necessary. But the constant new invention in the latter part of the movement largely circumvents the problem.

One of Rubbra's great obsessional pieces follows (Molto adagio ma liberamente, B minor, 3/4, no metronome marking). Here the work's 'more lyrical' nature is deep in the background, for this movement could well be described as tragic, or at least elegiac in the extreme, like the sinfonia to a Bach funeral cantata commissioned by the Almighty for some state occasion in the Hereafter. In 1939 many fair hopes finally had to be interred, at least 'for the duration' and perhaps, if all went ill, for ever. The movement opens with a ceaseless question-and-answer succession of three-note falling figures over a pedal. Like the finale of the first Symphony, this has the air of a cortège, an impression enhanced by the bareness of the accompaniment, with sustained chords and a throbbing repeated note in the bass, another of Rubbra's inescapable 'drums' though in fact played pizzicato by the double basses. One feels as if confronted by a mind asking itself the same troublesome question, time after time, and getting no further. The emotions behind the music seem far more intense than in the First Symphony, and to keep them in check Rubbra constructs the earlier part of the movement with strict formality, in eight-bar paragraphs (one or two of them isolated by an extra bar acting as a 'buffer'). Each is homogeneous and slightly different, taking at this tempo some forty seconds to play. The effect is rather that of a majestic dance over a repeated bass – a chaconne or passacaglia – but without the recurring pattern of harmonies those bring with them.

The second eight bars make a minimal alteration to the rhythm of the melodic line, and explore the key very cautiously. The third and fourth 'eights' offer an expressive line high up on the oboe and then the violins, and replace the throbbing bass notes with a counterpointing line. The falling figures briefly disappear, but are back for the fifth 'eight', a miniature *da capo* where they resume more or less their original form, with the deep 'drum-notes' also there again. The emotional continuity of all this is so striking that one is liable to overlook the structure.

It is possible after one more slightly extended 'entry', marked by a flowing pizzicato bass line, to make out the end of a first section and the presence of a new, contrasting and Elgarian tune in the major on the violins. The metre changes to 4/4. After a further eight bars the falling figures are back, but within the new four-time – the basic three-group adjusts to this by doubling the length of its final note, which seems to make it neither less nor more elegiac. Any slightly more ongoing quality is due to the quicker bass line. The strict eight-bar corset finally relaxes (5′ 30″), and the music slips back into the original three-time as it moves more freely towards a climax that it never really achieves. It fades away into a quiet final subsection looking back to that all-too brief Elgarian 4/4 interlude. The night is darkest before the dawn, which can now at least be sensed somewhere below the horizon in another move to the major (in fact D, which is simply one of the 'major versions' of the initial B minor). In this ending, as so often, Rubbra seems to ask himself 'What next?', with a transformation of the mood, this time from dark towards brighter; to hear the eminently 'minor-mode' opening figures recalled in the major is balm to the ear and a harbinger of better things to come. The reversion to 4/4 at this point is both for the sake of symmetry and, perhaps, because the theme of the ensuing variations will be in three, so that Rubbra wanted to avoid going on in the same time-signature.

There is truly light in the finale (E major, no tempo marking, initially $\quarternote = 76$, which would be around 'Andante'). It takes as the theme for variations an engaging, again slightly Elgarian melody to match the one in the preceding movement, and in keeping with the general 'domestic disagreement' that pervades this symphony it opens in E major and ends on that key's 'relative minor', C♯, though in the major mode. The tune seems to grow naturally out of the major-mode tunes that lightened the preceding darkness. Rubbra's handling of variation form here is unusual, with a curious alternation between 'manifest variations' increasing steadily in length, and brief interpolations so different as to feel more like the episodes in a rondo. The industrious analyst could dig out derivations, but the feeling is amazingly other, and this symphony's mercurial nature here becomes intrinsic to the very structure of one of its movements. It is emphasised by the instruction in the score, 'There should be the least possible break between the variations.' What becomes apparent on repeated hearing is that the composer seems to be going through very much the succession of moods that marked the opening minutes of his symphony; the variations are like a synthesis after the first movement's thesis and antithesis. Rubbra reused the 'variation/episode' pattern twenty-two years later in his *Variations on a Phrygian Theme* for solo violin, Op. 105 (1961), about which Grover commented that the odd men out (there not alternating but making up nos. 5, 7–10 and 12 of twelve) 'maintain very tenuous connections with the theme'. Rubbra did, however, make it clear in the Third Symphony that the more tenuously connected sections, too, count as variations; he marked them as that, and his subtitle for the movement was 'Tema con 7 Variazioni e una Fuga'; however many ways he was pulled as he wrote it, he remained in charge.

The variations take us through a variety of tempi, the initial ♩ = 76 recurring for the first two 'true' variations, i.e. nos. 2 and 4. No. 2 already takes us back towards the elegiac, transforming and developing the quietly confident melody. This variation is a great deal longer than the theme it varies, and a background of slow drum-beats emphasises the drastic change in mood after the unruly Variation 1. The contrasting odd-numbered variations are progressively more colourful, with the second of them (Variation 3) distinctly lively ('Presto leggiero'). As an engaging and Schubertian detail, the note (B♭) at the end of the main phrase is harmonised in three different ways as the variation proceeds. Variation 4 turns the theme upside down, which could just possibly be an echo of Max Reger's *Variations on a Theme of Mozart*, where the composer inverts the melody of the first movement of the A major Piano Sonata, making it sound a shade gawky in the process. The inverted theme is followed a beat later by the bass moving in canon, which is the kind of thing Brahms liked to do, notably in the set of piano variations Rubbra orchestrated around that time. Both the Fourth Symphony and the Brahms end with fugues.

The mood initially takes up the sombre one from the end of the second variation, but a note of serenity creeps in as it proceeds. The third anti-variation, No. 5, takes up the briskness from the end of its odd-numbered predecessor, with another of Rubbra's pedal-notes tapping away in the bass. Here the ending is hardly an ending, for he goes straight on into a further anti-variation (6), with horn interjections in 5/8 tempo which Grover found 'positively abrupt'.

Variation 7 clearly reverts to the theme, but at a much slower tempo. The practice of preceding the finale with an expressive slow variation went back to countless classical examples, and here a twilit calm descends. But lest we feel it's safe to go back in the water or emerge from the air-raid shelter, the music then breaks into a resolute and sizeable fugue, the movement's longest single section by a long way. (This pattern, variations followed by a concluding fugue, would reappear in the immediately post-war Cello Sonata, though the fugue there is deeply reflective rather than vital and determined like the one in this symphony.) The fugue subject, while seemingly quite unlike the theme, does incorporate one of its most important ideas, the interval of the descending fifth. At the end Rubbra superimposes on the already complex texture a resounding statement of his variation theme, very much as Reger had done in his sets of orchestral variations on themes by J. A. Hiller and Mozart. The finale's variations, in addition to their range of speeds, have moved through the keys, from the initial E major/C♯ to A minor, D minor, G major, B♭ major, F♯ minor, E minor and major, and, at the opening of the final fugue, F♯ minor. The ending is in C♯ major, though as in the preceding symphony the effect is rather, and merely, that of a *tierce de Picardie*. As in the variation theme, C♯ minor prevails over E in the 'marital conflict in the house of four sharps', but with a compromise (so necessary if such conflicts are to be survived) – the major mode is taken up by that final C♯ chord.

The Fourth Symphony (Op. 53) was composed in 1940 and orchestrated whenever army service left Rubbra time and leisure before its première with the BBC Symphony Orchestra at the 1942 Promenade Concerts. (The season had by then, of necessity, been moved to the Royal Albert Hall.) The army rather reluctantly granted Rubbra leave to conduct, on condition that he appear in his sergeant's uniform. (The orchestra had, after all, recently worked under Toscanini.) Three conductors shared the programme, whose first half alone was as long as most present-day concerts. Friday was by hallowed tradition Beethoven Night, on this occasion with the *Coriolan* Overture, Fourth Piano Concerto (the soloist being Irene Scharrer) and 'Pastoral' Symphony conducted by Sir Henry Wood. After Rubbra conducted his symphony Sir

Adrian Boult rounded off the programme with 'Mercury', 'Saturn' and 'Jupiter' from Holst's *The Planets*. The concert began at six in the evening, and a stoical note at the bottom of the programme page told the audience that in the event of an air raid warning they would be informed immediately so that those who wished to take shelter, either in the hall or in shelters outside, might do so. 'The concert will then continue' – what a way to go.

For the first time in Rubbra's symphonic output, the new work came out under half an hour, almost half of its twenty-seven minutes being taken up by the first movement, another enormous, obsessively monothematic piece to match the slow movement of the Third Symphony. The feeling, at least at the start, is less 'down', given the major mode and the greater length of the basic melodic idea. Where the earlier piece moved like a group under spiritual instruction walking carefully down the middle of the road with eyes downcast, in this one they are at least free to take bigger steps and look around them – and Rubbra wrote that the work's 'long harmonic paragraphs open out like a landscape', so there is something worth looking at.

Rubbra stressed that in this work, the one he called 'more chordal', he finally decided to defy Holst's injunction about never using the dominant seventh:[14] he opened up with it, and 'used it very, very often. After twenty years of suppression it came out in a rash!' ('A Symphonic Credo'). (The numerous comments by Rubbra on his Sixth Symphony, to be found in Chapter 6, come from the same lecture.) Sober scrutiny of the Fourth Symphony's fifty-two predecessors could leave one with the impression that Holst was already pretty firmly shaken off, but over this particular chord Rubbra evidently had to bide his time.

The dominant seventh's traditional function is to lead into a tonic chord, so that to open a work with it, rather than the tonic chord itself, is to create the immediate expectation of a change of key, indeed one toward the (more submissive) flat side. What by virtue of its 'first-up' position should be a firm statement of intent becomes at once a concession of weakness or sign of doubt, suggesting an impending move to the subdominant before there is time even to establish a tonic. Examples are rare in classical music, the most famous being the dominant seventh at the opening of Beethoven's First Symphony; another comes (rather curiously in a work supposed to celebrate the start of a lifelong partnership!) in Bach's wedding cantata *O holder Tag*, BWV 208. Rubbra's in the Fourth Symphony does the same, still more drastically since where Bach and Beethoven had at least used the chord in its most recognisable layout, with the tonic as the lowest note ('root position') Rubbra makes his bass note the contentious seventh ('third inversion', Ex. 18), rendering the chord that much less stable still. It should be observed that the 'dominant seventh' is really only that if used to lead, as its title implies, from the dominant to a tonic or at least to a cadence, whether perfect, i.e. resolving in the expected way onto the tonic, or interrupted.[15] When Holst advised Rubbra not to use it, he may really have been saying 'avoid perfect cadences, we're into the age of modal harmony' (which tended, unlike the perfect cadence, not to sharpen the third in the penultimate chord). It was the time when the old church modes had been resurrected as a sign of English independence from the traditional chromatic harmony developed and refined in German music during the nineteenth century. The perfect cadence was something Rubbra knew all about; in 1962 he edited for its republication an Italian book by another formidable composer-pianist, Alfredo Casella,[16] *The Evolution of Music throughout the History of the Perfect Cadence*. His already-quoted remarks about a different basis for the British Symphony show which way the wind was blowing, and he eventually had to take his own line over something as basic as the dominant seventh.

Wilfrid Mellers' analysis of the Fourth Symphony in *The Music Review* the year after the première brilliantly analysed the nature of Rubbra's use of that chord, referring to 'the subtlety and serenity of spirit which it plays its part in incarnating (a serenity so rare in the music of today and so increasingly valuable)'. Mellers evidently had a hot-line to Rubbra, for a passage in his article, dealt with in more detail apropos the Fifth, shows that he had already seen some of the sketches for a further symphony.

The Fourth's opening dominant seventh leads nowhere, and its successors only rarely lead to a perfect or even an interrupted cadence: they are simply one touch of harmonic colour among many, along the lines of a chord with an identical structure (major third plus minor third plus minor third) which when not fulfilling a cadential function is called the German Sixth.[17]

So much – too much perhaps – for the symphony's first chord. In such single-minded music the danger of monotony is played off against the rhetoric inherent in constant repetition. (Similar effects are found in other composers, for example in the first of Dvořak's *Four Romantic Pieces*, Op. 75, for violin and piano, and in much Schumann.) With Rubbra such dialectic will reach its climax in the passacaglia finale of the Seventh Symphony. The Fourth's opening (Con moto, 4/4, G major) has in common with the slow movement of the preceding symphony falling figures, one harmony to (in this case) each pair of bars, and a throbbing accompaniment, this time through the chords that go with the melodic idea rather than as a drumming bass (Ex. 18). Accompaniments are again particularly persistent, the same rhythm coming time after time under lapidary statements of one version after another of the opening melodic cell. After all of two minutes, the melody doubles its rate of strike, with a new and more rhythmically profiled figure to each bar (Ex. 19), the accompaniment for the moment going on as it was. After a further minute of setting itself up, the music is ready to embark on its journey. (The feeling is not unlike that at the start of the finale.) From here on Rubbra improvises one variant after another of his two basic ideas, and explores a range of moods. Although he is, as ever, 'feeling his way', he does it with such sureness of touch and sense of direction that the process is totally fascinating.

Ex. 18 Symphony no. 4, first movement

Ex. 19 Symphony no. 4, first movement, bar 27

Ex. 20 is a literal repetition of Ex. 19, entering in the bass as a counterpoint, but at twice the original speed and with aggressive dynamic and articulation markings it makes a surprisingly new impression. It is soon taken up by the higher instruments, just before the pulsing drums so often found in Rubbra begin to push towards a climax. Ex. 21 shows yet another variant, heard soon afterwards with the music going briefly into 6/8 and flowing more. But soon we are in 2/4, with yet another 'new' idea, Ex. 22, which is again a derivative, in this case from the accompanimental rhythm at the opening. (One may detect here an echo of a very popular Sibelius work, his Fifth Symphony.) In this closing stage of the middle section, where the brass instruments run riot with ever quicker versions of Ex. 22, something has to keep things on an even keel, and the bass line does so with a running scale that appears no fewer than twenty times, at different lengths and starting and ending on different notes. Here is another harbinger of the finale.

Ex. 20 Symphony no. 4, first movement, bar 61

Ex. 21 Symphony no. 4, first movement, bar 77

Ex. 22 Symphony no. 4, first movement, bars 84–5

Eventually the opening is ready to return as a fairly literal repeat, with both Ex. 18 and Ex. 19. Just as it was technically possible to talk earlier of a 'development' section, so the mood of retrospection and perhaps regret could make this feel more like a coda than a recapitulation, however monothematic the entire piece; but, as Saxton aptly observes, the symphony as a whole is 'a fine example of the composer's absorption in the process of forming, as opposed to a conception of form as a pre-existent mould'. Here the form is obstinate enough to end where it started – something that will recur in the eminently mysterious 'Teilhard de Chardin' symphony (No. 8). The final major chord, coming from the submediant (the chord of B♭) in what counts as a 'plagal cadence', is clearly just a pointer to whatever comes next.

'What comes next' in fact picks up that submediant, in a transition that is aurally less than obvious; the major mode of the submediant chord is replaced by minor, and bearing in mind the tonic chord that intervenes, the succession of harmonies is quite hard for the ear to make sense of.[18] Here again Rubbra shows that, whatever his predilection for counterpoint, he is a master of the things harmony can do to enlighten or confuse.

Mellers called the second movement (Intermezzo, Allegretto grazioso, 3/4, B♭ minor) 'an idyllic marriage of the principles of voice and dance'. Rubbra, as ever prosaic and averse to 'fine writing', spoke of it as 'a five-minute piece sandwiched between two fifteen-minute pieces' [he regarded the third and fourth movements, which are played continuously, as a single entity], 'designed to give mental relief and refreshment between movements full of tension'. A recording of the 1942 première shows him endowing it with some of the urgency he brought to the entire work; there was much to be said for getting through things as briskly as art permitted – had not the Queen's Hall, home of the Proms, already gone the way of all too much other bricks and mortar in the age of aerial bombardment? And if Richard Strauss could indulge in impossible accelerandos merely to get to his skat game sooner, what might a composer under threat of high explosive do, knowingly or unwittingly?[19] The 'five minutes' mentioned in Rubbra's broadcast introduction (see Appendix 1) shrank to little more than three, and it would have made a distinctly brisk waltz. A more docile side can be brought out at a more leisurely tempo; such lyrical music needs, above all, time to breathe, though not at the risk of having a bomb dropped on one.

At the Prom the outer movements, too, came out shorter than Rubbra had led his audience to expect, but that must have been more of a mental miscalculation all along; in no subsequent recording of the symphony does either outer movement last as long as fifteen minutes. The recording of the première shows, however, that circumstances in August 1942 brought out in the work a stature and intensity less evident from either of the commercial recordings produced over the ensuing slightly more peaceable half century. When 'revived' for Rubbra's centenary under Richard Hickox at the 2001 Proms (a matter of weeks before the watershed now referred to as '9/11'), the work was coolly reviewed. No performance has everything! Rubbra later wrote that the only 'ideal' one had been given by a little-known West Country conductor, Reginald Redman, who was in charge of the BBC West of England Light Orchestra during the 1940s and 50s.

In his new key Rubbra spins a graceful triple-time theme (Ex. 23) that could at first hearing be by Brahms or some talented disciple such as Heinrich von Herzogenberg. In particular, Brahms' Second Symphony may spring to mind; apart from the Rubbra Fourth's nearness in time to the Brahms-Handel orchestration, Brahms 2 had been the companion piece in the concert with the

Ex. 23 Symphony no. 4, second movement: basic four-bar idea

première of Rubbra 3. Curiously, one very short passage – bars 21–4 – changes harmonies in such a way as to sound like a composer for whom Brahms had very little use, Bruckner! The movement begins and ends in different keys – 'progressive tonality' again, and all part and parcel of the composer's constant sense of being under way, with a movement no longer a self-sufficient entity but part of a larger plan[20] that permits or even demands a Janus face. In other ways, too, the movement is less simple than it might appear. Built mostly out of four-bar phrases, it has a spell in the middle where they are replaced by units of three bars (Ex. 24); for a while the two vie amiably for first place, the four-bar pattern eventually reasserting itself. Rubbra's way of working with repeated, self-echoing single bars is from here on an inevitable reminder of the work's debt to Sibelius. In the course of this movement's few minutes the mood darkens a little, but its final few bars suddenly look inward with a memorably Elgarian serenity. The next movement is now 'set up', or it seems so, for what actually ensues is anything but serene.

Ex. 24 Symphony no. 4, second movement: three-bar continuation at bar 51 (fig. 22+1)

The remainder of the symphony moves gradually from A minor to E major; it balances the enormous opening disquisition, though here the time is split between a section which despite its making up almost half of the ten-minute movement Rubbra justifiably calls an Introduction (Grave e molto calmo, 4/4), and an Allegro maestoso (still beginning in A minor, 2/2). The Introduction is as 'grave' as the tempo marking suggests. At this point a reference to 'pervasive intervals' is unavoidable. (At least there are a lot of them so they are that much less pervasive!) The start (Ex. 25) is dominated by sixths which mostly rise, preceded and followed by the narrowest interval, a second – at the start there is a semitone (*) and after the sixth a whole tone (***), but this will vary as the melody's logic dictates. There is aspiration about the relatively wide interval of the rising sixth, but the implications can be anything from supreme confidence (not the case here!) to supplication (which seems nearer the mark). A brief, more consolatory section in a different metre (6/4) soon gives way, three minutes in, to a striking reference back to the work's very opening; the introduction's initial theme returns, of course in a rhythmically tightened-up form, now accompanied by much the rhythms that marked the accompaniment as the symphony began. They were then almost more dominant than the very broken-up melody they were supposed to 'accompany', so their return has a strong emotional impact. All in all, the Introduction is a cumulative section, a mighty paragraph working up to and dying away from a climax in a way that makes it both impressive in its own right and a challenge to the imagination: yet again, 'Where next?'

Ex. 25 Symphony no. 4, third movement

The answer comes as a strong contrast to all the elegiac music in the symphonies so far: the finale, completed as the full weight of war began to bear down on Rubbra's native land, is by some distance the most unbrokenly diatonic music found in them, with a hint of a different side of Elgar, a feeling of resolve suggesting determination to see things through. It's by no means a matter of 'Might is Right', rather of 'Right is Might': good is to prevail in the end, simply because it is good. A patriotic Soviet composer could have done it no better and would almost certainly have done it worse, because under political pressure and far more self-consciously. Shostakovich's Seventh Symphony, written at exactly the same time, reflected the drama of the siege of Leningrad in a way crude enough to get itself parodied by Bartók in the 'Intermezzo Interrotto' of his Concerto for Orchestra; Rubbra's Fourth lends itself to no such travesty. Finzi described Rubbra around the time of this symphony's composition as 'a ruthless spirit in an ageless body'.[21] One would gladly nickname the work 'The Alamein', were it not that the pivotal battle didn't take place until three months after the symphony's première. To that extent it is prophetic. It is in this symphony that Rubbra comes closest to the pattern found in

Shostakovich, with a long-drawn-out, at-first-hearing monotonous first movement making no concessions to a listener's wish for immediate contrast, and
a determined, vigorous finale. The resemblance, despite Rubbra's admiration
for the Soviet composer, does not extend to the kind of bitingly brutal scherzo
found in Shostakovich. An additional virtue of Rubbra's symphony is the concise way in which the whole thing is done.

The main theme (Ex. 26) opens up with the 'structural' fifth (*). Mellers
commented on its diversity, calling it

> one of the most remarkable and distinguished he has created. It has a
> bold, heroic quality in its enormous sweep and rhythmic vitality and
> freedom, while at the same time its subtly plastic tonal feeling, shift-
> ing between Aeolian, Phrygian, major and minor 3rds [Ex. 26^ and
> ^^ respectively], and occasional pungent tritones [Ex. 26**], seems to
> imbue its lyricism with an emotion deeply melancholy.

Ex. 26 Symphony no. 4, fourth movement

The enormous opening paragraph or chapter is underlaid by the most
extended of all Rubbra's ostinatos, a descending scale down from the dominant, E, to its lower octave, and, as the paragraph runs without hesitation to
sixty-two bars, the scale is repeated no fewer than thirty-one times. As with
any good backbone, its form changes halfway through; there is a turn from
minor to major, underpinning the E major towards which the music is tending.
One could expect any such repeated scale eventually to go still lower, and this
one finally does, first to E♭ and then to D, where it acts as the lowest note of
the very same dominant seventh chord on which the entire symphony started.
This must be either largest-scale planning or the special providence that looks
after sleepwalkers. Knowing Rubbra as we do by now, we may find it not too
difficult to have an opinion.

That initiates the climactic passage for the first part of the movement. Here a refinement on the frequently found Rubbra drum-beats, which were already noticeable in the Introduction, is that they change to a pattern of three upbeats and a longer final note, which could reflect the morse-code 'V for Victory' rhythm the Allies appropriated from the German Beethoven's Fifth Symphony to assert their belief that they would finally win. One might in the light of this, and notwithstanding Mellers' 'deeply melancholy emotion', describe the striding, assertive main subject as Churchillian.

A brief slower middle section applies the brakes, suggesting a reversion to the first movement's private and anguished thoughts, with a most expressive flute solo as reminder of a memorable variation in the passacaglia finale of Brahms's Fourth Symphony. When the first theme reappears, the sense of transfiguration is all the stronger. A final four-square melody ('Meno mosso, Trionfale') could be out of Elgar or Holst, recalling the celebrated or notorious ones at the heart of the third 'Pomp and Circumstance' March and 'Jupiter', which to the composers' dismay lent themselves to adaptation as patriotic hymns. Rubbra's tune has been spared that, calling less attention to itself because, true to the habits of a lifetime, he makes it just one of two heard simultaneously. All the same the ending, despite his general disclaimer, could seem some kind of political statement, and were that hunch correct, such music would suitably round off the entire first period in the productive career of a man who began life as anything but a serene, abstracted figure, whatever he later became.

Technical aspects apart, one sense in which the first four symphonies (as Rubbra himself said, meaning something else) 'refer one to another' is that the road from the near-panic at the start of the First to the resolve at the end of the Fourth is long and winding. It covers, perhaps, the 'seven lean years' of which Pharaoh dreamed, and the journey along it was something the composer can have seen clearly only once it lay safely behind him. Saxton's comment about the ending of the Fourth Symphony, that 'the journey to light and triumph has been far from straightforward', is a formulation applicable by extension to this whole first part of Rubbra's career. Indeed, light (not to mention 'that impostor triumph') was yet to be attained, as it would be, intermittently, in the symphonies from No. 5 onward. And in No. 4 in particular the change in mood from one end of the work to the other might be taken as among other things a sign of Rubbra's full emergence from private to public figure, as of his realisation that for the duration, as we used to say, quietist pacifism must concede centre-stage to a stiffening of the sinews and a summoning-up of the blood. No one, and least of all a major composer, spends or should spend his whole time dwelling on politics, but part of Rubbra's maturing process over the first four symphonies was a procession from 'the apprehension of war' to the knowledge that 'Now it's here we'd better win it, for God help us otherwise.'

Having set out as a fine pianist whose songs and chamber music often used the instrument as accompaniment (however imaginative) to a dominant line, Rubbra needed the true interplay of equal and independent parts to free him and show him at his best. Graduation to symphonic composing posed a supreme challenge to his use of counterpoint as prime agent in musical coherence. Chamber music could be an intermediate stage (just as Schubert had hoped that what we now regard as truly great works of chamber music would 'pave the way to a grand symphony') but in fact there is very little musical overlap between the Second Violin Sonata or First String Quartet and anything in the symphonies. Rubbra's four string quartets, unlike the great Schubert works just mentioned, were spread evenly over widely distant stages in a long career. His 'early' symphonies do nonetheless show the way as well and truly 'paved'; all his preparatory work culminated in memorable symphonic music, which would be surpassed only when he returned to the genre after the war.

CHAPTER 4

The Fifth Symphony

Before good could prevail, the war had to be survived and won. For a while, Rubbra's pacifism kept him doing 'war work'; once recruited, then promoted from private to sergeant, he ran the Army Classical Chamber Music Group, in particular a piano trio with the violinist Joshua Glazier (who had so far served as a driver) and as cellist Signalman William Pleeth. Like many other families at that time, his two sons born in the 1930s saw very little of him for several years. The trio's tours to the forces took it as far as Germany around the time the war ended. It continued after the war, with Glazier replaced briefly by Norbert Brainin just before the start of the latter's career as leader of the Amadeus String Quartet, and then over a much longer period by another Viennese-born violinist, Erich Gruenberg.

Writing his article on the Fourth Symphony, Wilfrid Mellers evidently had a good line to Rubbra. He mentioned a forthcoming further symphony in which that work's 'subtlety and serenity of spirit' were 'certainly explored further in the marvellous opening' of a piece 'in which the voice (a mainspring of texture in music) may explicitly come into its own, for Rubbra tells me that the symphony will probably be choral, with words by Henry Vaughan'. The sketches were eventually turned into a work for mixed chorus and orchestra in which Rubbra dared to upstage his teacher Holst by setting the ecstatically mystical Vaughan text *The Morning Watch*. Unusually, he found Holst's setting inadequate – according to his pupil Gary Higginson, 'One day he played over Holst's "Morning Watch" with me. He kept shaking his head and murmuring "Oh dear – rather weak", or "Where is the movement?" or "Not one of his best pieces".'[1] He said on one of the Grover tapes that

> In 1941 my Fourth Symphony was already finished, although not fully scored, and projects had been made for a fifth (choral) symphony. Preliminary sketches were actually noted down in 1942, but army life proved not to be the ideal milieu for symphonic thinking ... In 1946 I was free to take up the abandoned threads, but my enthusiasm for a choral symphony had waned ...

It took thirty years to wax again, but then produced a work Rubbra considered his finest, the *Sinfonia Sacra*.

He sketched a few other things for the future, and with difficulty secured leave to go and conduct the Promenade Concert première of the Fourth Symphony.[2] During 1942 he succeeded in completing a short orchestral *Introduzione e danza alla fuga*, one of a set of pieces by a trio of composers in celebration of Vaughan Williams's seventieth birthday. The others were Constant Lambert's *Aubade*, and Patrick Hadley's *One Morning in Spring*, and their first performance was in a BBC broadcast conducted by Clarence Raybould on 12 October 1942. Unlike Bach's 'Jig Fugue', BWV 577, the 'dance in fugal style' is in no sense a fugue, which led Grover to surmise that Rubbra at some point revised the work. It then acquired the less cumbersome title *A Tribute*. Its slow first part shows his mind still in the vein of the Fourth Symphony's opening, while the engagingly gawky dance must seem fitting to anyone old enough to remember the druidic figure cut by the elderly RVW!

A similar pattern is found in the long orchestral opening of *The Morning Watch*, though there is a great deal more subtlety as the music turns into a dance to match the text's first image of the soul 'breaking and budding' with 'flowers and shoots of glory'. The continuity of thought from the Fourth Symphony (Op. 53) to *The Morning Watch* (Op. 55) and *A Tribute* (Op. 56) is striking, with none of Rubbra's typical reaction against a new work's predecessor. On the other hand, the master of the convincing ending is much more abrupt in one or two works written with his mind 'elsewhere', such as *A Tribute* and *The Morning Watch* with their background of war service, or the *Ode to the Queen*, whose composition was complicated by a simultaneous commission from Aldeburgh so that deadlines came into it (see comment on the Seventh Symphony). They simply leave off.

After a transition suggesting that he had been absorbing the rapt counterpoint in Beethoven's late string quartets and *Missa Solemnis*, the second half of *The Morning Watch* ('Prayer is the world in tune ... O let me climb/When I lie down!') unfolds with the massive nobility and resonance of works in the Three Choirs Festival tradition going back to Parry and Elgar; here is music fit to roll around the great cathedral spaces of Gloucester, Hereford or Worcester – though the work's final form came about in response to a commission from the Musicians' Benevolent Fund for a newly founded St Cecilia Festival, which endures to this day. When Boult first conducted it on 22 November 1946 he used two orchestras. It is an altogether mighty piece, quite unlike Holst's modest but touching setting, and one wonders whether Rubbra had to be quite so hard on his old teacher!

There was also his first work written with Pleeth in mind, *Soliloquy* (Op. 57, 1943–4) for cello and orchestra (originally string quartet). Another piece commissioned while he was still in the army, and completed around the time the war ended, was a Mass for the Anglican Canterbury Cathedral, the *Missa cantuarensis* (Op. 59). For a while Rubbra was stationed near Canterbury, finding time to work on the Mass at the Cathedral Choir School.

His demobilisation papers came through just as the trio had played for the Forces occupying the British sector of Berlin, and his first move involved a visit to Northampton to collect the 'demob suit' that was the perquisite of all newly discharged servicemen. On the train afterwards, bound for Speen, family and cottage a musical idea (so far unidentified) occurred to him, which soon gave rise to a Cello Sonata (in G minor, Op. 60). The sonata was written very quickly; as a veteran, if not of armoured battles then certainly of many a breathless retreat endured as military audiences found themselves threatened with 'a piano trio by Haydn' rather than 'The White Cliffs of Dover', Rubbra must have rejoiced in his new-found freedom, not to mention the sheer fact of still being alive and in a world where pianos, even if brought in from outside, tended to arrive complete with their legs. (His reminiscences in *ERC* contain amusing stories of vicissitudes with wartime instruments!)[3] Hugh Ottaway called the Cello Sonata 'one of the finest ... by an English composer', high and justified praise placing it on a par with the superb ones by Frank Bridge and John Ireland. William Pleeth was its first performer, with Rubbra at the piano.

The sonata was followed by a set of *Three Psalms* (Op. 61) for low voice and piano, written with the new star among British singers, Kathleen Ferrier, in mind. He wrote for her voice again in the *Ode to the Queen*, though by the time of its performance she was too ill to take part; she died a few months after the Coronation, in October 1953, and the soloist at the first performance was Anne Wood. Rubbra's thoughts were, however, soon back with the challenges of symphonic composition. Musically speaking, the Fifth and Sixth symphonies (1947–54) take us into Joseph's 'seven fat years'. In his economics and Pharaoh's, those came first, as the time for stockpiling grain to get Egypt through the years of famine predicted by the 'lean kine' of the royal dream; in the economics of spiritual growth, hardship and trials come first so that when good times arrive the soul has knowledge out of which to grow and deepen.

During the immediately post-war years three crucial things happened in Rubbra's life. In 1948 he moved from nonconformism to ultra-High Church with his conversion to Roman Catholicism. It was Antoinette's religion, yet the 1950s saw their marriage crumble; they finally separated in 1957. And soon after the end of the war J. A. Westrup, Rubbra's former editor at the *Monthly Musical Record*, became Heather Professor of Music at Oxford; he instituted an honours music course and lost no time in inviting Rubbra to become a lecturer, though Rubbra took his time accepting. His students (who between 1950 and 1953 included myself) benefited from, among other things, his deep reflection on Bach's '48'. We young fresh folk were tickled that he could sometimes spend a full hour without getting beyond the third bar, but the few notes I made show how close his mind came to the inner logic of one of the greatest composers (see also p. 193).[4]

One important development just after the war was that Rubbra finally found a publisher with whom he would stay for the rest of his life. Maurice Jacobson, by then running the publisher Curwen, introduced him to Bernard de Nevers of the firm of Lengnick. Order gradually returned to his published works. Virtually all those assigned to Universal had during the war been administered for the English-speaking territories by Boosey & Hawkes and were now reassigned to Lengnick; the Second Symphony, whose score had not been engraved, was published as a miniature score based on a full score prepared for performances, while No. 4 still had to wait some time before it, too, was finally engraved. The one work to remain with Boosey & Hawkes, before Dr Kalmus's return from there to Universal Edition, was the money-spinner, the Brahms-Handel orchestration.

Discussing music composed around 1950, one needs to recapture a time when Strauss and Pfitzner were still alive and composing, or only recently deceased, Bruckner and Mahler intimidating and largely unknown figures, and the mind-set of Schönberg and his disciples the province of a tiny minority of mostly immigrant musicians. In 1933 Rubbra's *Monthly Musical Record* article on Debussy described Schönberg as 'ploughing a lonely furrow. A few disciples he has who are bent upon taking his theories to their logical conclusion, but the resulting music is not very satisfactory, to judge by what one has heard of Webern and Berg'. In the late 1940s, when a radical inter-war figure such as Hindemith was in retreat from his more exuberant ideas, the productive British time-lag (see p. 10) still applied, with *Peter Grimes* the new sensation and Racine Fricker going in to bat for Europe. Schönberg's famous remark 'There is still a lot of good music to be written in C major' could scarcely apply more precisely than it does to Rubbra, who within a few years of Schönberg's death made it come literally true at the end of his Sixth and Seventh symphonies.

1947 saw the start of work on another symphony, which he completed the following year. Rubbra's Opus 63, it was first performed a further year later by the the same combination of forces that had a decade earlier played and conducted the premières of the first two – the BBC Symphony Orchestra and

Sir Adrian Boult, as he now was. Rubbra was thankful for the break that had kept him away from symphonic composition, saying in his reminiscences for Grover

> It was not until 1947 that I was able to turn my thoughts to a new, purely orchestral, symphony. This gap of six years had enormous importance in determining the form and content of No. 5 ... It was sufficient to obliterate the previous symphonic period, and when at last I came to grips with No. 5 I did so with no sense of reference to the other four.

Any 'reference' in the new work was rather 'to the chamber music written in the interim' (which could only mean the Cello Sonata). In 'A Symphonic Credo' he said his necessary concentration on chamber and choral music during the wartime and immediately post-war years had its influence on the Fifth, felt in its 'greater transparency' stemming from his stricter adherence to the rule that 'at any one moment there should be not more than *one* predominating line'. A commentator is obviously tempted to find reflected in this music the post-war sense of release from danger and of freedom to act, so it is sobering to find Rubbra putting his finger on a purely technical consideration that helped him attain a new level.

In those 'other four' symphonies there was any amount of music to respect and warm to, but after hearing a great performance of the Fifth's opening movement, such as the one recorded by the Hallé Orchestra under Barbirolli as early as 1950 and still available from time to time, the listener may be more inclined simply to get his breath back, then say 'Masterpiece!' A new world is apparent. This is yet another nine-minute movement, but the speed at which it develops and therefore the amount that can happen are something new. Until now, the 'breath of a symphonist' saw Rubbra safely through long cross-country runs in which the distance counted for as much as the competition or the scenery; now he adds the breath of a great middle-distance runner dictating the course of a race with unfailing tactical flair and even finding time to look around. Grover summed up the new quality perceptively, writing of a new 'control the composer has imposed on his material; it does his bidding.[5] This has not always been the case in the fast movements of some of his earlier symphonies.'

Features of the earlier works are still present, but there is no longer an opening for the composer's worst enemy to say that (like Shostakovich at times) 'He does go on a bit!' 'Go on' is the crucial phrase, thanks to a new suppleness of invention and Rubbra's miraculous ability to take one instantly elsewhere.

Much about the first four symphonies might be thought leaden-footed in comparison, but that would miss the point, for they were of their time – Rubbra's time and the world's. The expectation and experience of war safely behind him, the ultra-sensitive creator has shed his army boots and is free to dance, the stronger for having trained all those years with them on.

The Fifth Symphony dates from around the time of Rubbra's conversion to Roman Catholicism, and he summed up its form in a term associated with religious art, 'triptych':

> the three 'panels' … are as follows:
>> Adagio – Allegro energico: Allegro moderato
>> Grave – Allegro vivo.
> From this it will be seen that the first movement, with its long *Adagio* introduction, exactly balances the final two movements (for these are played without a real break), the middle movement (a scherzo) affording the necessary bright relief.

Rubbra's faith, manifest in a wealth of liturgical music and implicit in much of his secular output, did not influence the actual construction of his compositions, as would that of a fellow-Catholic, Anthony Milner, in a 1958 set of orchestral variations modelled in great detail on the Mysteries of the Rosary, whose division into three groups of five – Joyful, Sorrowful, Glorious – offered an obvious hint of a three-section form. But then almost every work-title in the earlier part of Milner's career bespeaks the importance of his faith; Rubbra wore his less close to his sleeve when composing.

The Fifth Symphony's first 'panel', described by the composer as 'in B♭ major', begins in E♭ minor (Adagio, 4/4), but since B♭ minor dominates the first movement and the work ends in B♭ major this is not one of Rubbra's progressive-tonality pieces; it is merely that a tonality is quite slow to establish itself. Rubbra 'saw' its opening in a bus queue (see p. 109) – 'a brass texture, then a chain of descending fifths in the horns, all held together by a pedal until they became a dominant ninth' (*BCI*). Said 'brass texture' is in fact a good old Sibelian snarl! – but of the 'chain of descending fifths in the horns' there is now no trace; over the first two bars they hold (in octaves) a note that goes on to become the ninth of the (dominant) harmony, then descends a mere semitone to match what is going on below. The first two minutes of 'long Adagio introduction' offer the first fully formed example in Rubbra's symphonies of a pattern hinted at in the *Sinfonia Concertante* and the opening movement of the Second. It will recur in all the remaining ones save the *Sinfonia Sacra*.

The slow, mysterious opening with its low brass is for the moment ambiguous as to mode (minor? major?). Clear-cut brief snatches of melody (in the minor) on the first oboe are soon taken up by the high violins in a major-mode line whose flowering brings, so early in the work, one of its great moments. Ex. 27 gives an outline of all this, breaking off as the low instruments introduce a scale that will return to wondrous effect later on. Rubbra described his first idea as the work's 'motivating figure' and commented that its return at the end was part and parcel of the triptych's formal balance. What is hard to describe is that, as ever, his mind works contrapuntally, producing a weave like that in older liturgical works which has, reasonably enough, been called a 'motet texture'. There may well be just 'one predominating line', but the others are worth hearing too – there is no padding. Soon after the violin melody's expansion an accelerando leads to a big tempo-change ($\downarrow$ = 92, at which point B♭ minor definitely establishes itself) and a new, endearing and more conjunct melody which still, however, uses the semitone-plus-fifth figure that has been there in some form since the start (Ex. 28). Hearing the Fourth and Fifth symphonies in close succession, one may be struck (though Rubbra evidently wasn't!) by the similarity between this tune and the one in the finale of the Fourth (Ex. 26). The 'main section' is now under way, but before long the opening music returns on a quiet and distant-seeming oboe. This is the old formula, 'first idea briefly returning as codetta', but given the contrast of tempo with what has just been happening, the effect is dramatic, making one wonder 'What next?'

Ex. 27 Symphony no. 5, first movement, bars 3–6, 11–18

The middle section reveals striking things. The tempo slows further and the scale figure from Ex. 27 leads the music into a heartfelt song ('Teneramente') from the strings, reminiscent of Mahler's quietly reflective strain. Grover detected three 'visionary' passages in the Eleventh Symphony (see pp. 194–6);

Ex. 28 Symphony no. 5, first movement

this music in the Fifth is perhaps the first in which Rubbra shows what he meant by his religious term 'triptych'.

But quietude lasts no time at all, giving way to some predominantly rhythmical and slightly bizarre events at an Allegro energico tempo. Rubbra can conjure up a tornado out of a clear sky, as in the First Symphony and the opening movements of the Second and Third. He does it again here, with a dotted-note rhythm rampaging the length and breadth of the orchestra and the violins trying to assert their independence by playing three in the time of two. There follows a first echo of the 'non-variations' in the Third Symphony's finale, an incisive repeated-note figure taking the music into triple time. The second comes in another curious, *Beni Mora*-like passage marked 'Grazioso'. One way and another, Rubbra's long-lost Spanish ancestor is making himself felt. Conflict reaches a peak of intensity as the triple-time section comes to a head; the introduction flashes by again at breakneck speed, with a touch of the main section's theme thrown in. The climax seems to echo the Fourth Symphony by Rubbra's patron and admirer Vaughan Williams, a work that had been to the fore as Rubbra set out on his symphonic journey. Much of this middle section is derived from a slightly quieter passage that briefly held up the first section's progress about three minutes in.

At last 4/4 returns, at the movement's maximum marked speed ($\quarternote$ = 192: the 'main section' set out at $\quarternote$ = 92), with a broad, diatonic, seemingly new melody cast as the 'fulfilment' of the movement; the accompaniment, however, groups itself into 3/4 bars to maintain the tension. Finally the wave breaks, exposing again the quiet 'rock-of-ages' that was our entrée into another world at the start of the middle section. This is one of Rubbra's outrageously convincing big changes of tempo, right down to $\eighthnote$ = 60 for his sudden quiet ending with its final oboe reminiscence. The harp had little to do in the first two symphonies and was not required for the next pair; it is, however, to play a significant role in Rubbra's symphonic music, and at this point has a striking entry, only its third in the piece so far. The movement has moved from the initial E♭ and B♭

minor to D♭ major. With all its vicissitudes, it takes less than ten minutes to play; a Bruckner or Mahler would have spun it out to half an hour.[6]

The scherzo (Allegro moderato, D major, 2/2) again shows us Rubbra in cheerful-melody mode, with a four-square-sounding horn-tune for which his naturally contrapuntal mind soon generates plenty of competition. He cited this scherzo in 'A Symphonic Credo' as an example of music with 'a *graded* web of sounds in which there is one dominating voice, the others creating a background to it, but a background that is, nevertheless, tightly organised'. A lecture entitled 'Differences', mostly comparing music and the visual arts, contains the words

> The opening unaccompanied theme, or fragment of it, is *never* absent. Now this by no means implies that whenever the theme occurs you have to fasten on to it, as you would to a life-belt. The theme in this case gives formal cohesion, and its presence should be felt even if other things surrounding it are temporarily more important. The tendency for a lazy ear is to listen always to what happens at the top or bottom of the texture. May I remind you here that interesting things *do* sometimes occur inside! The outer parts are often only a framework for an inner content.

The first counter-subject, a simple snatch of descending scale, quite transforms the figure (based on the end of Ex. 27) that was so prominent and touchingly effective towards the end of the preceding movement. The scherzo is a vigorous, at times playful piece with a few quieter passages, and the basic tune, as the composer pointed out, happens to appear in keys based on all the twelve notes of the chromatic scale, including one in the minor mode. The cloud that so often brooded over the pre-war symphonies has lifted. In 1940 Finzi had referred to Rubbra as 'a ruthless spirit in an ageless body',[7] and though by 1947 he was no longer young as chronology measures youth, the saying 'You're as young as you feel' was seldom truer. While his private life over the ensuing years was to show how double-edged that can be, such music has an irresistibly youthful vigour and even charm. In the third movement of *Das Lied von der Erde* Mahler celebrated youth, but his bitter-sweet glance at something no longer approachable is absent from Rubbra's whole-hearted scherzo, which could rather be summarised in Peter Warlock's song-title *Lusty Juventus*.

Mahler's enormous influence on major twentieth-century composers scarcely extended to Rubbra, whose prediction in that 1933 article on Debussy was that Mahler's music 'could not be prophetic, his mind was too thoroughly steeped in and identified with the giant creations of nineteenth-century

Germany'. Grover's associative ear found 'a gentle Mahlerian irony' in *A Tribute*, though a less suitable dedicatee for a work with Mahlerian overtones could scarcely be imagined, given Vaughan Williams's notorious dismissal of him as 'a tolerable imitation of a composer'. In the Fifth Symphony from five years later the scherzo's resemblances to the *Wunderhorn* song 'Ging heut' Morgen übers Feld', which forms part of Mahler's *Lieder eines fahrenden Gesellen* and whose main melody figures as first subject of his First Symphony's opening movement, could suggest that Rubbra at least knew and was drawn to that aspect of Mahler.

A comparison with Mahler occurred to Stephen Banfield, a convinced admirer of Rubbra reviewing Hans Hubert Schönzeler's recording of the symphony in *The Musical Times* in January 1982; he felt that the movement's 'jaunty feudal tune ... can seem rather anaemic and irritating beside the more pungent peasantries of Mahler'. Similarly, Grover felt this scherzo 'cannot compare for boisterousness and impetuosity with those in Symphonies 2, 6, and 7'. It never does to wish a piece different from what it is; one can only respond to the first comment with 'perhaps in a "triptych" he wasn't after pungency' (but that counted throughout the second half of the twentieth century as an incontrovertible, even indispensable virtue), 'and does England in any case have peasants?'; and, to the second, 'perhaps his inner plan for the symphony, coming at that moment in time, required an easier-going movement than did those other symphonies at their moments in time'. A symphony was, after all, an 'essence' bound to no stereotype, and also, to quote Rubbra's broadcast talk on The Symphony, 'a universal form, not the objectification in music of a dark corner in the composer's psyche'. The main theme's constant presence gives this movement a Haydnesque monothematic quality; a seemingly contrasted two-bar figure in skipping triplets three minutes in turns out to be a variant of the tune, whose main function is to act as another of Rubbra's ostinatos, appearing ten times on the trot as soon as heard. A minute later the end of the movement is a *da capo* slightly compressing the first two minutes' music and fine-tuning its sequence of keys. (Rubbra began the section in D♭ major and now wants to get back to the movement's home key of D major without too much obvious alteration.)

The slow movement (Grave, 4/2, no key-signature) takes a long time to settle, the nomination eventually going to D major, where the scherzo ended. In a several-movement work it would be almost the rarest thing for the composer to revert to his opening as the starting point for slow movement rather than finale. But the third panel of a triptych should balance the first; moreover one vain dream in life is that one has been allowed a fresh start knowing everything learned first time round. That, in Hans Sachs's terminology, seems to be what Rubbra is dreaming here, after his 'Von der Jugend' phase. The score yields rather little to confirm such an impression, yet it persists. The two openings have in common a very deep, sombre initial texture (in the first movement, brass; in the third, double basses, horns and bass tuba), over which a slow melody feels its way towards the light, with the first oboe prominent. The similarity to the work's opening is partially concealed when one reads the score, since the first note heard above the deep brass is in the first movement another preparatory note, whereas here it turns out to be the opening of the cellos' melody – but one hears it in much the same way. The texture is lighter than at the start of the symphony, the melodies built differently.

In a typescript about church music from some time after the composition of his first two Masses Rubbra called the interval of the fifth 'at the same time the most *positive* interval we have (it immediately *affirms*) and the most mysterious. It seems to me to be an enclosed circle of sound that the listener and composer is free to fill.' In this movement, the heart of the symphony, Rubbra's love of the fifth is well in evidence. Notes a fifth apart likewise dominated the first movement's opening melodies, but the crucial difference lies in the ones a semitone away from them. In the first movement (see Ex. 27) the critical note, the very first heard as the oboe begins its melody, is the augmented fourth of the scale, a semitone below the dominant and so an immediate cause of dissonance and tension. It casts a shadow over the 'open' interval of the fifth which soon follows. At the start of the third movement (Ex. 29), the semitone is outside and above the magic fifth, and is consonant (minor sixth or minor third of the scale). When it moves on downward, the fifth's purity is unchallenged. Hence the feeling of 'the same and yet different' – and the figure that opens Ex. 29 is there for most of the slow movement, if not as melody then as accompaniment. At this point Rubbra's way of making a melody follow the dictates of its accompaniment anticipates something he was to do still more

Ex. 29 Symphony no. 5, third movement

memorably in the corresponding movement of his next symphony (see Ex. 37). The descending conjunct continuation (bars 5–9 of Ex. 29) is also rich in possibilities, and all the more so when inverted.

A minute in, long high violin lines emphasise the two notes a fifth apart that define tonality, the tonic and dominant (here D and A). Rising and rising, they are like arms held high and wide in welcome and blessing (Ex. 30). We could again be hearing Mahler, but without that composer's total immersion in his emotions. Cormac Rigby wrote of his times of religious contemplation, when he was not 'going deeply into' himself, but 'leaving himself behind'[8] – and that is what Rubbra does here. Exx. 29 and 30 and their developments throughout the movement embody not one of those famous 'omnipresent intervals' but an almost omnipresent melodic idea, heard in various versions at different speeds and with different functions. Rarely has Rubbra's improvisatory genius been so movingly in evidence.

Ex. 30 Symphony no. 5, third movement, bar 13 (fig. A+2)

An anomalous aspect of this important violin line has a bearing on the very nature of Rubbra's music, and on the way we hear it. As recorded by Barbirolli in 1950, the movement comes out almost 50 per cent longer than in the complete recording of the symphonies under Hickox. With Rubbra present, Barbirolli took his metronome markings literally; Hickox's more on-going tempo made the music curiously 'user-friendly'. It flowed and the orchestra sounded comfortable, whereas in the early recording it floated and hovered (which Rubbra presumably wanted), while the violins at times seemed over-taxed by their high sustained slow lines (which he wouldn't have wanted, but had to accept as part of the bargain). Barbirolli, in the words of an ex-member of the Hallé, 'made you play better than you could'; there were, however, limits. Still more important was his sixth sense that told him, beyond considerations of euphony and difficulty, what made Rubbra write as he did. Anthony Bennett, who has conducted Rubbra's Eighth Symphony, points out[9] that

> Conductors instinctively find a tempo at which Rubbra's musical gestures can be heard/felt with direct, almost physical impact; whereas the

composer's markings undermine that direct impact. The gestural quality seems to be suspended, and we find ourselves listening in a different way, from a great height as it were, with a sort of 'spaced-out' awareness.

Once the long violin lines have been fully developed, the semitone-plus-fifth figure adapts itself to become an accompaniment, forming the basis of one of Rubbra's ostinatos, which moves in groups of twelve even quavers amounting to 3/2 bars and so running counter to the ongoing 4/2 of the melody above them. The climax of the first movement showed something similar. There will be two varied restatements of Ex. 30, one quiet, the other still quieter another minute on.

The movement's accompaniments often move gradually, almost unnoticeably; at the start they drift upwards, like a cloudscape which may seem still but proves to have changed each time one's eye comes back to it. Yet another feature is a quiet series of drum-beats; this we have already met at various points in previous Rubbra symphonies, and it will be found again in more drastic form at the climax of the Sixth Symphony's slow movement and the outset of the Violin Concerto. Here three such beats lead up to a further one on an accented part of the bar; so knowledgeable a Brahmsian as Rubbra must certainly have recalled the part played by that quiet background rhythm in the wonderful *Schicksalslied* (Song of Destiny), where it could stand for the sensed and constant presence of the Divine, also the trace of menace it can carry for frail humanity. The drum-beats set in midway through the Fifth Symphony's slow movement, after a first welling-up of passion, beneath another sustained oboe melody and before a variant of the first tune. That in turn leads, some five minutes in, to an alarming explosion, an incredibly sudden and disturbing outburst with a fierce figure (Ex. 31), seemingly unrelated to anything before and impressive even though it's there for only a single bar, blasted out on horns and trombones. This is the most violent 'climax' in Rubbra before the *Sinfonia Sacra*'s explosion of sound to mark the moment of Christ's passing. It might be unwise to look for programmatic intentions; the mini-tornado passes as quickly as it came, and the main violin melody, plus its accompanying clarinets, is with us again. The various stages in the dream are meticulously signposted with metronome markings, the initial ♩ = 76 slowing down to 60, then

Ex. 31 Symphony no. 5, third movement, bar 56 (fig. E+2)

being replaced by quavers which steadily slow from 63/66 through 60, 50, 42, to 38; the latter marking amounts to a differently notated 'Tempo 1', and the opening mood duly returns, somewhere between D♭ major and B♭ minor.

Given the occasional sense of unrest that still makes itself felt, matching the first movement's Third-Symphony echoes, total peace of mind has yet to be achieved; with the second return of Ex. 30 it is almost there, give or take a strange snarl from muted horns which questions the peace of the closing bars. And yet there is something provisional about this final music, a reluctance to dwell; one expects a continuation. One stage is over, another follows.

That is to say, Rubbra specifies, as he did in the Fourth Symphony, that the finale (Allegro vivo, 6/8, B♭ minor) is to follow 'attacca', and it does, with a skip and a jump and a catchy melody. So organised is his mind that even the skip and jump echo the outline and rhythm of the music just heard. Here the traditional long, 'triumphant' finale might have been out of place; Bruckner won his spiritual battles in his finales, Rubbra's seems already won – maybe that intense if brief clamour a couple of minutes back was the final skirmish – and his finale begins as a celebration, another movement based on something like a dance. The preceding D♭ major now emerges as the relative major of B♭ minor, so that we are pretty close to the work's basic B♭ tonality again.

This is by some way the shortest movement, lasting a mere four minutes. Unduly short finales can have about them a touch of pathos; for example Mozart's late string quartet in B♭ (K589) leaves one with the impression that he gave up before the end, out of world-weariness or sheer disinclination to 'go the extra mile' on behalf of a cello-playing King of Prussia whose rewards for a composer's efforts had disappointed him. Despite shadows there is nothing pathetic about this Rubbra finale, even if one is left puzzled by its foreshortened conclusion. Grover invoked for it the Psalmist's phrase 'Make a joyful noise unto God'; the joy is in a minor key and curiously abbreviated, but there is something in that.

Within a fairly continuous skein of melody a variety of related but distinct figures jostle to be heard, but the movement is also a jewel of contrapuntal ingenuity with other thematic ideas constantly heard as 'accompaniment'. Since Rubbra singled out this symphony as the one where he consciously applied the principle, 'at any one moment there should be not more than *one* predominating line', it is worth wondering precisely what he meant by 'predominating' – for the web of ideas rarely contains one that is not in some way related to important things heard earlier in the work. This is much what Schönberg meant with his *Hauptnebenstimmen*, and it is part of the music's fascination.

The first main figure, with its three upbeat quavers (Ex. 32*), recalls the one in the Third Symphony's Intermezzo with its four-quaver upbeat group, though here the upbeat leads to no immediate 'downbeat'; the second main figure begins twenty seconds in, has all of forty-six bars to spread itself, and appears in a variety of forms, most of which reflect the slow movement's semitone-plus-fifth figure idea in one way or another, plus a more conjunct continuation. Ex. 32 also shows a selection from these ideas. A string melody marked 'sonoro' (Rubbra's marking for the 'episode' figure in the Cello Sonata's first movement, second time round, and for Ex. 28 in this symphony) briefly calls to mind the full stride of Mahler at his most euphoric. Here, a minute into the movement, the first tune appears as a counter-melody, and once again three and four begin to vie with each other. Brief passages take us back to the curious interpolations recalling the Third Symphony, the second and more rumbustious of them being quite bizarre. But the music's momentum carries us irresistibly on to a climax that surpasses the third movement's frantic few seconds with what seems a tremendous peal of bells (something essayed again, with far more slender resources, at the end of the First Piano Trio two years later). Rubbra's own feeling about the joyously repetitive falling half-scale (one of the longest of his memorable ostinatos) was that it is like 'Alleluia!'

Ex. 32 Symphony no. 5, fourth movement, bars 2–14, 22–34 (fig. A+12), 46–50 (fig. C+4), 58–62 (fig. D–1)

At this point there is a hint of Ex. 27 that set the whole work going, as the tempo slows – something is casting its shadow, and we are into the run-down to the first quiet ending to a Rubbra symphony. After this work, only the Sixth and the *Sinfonia Sacra* will end loudly. The opening dance makes one more appearance, in a recapitulation which for twenty-one bars is exact but then suddenly gives up. The mood of the work's opening tries again, and this time it wins, so that the symphony bows out on a version of that sombre music, principally Ex. 27, now given to the even darker-sounding cor anglais. Rubbra added in the drum-beats from the slow movement. So distinguished a sympa-thiser as Hugh Ottaway, who found the Fifth Symphony a 'transitional work' both before and after getting to know its successor, thought this sudden slow ending out of place; it didn't seem to him to arise from anything earlier in the finale. It does, however, reflect, and almost reproduce something earlier in the whole work, and why should that not reappear regardless of what has more immediately preceded it? Rubbra's own further comment in his introduction to the symphony for the BBC was 'Full circle is thus made', leaving open the crucial question, 'Why?' An attempt at an answer can be found in the next chapter; for the moment, it can be said that the listener may feel himself to be passing, for the second time but in the opposite direction, through a dig-nified portal by which he entered some daunting, overcast city, now to meet with radiant blue skies – for whereas at the start the mode was in doubt, here there is resolution. At last, a 'major' ending to a Rubbra symphony is no mere *tierce de Picardie*, but a statement, however quiet, of something achieved: a departure that is also an arrival.

CHAPTER 5

A Question of Mysticism – I

Rubbra's expression 'triptych' to characterise his Fifth Symphony is a reminder of the part religion played in his life. The crucial quality determining a religious nature was summed up by Pavese in his aphorism about belief in the importance of everything that happens in the world. Rubbra's copious reading would have shown him comparable things in Christian thought and in Buddhist maxims such as 'the dharma-body of the Buddha is the hedge at the bottom of the garden', and some of his most characteristic features can be read as manifestations of an innermost religious nature. There was his extreme care over a starting-point, reminiscent of the pioneer twelve-tone composers' scruples about settling for a tone-row on which to base any given piece. Such concern for a firm foundation (which extended to making sure themes would also work in inversion, according to his recollection of the 'light reversal' episode) was in part a highly effective counter to self-doubt, or so Benedict's memoir suggests: on the one hand he happily admitted to letting himself be led by his inspiration, on the other he was known to spend days getting a single bar right and doing what Cyril Scott had called 'rejecting from [his] creative arena all the obvious and unsuitable and weaker ideas which continually flowed into it'.

As one immerses oneself in Rubbra it begins to become clear that for all their differences in idiom he shares character-traits with Schönberg, as with Webern, behind whose musical bareness lay a sense of annihilation followed by rebirth which he compared to experiences related by the mystic Jakob Böhme. Rubbra could well have written, of his all-pervading intervals and his care in choosing them as a starting-point, 'this compulsion, adherence, is so powerful that one has to consider very carefully before finally committing oneself to it for a prolonged period, almost as if taking the decision to marry; a difficult moment!' Those words are in fact from one of Webern's 1932 lectures *The Path to Twelve-Note Composition*, and continue 'our [tone-]rows mostly came into existence when an idea occurred to us, linked with an intuitive vision of the work as a whole; the idea was then subjected to careful thought, just as one can follow the gradual emergence of themes in Beethoven's sketchbooks. Inspiration, if you like'. Here Rubbra's 'sifted out of the initial idea after it has been stated as a single melodic motif' becomes important; the time-sequence is different, the principle comparable.

And there is Rubbra's concept of 'achieving full circle' as one way to ensure and convey unity. 'Unity ... is the establishment of the utmost relatedness between all component parts. So in music, as in all other human utterance, the aim is to make as clear as possible the relationships between parts of the unity; in short to show how one thing leads to another'. Those words, again Webern's, apply wonderfully, not only to Rubbra's ability to make clear the inner logic of Bach's '48', but equally to the sense of wholeness found in his own music, its sense of 'one thing leading to another' and the extraordinary degree of motivic interrelatedness Grover was at such pains to demonstrate. Schönberg invented the expression 'tönend-bewegte Raum' – a sounding and moving space – which he conceived to be 'as it is in Swedenborg's heaven (as it appears described in Balzac's *Seraphita*), with no absolute underneath, neither right nor left, forward or backward'; Rubbra's childhood experience with the reversal of up and down, light and dark, came close to that, just as his 'visual impression simply of a musical shape without knowing the actual notes' (see p. 101) touches on Schönberg's 'moving masses whose shape is unnameable and not amenable to comparison'.[1] No wonder that in his article 'Letter to a Young Composer' Rubbra was emphatic that composing entails not a choice between styles but having something of 'stature' to say. That is as characteristic of his religious nature as of Schönberg's (or, indeed, Beethoven's in music such as the end of the Credo in the *Missa Solemnis*). The intense, metaphysical seriousness of Rubbra's best music is part and parcel of his 'lack of the common touch'; it will probably mean he remains permanently a minority, acquired taste – something that applies equally to the intense and serious Schönberg and Webern. (It does not apply to the intense and serious Beethoven, though all such statements depend on what one means by a minority).

Few people can have got to know Rubbra's music better than Grover, whose research began while the composer was still alive, offering the opportunity of full-scale conversations with him. Grover's note on Rubbra in the 2001 edition of *New Grove* sums him up as follows:

Rubbra's output reveals a unity on two levels: the musical, which is readily demonstrable, and the less easily perceived religious/philosophical, which overrides the musical and encompasses almost everything he wrote. It is universal rather than sectarian, an instinctive blend of the most spiritual and mystical elements of Buddhism and Catholicism. It led to a music that overflows with optimism and a sense of well-being, though the, at times, dramatic and conflictual aspects attest to the hard-won nature of that ultimate peace and reassurance'.

One might just wonder whether the relationship between 'well-being/ optimism' and 'a blend of religions' was the other way about, with Rubbra's genes leading him first to write joyful music for which he only later arrived at an intellectual correlative through reading and reflection. One might also ask how 'demonstrable' anything about a composer – unity or whatever else of such a general nature – ever really is, short of going to the lengths Hans Keller went to in his system of wordless Functional Analysis.

A crucial element in Rubbra's 'inner life' was his relationship with the experience known as 'mysticism'. Religious he undoubtedly was; most great composers are, in one way or another, while infinitely few religious people are great composers. Both the great composer and the mystic live in consuming 'communion with a living reality, an object of love, capable of response, which demands and receives from him a total self-donation',[2] but the composer's Zliving reality is music. That is not to imply that all mystics live solely with their 'dear God' for company, cut off from the world, for many of the greatest have also been amazing organisers and dominating personalities – St Francis of Assisi founding the Franciscan order, St Teresa of Avila reforming the Carmelites, St Catherine of Genoa ministering to the sick. The moment of illumination is brief and unsought, its resonance profound and often practical.

Stripped of confusing assonances with words like 'mystery', mysticism signifies direct contact with divinity (infinity, eternity and very often a Creator), not mediated by any institution or other person. Different accounts stress its different sides: Rubbra was interested by a book *Tertium Organum* (modestly subtitled 'The Third Canon of Thought: A Key to the Enigma of the World') by P. D. Ouspensky, who pointed to mysticism's totally different 'logic' as against that of the 'real' world, while around the same time Evelyn Underhill, the leading British writer on the subject in the first half of the twentieth century, stressed its sense of a burning love for and on the part of a divinity that might or might not be incorporated in a personage. It would take a brave scholar to risk an enumeration of specific musical features pointing to the mystical experience, but the Rubbra enthusiast Dr Elsie Payne was prepared to try. Her initial exposition of mysticism in connection with his work came in her article on the non-liturgical vocal music (*ERC*):

> what most people mean by a mystical experience is an experience of reality that is direct, an end in itself, some sort of sudden illumination. It never comes as a result of deliberation, nor does it lead to explanation or to any kind of practical activity, but only to itself ... That which

is mystically inclined … uses the data of music deliberately to symbolise the immediacy and completeness of a mystical experience and to suggest an atmosphere of other-worldliness.

Which covers some of the ground, though not an often-vital element, the sense of a personal, one-to-one relationship with 'the Divine'. That is especially strong in Jewish mysticism, where it is summed up by Martin Buber's formulation, 'I and Thou'. W. H. Auden's comments on mysticism drew attention to a range of phenomena falling into four categories – The Vision of God, The Vision of Agape ('the classic Christian example of this is, of course, the vision of Pentecost'), The Vision of Eros ('the glory of a single human being … [with] sexual desire always, and without any effort of will, subordinate to the feeling of awe and reverence'), and The Vision of Dame Kind, in which oneness with Nature is uppermost.[3] The second movement of Rubbra's Sixth Symphony has extraordinary qualities that aroused comment at the time, and a reviewer of his slightly earlier Piano Trio detected in it 'a genuine mysticism' (see pp. 115–16). The latter idea also appeared in 1955 in so obscure and ephemeral a source as a 2,000-word article for the Oxford student periodical *Isis* by a youthful graduate student, who could find nothing more tangible than an invocation of 'a timeless experience' as excuse for Rubbra's apparent nonconformity with the sociological criteria of the period. (See Appendix 2.)

A useful exposition of the difference in both nature and context between the 'everyday' consciousness and an 'other condition' ('anderer Zustand') comes in a 1925 book review by the great Austrian novelist Robert Musil. In his *Ansätze zu neuer Ästhetik: Bemerkungen über eine Dramaturgie des Films* (Towards a new aesthetic – remarks about a dramaturgy for film), assessing a new book by the Hungarian poet Béla Balázs, Musil summed up those differences:

> the state of mind influenced by the metrical, calculating, sceptical intellect has a counterpart, no less historically-demonstrable even if it has moulded our destiny less powerfully: it has been called many things which all boil down to much the same thing – the state of love, of goodness, unworldliness, contemplation, vision, closeness to God, ecstasy, abdication of the will, insight, and much else appertaining to a basic experience which in the religion, mysticism and ethics of every society in history reappears with a unanimity matching its remarkable omission to develop.

It would be crass to seek a reductive explanation for the all-important distinction between the two 'conditions', though it does have a physiological underpinning in the human body's two autonomic nervous systems – the sympathico-adrenal, which activates the body, and the parasympathetic, 'whose bodily manifestations are in every respect the opposite; pulse and breathing are slowed down, the muscles relax, the whole organism tends towards tranquillity and catharsis'.[4]

But there remains the crucial question, encapsulated in a different context by a question Schönberg posed in a draft for an essay: 'By what chord or chord-progression would one identify the Fascist confession, and by what the Communist?' By the same token, how is one to identify in what Elsie Payne called the 'data of music' – whose content, if one hopes to avoid hopeless banality, is by its nature not to be replicated in words – a state such as mysticism? By what chord or chord-progression would one identify 'an inward unfolding of a kind of oceanic feeling and its slow ebbing-away'?[5] Great mystics such as St John of the Cross have left in their poetry a series of profoundly impressive attempts to convey the nature of such moments; how is a composer to do anything comparable?

Rubbra's second setting of St John came at precisely the time when the Sixth Symphony began to take shape, 1953. Payne found *Song of the Soul* 'not only humanly passionate but also rarified or mystical', and tried valiantly to encompass both ends of the spectrum in her list of the music's features (the italics are mine, to underline the 'mystical' as distinct from the 'humanly passionate' qualities she specified): 'melody which is forthright, positive and rhythmical, yet *unmetrical and ambiguous in tonality and modality* ... harmony which is lavish and varied but again *insecure in tonality, and frequently made up of bottomless 6/4 chords*'. The ambiguous term 'bottomless' can mean 'infinitely profound', or 'unsupported by any part lower than themselves', or can simply refer to the fact that the 6-4 chord, like its companion the 6-3 or first inversion, does not rest on the firm foundation of the chord's root note, so that it makes a less stable impression than the same chord in 'root position'. Payne was presumably using the word in the last-named sense, a supposition backed up by Rubbra's own characterisation of the second inversion (*Music and Letters*, November 1955) as in itself 'always somewhat elusive in effect'.

Payne's further identifying features of mysticism were 'an instrumentation which, though colourful, is *light and ephemeral, with much exploitation of harp timbre*;[6] and an overall vivacity and sense of continuity, in spite of a *fluctuating momentum and a basically episodic formality*'. Her criteria were formulated apropos a vocal work with a mystical text, so there is again a risk

of confusing the verbal and the musical. In search of some higher category
that subsumes both, one may be helped by Rubbra's interest in Ouspensky.
Tertium's 'key to the enigma of the world' was a 'third mode of thinking' (a reference to Aristotle's *Organon* and Francis Bacon's *Secondum Organum* – 'but
the third existed before the first ... and is a key to the hidden side of life'). That
was equivalent to mysticism, in which the classical postulates such as 'Each
thing is either A or not A' no longer applied. In the third mode of thinking, A
is everything and therefore both A and not A: the religion of world mysticism
sums up the same thought in different terms – the Upanishads' 'Thou art That',
Lao-Tse's 'The Tao which can be expressed in words is not the eternal Tao', St
Paul's 'In Him we live and have our being'. Mystical thinking's nonsensicality
and irreconcilability with normal logic was precisely what Ouspensky found so
important about it. Hans Keller would half a century later turn a comparable
distinction to advantage in considering the nature of great music:

> The Law of Identity says that A is A ... It is a musical axiom that A must
> become more than A. The Law of Contradiction says that A is not both B
> and not B; in music it must, axiomatically, be both. The Law of Excluded
> Middle says that A either is or is not B, whereas in music it goes without
> saying that A must have it both ways if it is to be meaningful.[7]

His Freudian mind did not run in the direction of mysticism, but the formulation is a significant pointer to the 'living reality' of great music. If that reality
is all too rarely sensed, the cause could be the countless preoccupations of
everyday life and the way in which truly concentrated listening suffers what
Ratzinger calls the fate of 'faith and the culture of faith in the interstice between
aesthetic elitism and industrial mass culture'.[8] The abrogation of the laws of
symbolic logic suggests that profound musical creativity is akin to mysticism,
but not that the two are or can be identical.

We have seen Rubbra warning his listeners, apropos the Fourth Symphony,
that 'The symphony is in the philosophical sense of the word a musical
essence, rounded, complete and independent – in other words, it forms its
own world.' That is hard to place in any context of traditional philosophy (a
subject on which the list of books in his library shows him to have read widely),
though it tallies with other assertions of music's autonomy, such as Mendelssohn's 'Music is untranslatable into words, not because it is too indefinite but
because it is too definite.' The concept of 'essence' goes back to Socrates and
Plato, as a higher category taking in all individual examples of an object or
form; in their sense, any given symphony would be one of countless different

manifestations of an 'essential' symphony. Rubbra's formulation might have more correctly run 'a concretisation of an essence, namely The Symphony', but that would have been too high-flown for a post-Reith radio audience. What he did enlarge on, once again in 'A Symphonic Credo', was the distinction of St Thomas Aquinas (1227–74) between 'accident' ('an attribute that is not part of the essence') and 'substance'. The latter appears to be what Rubbra had in mind when he spoke of 'essence'. A composer, in his view, *must* be indebted to the past, but the debt can be to the 'accidents' of music (the distinguishing features and superficial appearances that, for Aquinas, serve to describe what man is, without being essential), or to what *is* essential, the 'substance'. Aquinas called that 'the primary realities', and Rubbra's quotation from him continues: 'Were all substances mortal and none of them everlasting, nothing would be permanent and everything would be transient. This is inconceivable' – if not to the Buddhist that Rubbra briefly became, soon after he first delivered the lecture. He said that musical history was full of secondary figures whose indebtedness was merely to the 'accidents' of music, as against a few who 'built on the substances of music'. For the latter

> an individual style will be an *end-product* of creative thought and not a starting point, which is perhaps one reason for the usually slow recognition of an artist who starts from fundamentals, for he can make no immediately startling effect, owing to his awareness of being but a link in an age-old tradition; and the body of thought that does eventually recognise him has in a sense been built-up by his very insistence on primary things.

Proust wrote comparably about the unique and original masterworks which 'create for themselves something lacking at the time of their creation – an audience'. Rubbra declined to attempt any specification of music's 'substance': 'If I could answer that question there would be no more need for me to compose! Only music can reveal what substance is, and it is a continually expanding revelation because the underlying substance is infinite.' He was, however, clearly at one with Schopenhauer:

> What manner of perception can observe that one and only essential quality of the world, which is outside and independent of any relationship, the true content of its phenomena, subject to no process of change and therefore perceived for all time with equal truth – in a word, the ideas that make up the direct and adequate objectivity of the Thing in Itself? Art, the work of genius'.[9]

A 'unity of opposites' is implicit in what might be thought Rubbra's two irreconcilable views of music, as 'sociologically conditioned' and as an 'essence unrelated to events of everyday life'. Setting out from that thesis and antithesis, he arrived at a masterly synthesis, not in any words of his but in his music. It is a matter of the scale on which decisions are taken: the language of music is a 'given', but one amenable to further development in the work of a major creator, while the countless individual decisions taken at micro-level as a work comes into being are up to the mind creating that work. Life is full of such antitheses: nature/nurture, predestination/free will, man as individual/man in society, or, within Rubbra's church in his lifetime, continuity/reform. What is crucial is that each person or institution accept the need to find his, her or its own unique resolution and synthesis, with help wherever he or she or it can find it. Whether as composer or as performer, the musician has his concentration, so intense as to blot out anything in the outside world; but what is brought into the room before concentrating is a different question.

CHAPTER 6

The Sixth Symphony

The decade and a half after the end of the Second World War saw Rubbra increasingly regarded as one of Britain's major composers, not short of commissions and much performed. His generation was sometimes taken aback by the sudden post-war 'anointing' of Benjamin Britten as The Great New National Composer. Gerald Finzi felt strongly about that, and according to his first biographer Stephen Banfield someone who felt even more strongly was Rubbra, since at the time he found Britten's music lacking in 'inner core'; when *Billy Budd*'s première was broadcast, he rang Finzi in an interval, 'totally exasperated'.[1] They had not been among the young Britons favoured at pre-war festivals of the International Society for Contemporary Music, where Arthur Bliss, during his *enfant terrible* period, aroused interest, as did the prodigy Walton, with his String Quartet (soon repudiated!) at the very first series of concerts in Salzburg in 1923, and later his youthful masterpieces, the overture *Portsmouth Point* (Zurich, 1926) and the Viola Concerto (Liège, 1930). Neither Rubbra nor Finzi even met the Society's guiding spirit, Professor Edward Dent, until after the Second World War; the curious Dante quotation Rubbra appended at the start of his 1955–6 Piano Concerto (see p. 136) hints at a preoccupation with 'opportunism' in some shape or form. But at the time it was all relative, something to grouse about when not better occupied, and the energy and vitality sensed in Rubbra's music from the late 1940s and early 1950s were charmingly reflected in an account by Arthur Hutchings, dedicatee of the Third Symphony, of the 'arrival' at Durham University of the 1949 recorder piece *Meditazioni sopra 'Cœurs désolés'*. He played the piano part and sang the one for recorder, in his fortunately inimitable fashion, to two colleagues, and soon afterwards accompanied a recorder player in a proper performance. Of its enthusiastic listeners, 'two were technicians and analysts of music by profession, and the third a young man at that stage when young musicians are greedy for new music and new techniques. Yet each 'first reaction' expressed the *emotional* effect of the new work'.[2] That quite modest recorder piece forms merely part of the background to the Fifth and Sixth symphonies, but like them it helps to show that Rubbra's music had reached a plateau with the 1946 Cello Sonata. This recorder piece from three years later shows again the irresistible carolling found in the sonata's most exultant passages. The plateau opened out fully in the Sixth, Seventh and Eighth symphonies, despite strong differences in their character and tone.

British Composers in Interview (BCI) is now hard to come by; Rubbra's interview offered not only his views on many things to do with composition and musical taste, but also basic facts about his way of life (the interview, from as late as his early sixties, describes a long-established pattern). A normal day would see him working for six hours; he liked if possible to have a piano at hand, and a 'sitting' could produce anything from two to twenty bars. He composed his works straight through, 'working slowly to get things right before going on, and revising very little', and, as his most famous or notorious statement, he said 'I never know where a piece is going to go next … The excitement of discovery would be lost if I "graphed out" where certain climaxes, etc., would be.' Schönberg was quoted by Webern as saying 'the most important thing in composing is an eraser', and Rubbra too found that 'rubbing out can be as creative as adding'.[3] He also said he sometimes saw a new idea in his mind's eye; for example, the opening of the Fifth Symphony 'came to me while I was in a bus queue. Music often presents itself to me in a visual way as it did on this occasion. I mean, I see it written down before I actually hear it.' In that case his 'vision' was very precise (see p. 89), but

> often it is not so specific; I have a visual impression simply of a musical shape without knowing the actual notes. I know the kind of music it is, the mood and texture and timbre, but it lacks all precise details. These visual revelations are always brief – just a short germ – and it is only when I can get them down on paper that they reveal their true musical significance and potentialities to me. But then I have a theory about this. I believe music is in the subconscious waiting for us to discover it; that the composer's task is not the creation of something new, but actually the discovery of something that already exists.[4] That is probably why I am so little concerned with form in the broad sense of that word. My music seems to be complete within me from the moment I begin; composing is the conscious act of revealing it.

The public persona – dignified, spiritual, elevated above the common rut – was complemented by the ever-present private man and his passionate nature, which had already been apparent in the 1920s photograph. Hence, surely, the full emotional range of Rubbra's music On a personal level, however, extra-marital affairs from the middle 1940s onward fatally affected his marriage. When he first met Colette Yardley during the war she was a married woman with a young son. For a while Rubbras and Yardleys were neighbours at Highwood Bottom. In 1947, however, Colette and Rubbra had a brief liaison which left her pregnant. Their son, christened Adrian, was brought up with the Yardley family. Colette and Edmund remained separated but on friendly terms for some years, then from the 1960s onward his final years were spent with her after her amicable separation from her husband Hugo. In view of their shared Catholicism, marriage had to wait not only until Antoinette died in 1979, but three years longer, until after Hugo's death. Adrian Yardley reached his late twenties before being made aware that the distinguished musician sharing the family home was in fact his father; he is now the administrator of the Rubbra Estate.

Rubbra's mind having turned to religion and to composition for the Church, he produced more liturgical music after finishing work on the Fifth Symphony. His conversion was reflected in a second, Latin Mass (which he also adapted for Anglican use), the 1948 *Missa Sancti Dominici* (Op. 66/66a). Its title reflects the date, 4 August, i.e. St Dominic's Day), when he was received into the Roman Catholic Church; it was first performed the following year. His church music typescript refers to the difference between his first two Masses:

> The English Mass … was the result of a sort of *diffused Christianity* that I had always believed in; but when a few years later I was received into the Roman Catholic Church, my beliefs became crystallized and, I hope, expressed in the six movements of the Latin Mass. My particular problem in it was to express *myself* in the language that had become personal to me, *and yet* be sufficiently impersonal – or should I say, supra-personal, to add something to the participants' aspirations.[5]

There would be three further Masses, the *Missa a tre* (1958, see pp. 150–1), a *Missa Brevis* composed in the mid-1960s for the boys' choir at Trinity School, Croydon, and a very late one 'In Honour of St Teresa of Avila' from 1980–1 (see p. 113).

In both the first two Masses Rubbra wrote for the most part in a strictly homophonic style far removed from the elaborate counterpoint in his symphonies and Cello Sonata. That may seem strange, given the great contrapuntal traditions of liturgical music, but he was determined to help the churches renew their congregations through a new accessibility. While severely testing the upper register of the Canterbury boy-sopranos' voices in a movement such as the Gloria of the *Missa cantuarensis* – they were, after all, 'pros'! – he bore in mind that the typical choir could lift its level only so far in response to challenge. He would, however, certainly have wanted no part in what the major theologian of the time, Joseph Ratzinger, called 'the increasingly grim impoverishment which follows when beauty for its own sake is banished from the Church and all is subordinated to the principle of "utility"'.[6] Indeed, it is when writing religious music such as *Song of the Soul*, rather than in his symphonies, that he seems most intensely interested in the riches of harmony.

In his 'liturgical music' typescript Rubbra said of the *Kyrie* of the *Missa Sancti Dominici* that

> being now more harmonically minded, we apprehend the fifth as a *unit* of sound, and not the result of a fortuitous movement of two parts: so I *treat it as a unit* by having successions of consecutive 5ths. This is carried to great lengths on Page 2, where a chromatic movement of 5ths against suspended melodic notes in the alto and tenor give [*sic*] a fluidity which always however resolves on to the central A.

In that way the Mass movement anticipated one of the most memorable features of the Sixth Symphony's slow movement (see p. 124).

Two decades before the Second Vatican Council, which during its sessions lasting from 11 October 1962 till 7 December 1965 saw a new Pope, Paul VI (Cardinal Montini), elected to succeed John XXIII, Rubbra of course still set the Ordinary of the Mass in Latin rather than in the vernacular. The purest homophony is found in the Credo of the *Missa Sancti Dominici*, which from the words 'Et in Spiritum Sanctum' to 'Et exspecto resurrectionem mortuorum' moves exclusively in parallel diatonic triads, more than restoring the balance after an immediately preceding passage, 'Et ascendit in coelum', where for once the voices moved contrapuntally, in fact in two-part canon; and in the nine Tenebrae Motets, Op. 72 (1950–61).[7] There the liturgical circumstances of Maundy Thursday, approaching the darkest moment of the church year, demanded the strictest and most austere music, for which Rubbra had been set a daunting example in the output of the (otherwise predominantly cheerful!) Spanish composer Tomás Luis de Victoria (1548–1611). Counterpoint was ruled out *a priori*, harmony, to quote the composer Franz Schmidt, 'is something a seven-year-old can do', yet the motets (or to give them their correct title, nocturns: within the liturgy they served as responsories) impress by individual turns of harmonic phrase linked to their penitential texts. The very occasional indulgence in melisma, as at 'Vos fugam capietis, et ego vadam immolari pro vobis' (Ye shall run away, and I will go to be sacrificed for you) in the first Nocturn, is effective out of all proportion to its modesty.

A good deal happened in Roman Catholic church music during the decades after Rubbra's conversion. Ever since Christmas Day 1903, when Pope Pius X issued a *motu proprio* on liturgical music, *Tra le Sollecitudini*, the church had aimed for dignity and appropriateness in its music, after a period when Italian believers in particular had been exposed to sounds clearly taking their norms of expression from the world of opera. Pius at one point wrote that 'should Christ return to Earth, the money-changers wouldn't be the first people he expelled from the Temple!', though he elsewhere made it clear that 'I love music of all kinds, I love Bach and the great symphonists, and even the master-pieces of opera: but I want opera to stay in the theatre'. He wished church music to possess

> Sacredness – it abhors any profane influences;
> Nobility – which true and genuine arts should serve and foster;
> Universality – which, while safeguarding local and legitimate custom, reveals the Catholic unity of the church.[8]

and his reforms had brought, above all, a strong emphasis on Gregorian chant, also on classical polyphony, the name specifically mentioned in the latter con-nection being of course Palestrina, whom Rubbra acknowledged with a hint of reserve as the 'perfect church composer': 'he is extremely adventurous within the limits of the style, particularly in contrapuntal details, but there's always a rocklike adherence to central laws, and rarely is an unexpected musical vista revealed'. The sting in the tail explains his purely musical preference for Byrd, Victoria and 'the great Josquin des Près, perhaps because of their greater, or apparently greater, warmth'.

After the Second Vatican Council a post-conciliar commission was briefed to draw up detailed rules for further reform of church music, and in various fields the senior figures in charge exceeded the letter of the Council's dicta, implementing what they somewhat subjectively regarded as its 'spirit'. Their recommendations on church music were summarised by the 1984 *Dizionario Nuovo di Liturgia* in an article, 'Canto e Musica', but the reformers' ideas were subjected to stern comment from a strongly traditionalist standpoint in Ratz-inger's 1981 book *Das Fest des Glaubens* (translated as *The Feast of Faith*, chap-ter 'On the Theological Basis of Church Music'); younger brother of an out-standing Master of the Music at Regensburg's famous cathedral, the home of the celebrated 'Domspatzen' or Cathedral Sparrows, he spoke out in comments on the theologians Karl Rahner and Herbert Vorgrimler against the wilfulness with which some of the Constitution's clear dicta had been elaborated. The same authority's later *Dem Herrn ein Neues Lied* (New Song for the Lord) showed Ratzinger's more typical spirit of conciliation, drawing attention, for example, to the fact that Pius x's *Motu Proprio* and the post-Vatican-II reformers to some extent shared common aims. Another decade later he would be chosen by his peers to become Pius x's eighth successor.

A good deal thus changed in the Roman Church's attitude to its music during Rubbra's lifetime, but only the relatively unimportant *Missa Brevis* for treble voices and organ (Op. 137) and the late *Mass in Honour of St Teresa of Avila* were composed after Vatican II, still before the appearance of 'Canto e Musica'. By a nice artistic paradox, the post-Conciliar *St Teresa Mass* feels less 'reformist' than the ones from before the Council, indeed it is by some way the most sensuous of the four.

During a relatively short but important phase in his creative life, from 1949 until 1962, Rubbra several times used for works or movements the term 'Meditation'. That religious or deep-psychological practice is distantly related to the 'direct experience of divinity' found in mysticism.[9] All Rubbra's musical 'meditations' apart from the final one, *Meditations on a Byzantine Hymn*, date from the years leading up to the composition of the Sixth Symphony, with its possibly mystical passages in the slow movement. (In 'A Symphonic Credo' Rubbra called that movement 'a simple meditation'.) Grover pointed out apropos *Meditazioni sopra 'Cœurs désolés'* that 'the word should not always be interpreted as indicating sections that are slow, soft or pensive'; he cited Rubbra's markings 'Con moto', 'grazioso' and 'allegretto' for some of the piece's sections. On the other hand, when in the following year successive sections of his First Piano Trio were marked 'Meditazione', the term denoted music of a profound stillness and thoughtfulness. One can truly sense there a soul in solitude with its Maker, and the way the calm develops into a final tremendous peal of bells seems a reward for patience and devotion.

The finale of the 1952 Viola Concerto is a sequence of what Rubbra called 'nine interrelated meditations' (see pp. 119–20), while 1953 saw the composition of the short *Meditation* for organ (Op. 79) dedicated to one of his students, the young organist James Dalton (Rubbra being no snob in the matter of dedications). This piece offers a finely spun arch of melody over an unchanging deep pedal note. To acquire a first idea of the workings of Rubbra's methodical yet inventive mind, one can do worse than home in on short pieces such as the organ *Meditation* or the 1963 *Improvisation* for cello. They show simply and clearly how he achieves the classical blend between repetition and development of an initial idea. Given their brevity, there is no need even for a score;

repeated listening impresses on the mind the works' very brief ideas and their modicum of development. Meditation often involves progressive reflection on an initial idea, rather than total 'freedom from thought' or repetitive mantras; in religious thinking a 'meditation' can amount to a sermon, and Rubbra's development of his simple ideas in those 'meditations' is likewise a process of 'progressive reflection'. The final appearance of the word in his output came nine years later with the *Meditations on a Byzantine Hymn*, where the structure is rather more complex.

Rubbra was aware of being occasionally called 'austere' – an emotive word during the immediately post-war years when consumer goods were often quite basic, so that 'austerity' and (mostly for larger items such as furniture) its companion 'utility' came to be used as adjectives synonymous with 'minimal'! In 'A Symphonic Credo' he admitted to having occasionally

> tried to slacken the tight background by introducing non-thematic material, patterns and so-forth. But they have never been effective, perhaps because I was striving to remove the charge of 'austerity' by introducing devices contrary to my musical nature. That I no longer do so is because I am now [mid-1950s] confident that even if I do use a texture that is erroneously labelled 'intellectual', thus leading to the associated idea of 'austerity', my heart and senses are quite as warmly involved as are those of the composer of sensuous harmonic music.

There followed a remark about the need for performers to play with maximum expression.

'Austerity' is often the last thing present in the work of this composer who knows and can communicate the rarest of states, joy. As one example, Rubbra turned to advantage the instruction in both the 1662 and 1928 Anglican Prayer Books to place the Gloria at the end of the service, making it not the 'second movement', as in a Mass for the Roman rite, but the closing one; this offered the chance, in his 1945 *Missa cantuarensis*, to make his euphoria at the splendour of God's creation into a true finale. Both before and after that Mass, which consistently offers music of a purity and elegance worthy to save the cause of church music at any future 'Council of Trent', there are countless joyous climaxes and endings in his music.

Another fruitful line of activity after the war was the composition of no fewer than eight works for recorder, mostly written with the virtuoso Carl Dolmetsch and his harpsichordist partner Joseph Saxby in mind. The first was completed on Easter Monday 1949; *Meditazioni sopra 'Cœurs désolés'* (Op. 67)

matched the old idea of the 'Phantasy' much more closely than had the imma-
ture piece to which Rubbra gave that title twenty years earlier. Crisply concise
and contrasting sections follow one on another, as if in a tightly organised set
of variations, though Rubbra's own verdict on his handling of the 'theme' was
that the work had arisen through a process 'akin to the psychological law of free
association', and that resemblances to the chanson theme were 'in a sense for-
tuitous'. The touching melody from a four-part chanson by 'the great Josquin
des Près', on which the piece is based, receives a final dignified restatement.

Two major chamber works from the time immediately after the Fifth Symphony were a First Piano Trio (1949–50, Op. 68) and Second String Quartet
(1951–2, Op. 73). The Piano Trio, like the recorder *Meditazioni*, is a single-
movement piece, but lasts nearly twenty minutes and has many sections. The
sizeable opening one, taking up almost half the work, features the semitone-
plus-fifth idea so prominent in the Fifth Symphony a year or two earlier. This
'movement' comes to a decisive end, as a movement should, and only the ensuing scherzando's bold plunge in could make it count as part of a larger single-
movement composition. Like most such Rubbra pieces it is at times positively
rowdy, but a Theme and Three Variations which he called 'Prima', 'Seconda' and
'Terza Meditazione' totally change the work's direction, taking it into extreme
stillness. It does, however end, as did the opening 'movement', with one of his
most vigorous and stirring peals of bells. Passages in the 'Meditazioni', with
sustained string-instrument sound against incessant slow piano chords, might
suggest that Rubbra had been impressed by the comparable movements in
Olivier Messiaen's *Quatuor pour la fin du temps*; the 1957 'Portrait Gallery'
piece included the sentence 'A letter from Rubbra is more likely to contain
a vigorous appreciation of a work by Messiaen or Julius Harrison[10] than any
account of his own composing activity.' In his talk on Skryabin Rubbra named
Messiaen as that composer's one true heir, adding that both men had features
'some of which one may find agreeable, some repellent'.

Perhaps on the basis of those sectional subtitles, a review of the Trio by the
Austrian-born critic and pianist Paul Hamburger in the autumn 1950 issue
of *Music Survey* referred to its 'genuine mysticism'. The great post-1938 generation of musical immigrés from Germany and Austria took relatively little
notice of Rubbra, so the comments of a true intellectual and most distinguished
member of the band are of value. Hamburger called the 1946 Cello Sonata,
too, mystical music, 'but more inventive than the Trio', and there is certainly
enough in its finale's extremely still, perhaps meditative Theme and Variations
to show what he was hearing. Hamburger had some formal reservations about

the earlier part of the Trio, but found in its 'Tema' and 'Meditazioni' 'a deeply serious and God-fearing musicianship'.

The Second Quartet received its première from the leading British ensemble of the immediately pre- and post-war years, the Griller String Quartet. John Pickard's note for a recording of a later quartet, the Third, compares that work's relationship to Rubbra's First with that between Beethoven's Op. 18 set and its successors; the second stands between the two not merely in time but in manner, with only a trace of the Ravelian echoes found in its predecessor from two decades earlier, and already distinct traces of Beethoven's classic cycle. The brief and exciting 'Scherzo polymetrico', with its opening tune not unlike that in the scherzo of the Fifth Symphony, could put one in mind of the ethereal yet tumultuous Beethoven encountered in a piece such as the second movement of the F major Quartet, Op. 135.

The slow movement is subtitled 'Cavatina'; that was the title of a Cyril Scott piece much liked by Rubbra, who quoted it in his *Music Magazine* tribute,[11] but in the context of a string quartet it amounted to a conspicuous allusion to Beethoven, who had given the title to the deeply expressive slow movement of his late String Quartet in B♭, Op. 130. A composer working with such total respect for a supremely great predecessor would have called a movement 'Cavatina' only after the most careful thought, to show how much it meant to him. Expectation is aroused, nor is it disappointed. A cavatina can be either a short aria, without *da capo*, the slow, lyrical section of an extended 'scena', before the virtuoso 'cabaletta', or a songlike piece of instrumental music. The Beethoven has a *da capo* after the famously, uniquely emotional arioso-like passage marked 'beklemmt' (oppressed); Rubbra's cavatina shows a more continuous, seamless texture, without so starkly contrasting a middle section, and its profoundly meditative air hints at the rarefied, perhaps mystically detached music that followed a couple of years later in the slow movement of the Sixth Symphony.

In its simple beauty this quartet movement is one of Rubbra's finest, and in whatever it has by way of a middle section (not 'oppressed' like Beethoven's, rather transfigured) it reminds us of another significant melodic figure that played a major role in the Fifth Symphony's slow movement, the rising and falling line using the two basic pillars within the octave, tonic and dominant. A series of fifths up and down, another use of the 'most positive and mysterious interval', anticipates by almost thirty years what he called a 'culmination' of his symphonic thought in the Eleventh Symphony. These fifths accompanied Rubbra throughout his life, and were as much 'his' intervals as were, for

Schönberg, the major sevenths and minor ninths that gave his mature music its special 'distorting mirror' quality. The differences between those two not-dissimilar minds could hardly be better encapsulated than in their most typical intervals. Schönberg attributed the character of much of his music to a sense that he 'had fallen into an ocean of boiling water, and not knowing how to swim or get out in another manner, I tried with my legs and arms as best I could';[12] Rubbra did not entirely keep out of hot water, but he had been spared the experience of growing up amid the neurasthenia of fin-de-siècle Vienna. In her 1955 chapter for *ERC* Elsie Payne drew a further crucial distinction:

> The present age is nowhere conducive to complacency; but world-event has shaken more ruthlessly and continuously abroad than it has here. This is particularly so where Jewish people have been concerned. We have been angry, perturbed and afraid, but more in the capacity of spectators than of participators; and thus it is that all English modern music seems, on the whole, milder – including Rubbra's.

(The ensuing half-century was hardly to be foreseen.) The texture near the movement's end, with the two violins playing in parallel thirds and then sixths in their highest register, is astonishing, and something neither Beethoven nor that supreme master of quartet texture Haydn ever thought of. There follows, in the best Rubbra–Schönberg fashion, an echo of the melody from the start.

Another sizeable work from that time was a Viola Concerto (1952, Op. 75) commissioned by no less a figure than the leading virtuoso William Primrose, colleague of supreme instrumentalists such as Heifetz and Piatigorsky. It was complete by late June of 1952, when Rubbra played it through to Gerald Finzi at Highwood Bottom; the première, with the BBC Symphony Orchestra under Sir Malcolm Sargent, formed part of a Royal Philharmonic Society concert at London's Royal Festival Hall on 15 April 1953, with a further hearing on the Third Programme the following night. Rubbra would have been well aware of two concertos from the immediately preceding quarter of a century, the outstanding one by Walton from the late 1920s (though it is surely pure coincidence that in both that work and Rubbra's concerto the solo line opens with a rising minor third), and the very last music of a man he so admired, Béla Bartók, whose 1945 concerto Primrose had in fact commissioned. He gave the first performance in 1949, and now ordered concertos from Rubbra, Darius Milhaud and the thirty-year-old Peter Racine Fricker. In his memoirs he called the one by the last-named 'magnificent' and 'the finest in the repertoire', limiting himself to the barest mention of those by Rubbra and Milhaud. There was a different performance not long after the première, conducted by Sir Thomas Beecham with the principal violist in his Royal Philharmonic Orchestra, Frederick Riddle, as soloist. Rubbra was delighted with that, feeling that the unique Beecham magic had, as so often, brought about a great event after an uncertain start.

Primrose had settled in the USA on becoming principal viola of Toscanini's NBC Symphony Orchestra in 1937. During those years leading British instrumentalists fell into two categories, some keeping to a sober English way of playing, others more open to Continental or American influences. Among clarinettists, for example, Frederick Thurston represented the 'indigenous school', Reginald Kell with his more adventurous use of vibrato the other, and the viola saw a comparable distinction between the immensely influential, home-based Lionel Tertis and the cosmopolitan Primrose. Rubbra's concerto might have suited Tertis better than Primrose, who was a generation younger. He did at least go on playing the work; its composer travelled to the USA in October 1959 on an expenses-paid trip, to hear four performances with the New Jersey Symphony Orchestra in three unspecified cities in that state. Primrose was also keen to record the work with Boult, but in the early 1960s heart trouble curtailed his activities.

The concerto has a certain amount in common with the Sixth Symphony from a year later. In particular, a motive with a falling fifth, basic to the symphony, is a good deal in evidence in the concerto's scherzo. At the start, its first movement also anticipates two symphonic openings from later in Rubbra's life: a harp note and deep tremolando C look to the 1957 Seventh Symphony, while its deep solo stringed instrument over a still-lower-lying bass is reproduced another seventeen years later at the start of the Tenth. As so often in Rubbra, a livelier section begins about two minutes in – one can be no more exact, for by now one of his characteristics is a way of overlapping sections, like the links in a chain or necklace. (The concerto's finale is explicitly built in that way.) The new one here brings a further anticipation of the Seventh Symphony, this time of dancing, Tchaikovsky-like music at the same structural point. After a violent storm has blown up and blown over, one turn of phrase five minutes in is like a literal quotation from Tchaikovsky. The sober atmosphere, soon returning, is more than once dispelled by something almost frantic, but eventually prevails and is finally underlined in the cadenza. Despite a precedent in Elgar's violin concerto with its accompanied cadenza, the idea of couching what was by tradition the soloist's showpiece entirely over a brooding timpani roll was daring and dramatic and ran the risk of alienating its performer.

The scherzo sets out in what one could call a Lemminkäinen mood, with the soloist now joining in the heavyweight dance, now wending his own quieter way like Berlioz's viola-playing Harold shunning the Orgy of Brigands. As well he might, for some quite outlandish things go on in the background, where sinister birds seem to be rehearsing before an appearance in that remarkable Hitchcock film.[13] (In the Sixth Symphony they reappear, now totally happy.) The side drum gears itself up for its big moments in the Seventh Symphony five years later, and near the end there is another appearance by Rubbra's 'far-distant Spanish ancestor', who seems to be over on a flying visit – perhaps for the 1953 Coronation, since he is also distinctly in evidence in the orchestral opening of *Ode to the Queen*. One could be hearing one of the Spanish pieces from Walton's *Façade*, and there is almost a feeling of parody, comparable to Bartók's send-up of Shostakovich's 'Leningrad' Symphony in his Concerto for Orchestra. Like most Rubbra scherzos, this is for the most part uneasy music, the product of a very full mind, and like most of the concerto it raises again issues only partially resolved in the far more optimistic Fifth Symphony.

Rubbra called the concerto's finale a 'collana musicale', a musical necklace, saying that the music, based entirely on material from the viola's first thirteen bars, made up 'nine interrelated meditations ... without a central theme, but linked together in spirit'. Even Grover found the segments 'simply too small, and in many cases, too obscure to be recognizable', but the procedure helped Rubbra give the music the form he wanted. It could be that his 'interrelated' referred to such interlinking of the sections; so much in his music having always been interrelated in terms of intervals and motifs, he would hardly have thought to single that out for comment. With the distinctions between the meditations mostly softened by such overlapping of sections, the listener is more likely to perceive a gradually changing flux, within an atmosphere of intense concentration; Rubbra wrote into his score study figures from I to IX in addition to the more normal study figures in Arabic numerals or letters.

Meditations I and II are long and slow, minor then major, sombre then serene, and both strikingly beautiful ('from the heart it came, may it speak to people's hearts', in Beethoven's words). Another instrument Rubbra used with as much tact as economy was the harp, sometimes giving it music that suggested a clock ticking life away. That is so in the extremely still music that ends Meditation I, for viola and harp over the barest string accompaniment

– it suggests someone straining his perceptions almost to the point of pain[14] as he tries to recall something infinitely precious that is about to disappear. The rhythm changes to 6/8 (Meditation III), but the mood is still sombre, and some seven minutes in we find another Rubbra fingerprint, a series of drum beats that could be saying 'All flesh is as grass.' Meditation IV brings a milder *memento mori* from the harp, with a lovely added clarinet line that looks forward to a great moment in the slow movement of the Sixth Symphony. Quite abruptly (Meditation V) the music breaks into a brisker (though ephemeral) 6/8: we seem to be into a typical Rubbra form – slow first half, quick second half, in effect two movements rolled into one, a scheme he would return to in the Sixth Symphony. But the quick music all too soon turns back toward the minor mode and subsides (VI). In Meditation VII Old Mortality Harp again seems to pluck off the moments one by one. This varied restatement of II is followed (VIII) by another version of III, a new touch being a texture that figures in the slow movements of the preceding and ensuing symphonies (Nos. 5 and 6); the entire string section plays slowly moving chords, like an ever-changing cloudscape. A final flurry of life (Meditation IX) looks back to a theme that opened the upbeat, patriotic finale of the war-time Fourth Symphony; then it had been a public matter, here the composer is coming to terms with some private issue, perhaps of reassurance. And here, at least, the world-famous soloist can end on a flourish!

With its reversal of the usual pattern – two predominantly slow outer movements and central scherzo – the concerto must have been a puzzle to its commissioner, hoping for a display piece and finding himself almost an onlooker at some esoteric meditation! After the première it was also felt that problems of balance arising from a soloist so centrally placed in the texture had not been entirely overcome. Beecham must have managed that a good deal better than Sargent, but then he was an incomparably better conductor!

Despite the imminent break-up of Rubbra's marriage, the years at the end of the 1940s and the start of the 1950s were among the most outwardly fulfilled in his career. There are musical connections between the *Missa Sancti Dominici*, written to reflect his conversion, and the Sixth Symphony, for passages in the *Christe* look forward to similar music with moving fifths and 'suspended' notes in the symphony's slow movement.

One of Rubbra's most important choral works, *Song of the Soul*, was composed in 1953 for Paul Steinitz's London Bach Society. With its reflection of mystical ideas it belongs to the genre of Rubbra piece that most explicitly reminds one of his debt to the composer of works such as the *Hymn of Jesus*;

the constant use of overlapping diatonic chords brings about in both Holst and Rubbra a sense of both mystery and security. Here the St John of the Cross text is set in Roy Campbell's translation. In 'Edmund Rubbra Writes about the Development of his Choral Music' (*The Listener*, 6 June 1968) he told with amusement of the time when its text's vivid erotic imagery caused the headmaster of a music school to forbid his boys to perform it! The harmony's almost self-indulgent fullness again hints at Messiaen, but the rhythmic organisation could not be more different; just as Rubbra distanced himself from Bartók's 'irregular regularities', so Messiaen's 'non-retrogradable rhythms' would have been foreign to him. Whatever the double meanings in *Song of the Soul*'s text, the rich and euphonious music offers nothing that could be mistaken for the language of 'worldly' eroticism. The choral parts go their majestic and fairly unvarying way, the frequent instrumental interludes providing variety and a welcome lightening of the texture.

In 1953, five years after completing the Fifth Symphony, Rubbra began work on its successor (Op. 80), written to a BBC commission, which occupied him into the next year. The 1954 première was yet again by the BBC Symphony Orchestra, this time not under Boult but under its Chief Conductor of the day, Sir Malcolm Sargent. It met with strongly approving critical comment.[15]

Ex. 33 Symphony no. 6, first movement

The Sixth Symphony is a progressive-tonality work moving from F major to C major. As already remarked, Rubbra provoked a small controversy by placing at the top of the manuscript the four notes E, F, A, B (Ex. 33): he eventually settled the argument in *Musical Opinion* by saying all he had meant was that many of the work's ideas were based on 'a selection from these notes', and that E–F–A–B was in no sense a 'motto theme'. In 'A Symphonic Credo' he gave chapter and verse for his use of the notes in the group. Apart from the obvious thematic one in the finale (a cor anglais melody led off by the four notes, see also Ex. 39; it should be remembered that this movement was composed first), it took a period of patient waiting before 'a sudden light' showed him where the origins of the remaining movements lay. Ex. 34 shows how the first took shape 'from a chord containing the first three notes of the basic group, the second from a fifth consisting of A and E, and the scherzo from a melodic use of E and F'. Ex. 34 also shows more precisely the form in which E–F–A–B opens the finale.

Ex. 34 Symphony no. 6: some of the forms taken by E–F–A–B in the Sixth Symphony: (a) opening chord; (b) fifths at opening of slow movement; (c) opening rhythm of scherzo; (d) opening of finale

Rubbra did not specify what key the symphony is in. His quotation of the group above the first page of the score replaced a blanket indication of key for the whole work, which opens in D minor to end in C major. (More immediately, the music will move after seventeen bars to the relative major, F major, via a transition through D♭.) The symphony begins in 4/8, Lento, and the first melodic idea (Ex. 35) is heard against a sombre, sustained background, with low horns, bassoons and harp and a timpani roll. The uneasy quality of the opening chord reflects the fact that the E and F from Rubbra's four-note package are heard grating on one another (Ex. 34a), along with A and D. This is an immediate first instance of the four-note package giving rise to something other than a 'motto theme' or figure that might 'pervade' the symphony.

Ex. 35 Symphony no. 6, first movement

Ex. 35 suggests that, like the first four symphonies, the Fifth and Sixth, despite five years between them, are companion works, for in the Sixth we meet again the semitone-plus-fifth that began the previous symphony – only here the fifth comes first. The entire motive sounds more like the end of something than the beginning, a case of 'goodbye to all that' – an idea supported that the fact that it bears no relation to the work's basic E–F–A–B group beyond containing the note A.

At bar 18 tempo and metre change to Allegretto and 6/8, but the pulse remains the same. This is one of the times when Rubbra takes us somewhere instantly different, as if in a 'dissolve', as one of his apparently simple tunes strides out with elbows swinging. This might when first heard seem better suited to a divertimento than a symphony, indeed Lennox Berkeley's delightful orchestral *Divertimento* (1943) opens with a not totally dissimilar one. Though the F and A from the group still appear, the F is quite subordinate and touched only in passing; the other principal note around which the melody revolves is C, dominant of the new key, F major. B has yet to show its hand; it chooses its moment well, fourteen bars further in, appearing as a sharpened fourth that creates almost the first moment of tension.[16]

Much happens in this main section, which takes up the remaining eight minutes of the movement. It is tempting to try and make out here the traditional features of sonata form – exposition with contrasted first and second subjects, development, recapitulation, coda; elements of all that are present, and late in the movement the sweep of the music certainly leaves one with the impression that a vigorous recapitulation has been going on. Yet on closer examination one finds that the 'formal scheme' (an idea Rubbra by nature avoided) is handled loosely enough for the eventual satisfaction to come from sharing his sense of freedom in doing as he pleases, rather than from saying 'I've got it worked out.'

Which is to say that much of Rubbra's 'development' comes, like Schubert's, even as he expounds his themes, and that, so far as contrast is concerned, there is plenty of it but the best is found when what one might think the 'development' is already well under way. It comes in a wondrous episode featuring the woodwind about three and a half minutes in; they chirp away like happy birds against a continuation of rising and falling major scales from just before. Those scales will return to magical effect at the climax of the slow movement. To confuse us further, Rubbra eventually 'recapitulates' the episode as if it had really been a second subject. Where one ought by rights to be found, namely two minutes or so into the exposition, there is certainly new material, but it flows effortlessly out of the variants of the first tune that we have so far been hearing. There are two strands, the other starting soon after; the first is never heard again, which makes it more like an episode in a rondo. The second, with a way of starting after the beat and dying away on a feminine ending, is followed by a climax with an 'Alleluia' feeling, after which the magic birds have their say. The metre here changes from 6/8 to 3/4. This section lasts all of twenty-five bars, with the strings playing a more prominent role in its later stages.

Still in 3/4, but 'molto meno mosso', we come to the most relatively sombre music in this main section of the movement, with insistent trombone notes and another of Rubbra's obsessive series of drum-beats; the melody in the violas and cellos seems a variant or development of the second strand of that so-called 'second subject'. It is short lived, leading to a reassertion of the buoyant 6/8 from the start of the main section; at several points in this movement, Rubbra seems like the man who told Dr Johnson he tried to be philosophical but cheerfulness kept breaking in. What also breaks in precisely here is a new figure (Ex. 36) which is going to be very important in the scherzo.

Ex. 36 Symphony no. 6, first movement, bar 137 (fig. 15+5)

Before long we are in a passage which certainly feels like a recapitulation, the music from about six and a half minutes in more-or-less repeating what happened earlier. The feeling of a confident return to the starting-point is driven home at the outset by the one cymbal clash in the entire work. Similarly, the next music recalls the bird-song section and its ensuing 'Alleluia', in a fairly literal repetition that does, however, break off slightly sooner. As ever, Rubbra takes the long view, and from here on the music winds down, with a thoughtful 3/2 section in D♭ quoting the main theme and ending on the initial Ex. 35, now a semitone lower. That still sounds valedictory but has finally found a way to be what it should have been all along – an ending.

So quiet a close leaves one with the by-now-familiar Rubbra feeling, 'Where next?' Leading from a quick movement into a slow one through a final slow section must be far easier to bring off convincingly than its opposite, a quick section at the end of a slow movement anticipating things to come: the answer to the question is none the less miraculous – a second movement entitled 'Canto', headed by a quotation from the Italian poet Leopardi about 'this lonely hill/And this hedge that excludes so large a part / Of the ultimate horizon from my view'. It is marked Largo e sereno, 4/4, and there is no key-signature, the music returning from time to time to A minor and ending in or on A major.

At the start of the Sixth Symphony's slow movement distant horns move from one fifth to another, the first consisting of the notes A and E from the basic group; in a note for a 1963 performance of the work by the BBC Welsh Orchestra (as it then was), conducted by Sir Adrian Boult, Rubbra wrote of 'interweaving muted horns sounding like a distant male choir'. A floating clarinet (a distant female companion?) seems happy to go wherever they call; the way its notes are reinterpreted as the horns move on (Ex. 37, in which my arrows show how the clarinet follows their lead) is something already found five years earlier in the Christe of the choral *Missa Sancti Dominici*. Suddenly, at one of the great moments in this symphony, it plunges steeply down into the arms of the quadruply divided cellos, who have a wonderful Schubertian sound. (In the passage referred to, during the 'Great' C Major Symphony's introduction, Schubert himself looked back to the point in Haydn's *The Creation* where, to a

Ex. 37 Symphony no. 6, second movement

comparable halo of warm divided cellos, the beasts and birds are exhorted to go forth and multiply.) There is deep emotion here, felt again in the seven-fold descending-scale ostinato that comes as an all-embracing emotional gesture to dominate the latter part of the movement.

As at a similar point in the preceding symphony, the chordal accompaniment for the strings briefly takes on the character of a slowly changing cloudscape. The game of slow-motion follow-the-call comes four times, scored in a variety of ways. The first time, it is followed by a quite short section with an expressive oboe melody, while after the second an even shorter but 'intense' (Rubbra's marking) sentence for the strings leads to a third appearance, against which a high solo violin touches the heart with a fleeting phrase. Its final falling scale is the cue for the longer section at the heart of the movement and indeed of the entire symphony; taken up by one section of the orchestra after another, it becomes a slow ostinato against which the upper strings and woodwind develop new melodies. In these slowly descending scales we find once again the idea of disembodied bells.

After the seventh statement the climax is reached, with the scale, now the other way up, followed by an insistent dotted-note rhythm on the brass that is clearly another call, but this time a stern one, clearer and longer than the brief explosion at a comparable point in the Fifth Symphony. 'Follow-my-leader' has turned into 'Simon says': when He speaks, and only then, one jumps to it and does as commanded! The literature of religious experience speaks of God stretching out a hand to reclaim an errant soul. (A Catholic convert, Francis Thompson, left a poem, 'The Hound of Heaven', which vividly evokes that feeling. Rubbra was familiar with Thompson's work, and borrowed from him the term 'Corymbus' to characterise the first movement of his next major work, the 1955–6 Piano Concerto.)[17] The descending scale reappears to crown the climax, even as the bass instruments complicate matters with a cross-rhythm (three against four) based on our old friend semitone-plus-fifth. As the excitement dies away, the familiar held fifths on the horns reappear, almost as if they had been there the whole time, unheard, and straight away the clarinet dives again into the arms of the cellos. This faintly suggests something that would come into fashion in avant-garde music a decade later – a palindrome – for the opening's follow-my-leader of clarinet and horns is delayed until it is over.[18] Soon we reach the coda; the longest exposition of the 'open fifths' idea brings a memorable movement to a memorably long-drawn-out quiet conclusion. Most unusually for Rubbra, despite speedings-up and slowings-down there has not been a single change of metronome-marking; his total concentration can accommodate whatever goes on, without a flicker. The contrast with the sedulously notated procession of metronome markings in the previous symphony's slow movement is striking.

In 'Differences' Rubbra summed up this movement, and much else about his music, calling it 'extremely parsimonious in actual notes, but I do require the players to play everything with intense expression. It is really a landscape in sound'. That is reinforced by something he wrote in 'A Symphonic Credo' at the point where he was about to discuss this symphony in detail: 'It is really up to the individual players to extract all that is possible in expression and nuance from the particular thematic lines allotted to them. Only then will my meaning be made as clear as I intended.'

Apropos 'landscape', Rubbra said at the end of his lecture 'although Leopardi speaks of an Italian landscape, it is one that was also intimately mine from the window of my workroom' – which stresses the immediate surroundings and its associations at that troubled time, rather than the poet's 'space, silences and calm'. It could also be a reminder of those open fields bordering his childhood home, which according to his reminiscences in *ERC* had meant so much to him.

The scherzo (C major, Vivace impetuoso) brings us back down to earth with an invigorating bump. Rubbra described it as 'unbuttoned', a favourite word of his, though despite its bluff honest opening it is a mine of ingenious contrapuntal devices – Rubbra at his most Bach-like. The main theme (Ex. 38) is a four-square, dancing melody. Here the fifth is complemented by its inversion, the fourth (both go from dominant to tonic but in opposite directions), with the fifth ending the tune. Many statements of this main melody end with the idea introduced as the first movement reached its turning-point (Ex. 36); bars 16–17 are typical, and are followed in 18–19 by a typical Rubbra inversion.

Ex. 38 Symphony no. 6, third movement

Constant falling scale figures act as a regular counterpoint to the main melody, and in due course they will provide another of the composer's 'happy bells' climaxes.

A degree of relaxation comes in a passage beginning about three quarters of a minute in, offering what Payne called 'instrumentation which, though colourful, is light and ephemeral, with much exploitation of harp timbre'; the mild sounds of the celesta are heard, doubled by the harp, in a charmingly floating accompaniment which is almost another of the composer's ostinatos, except that its successive appearances change shape and length in a protean way. This, mystical or not, is certainly no 'middle section' or trio; to dispense with one in a scherzo was standard practice for Rubbra, who only came within striking distance of a trio in the Seventh and Eighth symphonies. A little under two minutes in, there are a few seconds of confirmatory 'codetta', then a substantial developmental passage lasting about a minute. Its latter part is notated in 2/2, but with so many cross-rhythms and appearances of the basic triple-time figure the listener may well notice no change. That is all the more so once Rubbra begins to notate 'three in the time of two'; the recapitulation in fact begins with the final three bars of the 2/2 section. One exceptional indulgence is the use of a xylophone's unmistakable cheeky sound, for exactly four beats, about a third of the way through this middle section; one is reminded of the way Brahms allowed himself a triangle in the boisterous scherzo of his Fourth Symphony, or Bruckner a single cymbal clash in the slow movement of his Seventh. Rubbra pointed to his use of the xylophone and celesta, 'instruments I have hitherto kept out of my symphonic palette'. The indulgence briefly seems to have been expensive; the xylophone does, after all, have *danse macabre* associations, and a momentary chill falls over the music.

By Rubbra's criteria, the unusual thing (though here in keeping with what happened in the first movement) is the clear recapitulation of a really long stretch of music from the outset; for 122 bars the music is identical with that heard for two minutes just after the opening of the movement, give or take five at the start in which a double bass *pizzicato* is added. In due course there is a striking change of mood, with Rubbra, as ever, thinking where to go next. In the main body of the movement the crotchet was moving at 228 to the minute, now it is slowed right down to 56 as the first horn sounds what could be a cautionary note, or rather three: the first flute answers with a distant echo of the dance tune, and we are ready for the finale.

That was in fact written first, with Rubbra under the impression that he was writing a first movement. In 'A Symphonic Credo' he wrote that

> The end of the movement, however, had such an air of finality, that I gradually came to realise that nothing could follow it. Added to which there was a practical difficulty in making this the first movement, for the unaccompanied theme beginning with [E–F–A–B], which opened the movement, was given to the English horn, an instrument notoriously difficult to play in tune unless well-warmed up beforehand. These considerations led me to make this, the first movement written, into the finale.

The movement sets out from A minor (Poco Andante, 3/2), ending in C major, which in view of the two keys' common signature is and isn't progressive tonality. The opening (Ex. 39) is one of Rubbra's most Sibelian passages, with the E–F–A–B on the cor anglais, perhaps a reminder of the older composer's *Swan of Tuonela*, responded to warmly by the lower strings. Both elements here are prominent through the remainder of the introduction, which

Ex. 39 Symphony no. 6, fourth movement

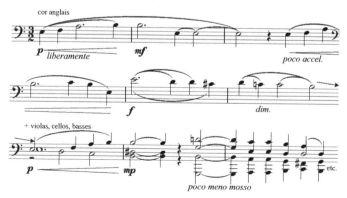

becomes a passionate outburst with the strings' answering and consoling phrase from Ex. 39 particularly prominent. (To show the precision with which Rubbra helped his performers to achieve the intensity he wanted, the example shows more of his expression and tempo markings than most of the others in this book.) Four minutes in, the fifth-plus-octave idea (Ex. 30) from the previous symphony (and meanwhile the Second String Quartet) reappears. It all dies away, and a quiet horn offers one more statement of the lower strings' 'answer' to E–F–A–B.

Half a minute later the music moves, with the unmediated directness found when one thing replaces another in a dream, into Allegro moderato and 3/4; by now we are in E♭ major, as far as one could be from the A minor of the opening, and Rubbra's never-far-distant vein of joy recalls music in 3/4 from the first movement. This section opens up with a jubilant tune on the first violins and trumpet, and soon another, in a quicker tempo, on the high woodwind. A further melody on the first violins is marked 'grazioso ed espress.', the gentler effect being emphasised by the drop in key from A to A♭. But the initial mood is soon restored, with the high woodwind skirling merrily over the strings' and trumpets' melody.

And that, in many a symphony, could be that – quick main section after quiet introduction, triumph after doubt. But it is never so simple with Rubbra, for this proves to be just an interim climax rounding off the first section. The course of the Viola Concerto's finale seems likely to repeat itself; the sky begins to darken, with various versions of the 'motto' idea guiding the music, and quite soon a strange new mood sets in; though the tempo is that of the movement's opening, a horn and trumpet feel their way into unknown territory. The strings, too, are eventually becalmed, in a brief and curiously Mahlerian passage. They soon reassert the basically joyful mood found in the main quick section; in a full-scale sonata form movement this would feel like the start of the recapitulation, but after seven recognisable bars from the opening of the Allegro moderato Rubbra drastically foreshortens the whole thing in order to close out the work at not-too-great length. The final bars are strong and affirmative; all the same, the journey from 'goodbye to all that' to 'I like it here' has been long and eventful.

Once one knows the Rubbra Sixth, a backward look at the Fifth confirms Ottaway's view that the latter, while certainly a major achievement and significant further step, was still in a sense a work of transition from the world of the first four to a new world. Mellers' prophetic words from 1950 spring to mind – 'Rubbra's achievement has depended on his being endowed with what is, for a man of the contemporary world, rather a peculiar spiritual make-up'. Such a nature appreciates the varied and tempting beauties of the world and yet longs to turn away from them towards something still truer and yet more lasting. That conflict is spelled out in the Fifth Symphony's uncertainties, but in the Sixth it seems no conflict at all – and certainly not of the kind so often thought essential to a symphony; reflectiveness and joy coexist, with no more conflict than lies in the knowledge that, come the end, one or the other must have the last word. Either could round it off equally convincingly, but he can't have both. The composer has discovered an inner space whose fullness it is his privilege to explore, undistracted. The stillness at the opening of the Sixth Symphony's slow movement is something quite different from the poignant beauty of the corresponding movement of the Fifth – nothing any longer threatens, though the eventual trumpet summons is irresistible. And elsewhere the later work is pervaded by sheer joy, Rubbra in what one may call his 'Alleluia' mood.

This symphony corresponds in Rubbra's output to another Sixth, the 'Pastoral', in Beethoven's; the rapt, relaxed thankfulness of the Shepherd's Hymn after the storm is as real and profound as the ecstatic joy evoked in the finale of the 'Choral' Symphony (and less likely to be confused with a samizdat plea for 'freedom'). Similarly, Rubbra achieves sublimity in this often cheerful symphony, balancing quiet rapture against forthright acceptance of all that is good about existence. Robert Simpson was known to muddy the waters of aesthetic discussion by calling the Second Viennese School's music 'anti-life'; the expression 'pro-life' has meanwhile become loaded, but the Rubbra Sixth can fairly be called life-asserting. Its ability also to summon up a psychic state that is detached from life rather than an assertion of it – its possible embodiment of mysticism in music – needs to be considered, as it will be in the ensuing chapter.

CHAPTER 7

A Question of Mysticism – II

After however much textual exegesis and background thinking one must, if one raises the idea of mysticism in Rubbra, finally turn to the music's inscrutable, ambiguous but all-important testimony. Probing the Sixth Symphony for the stigmata as identified by Elsie Payne, one can take its opening mood merely as a point of departure, from itself and from the past; the first movement's overriding vigour and variety would of itself hardly point to mystical thoughts. The melody is if anything less 'ambiguous in tonality' than others of Rubbra's, and bottomless 6-4 chords are not much in evidence, though the harp is used a good deal. The 'happy birds' interludes, like the running violins at 'Pleni sunt coeli et terra gloriae Tuae' in the Sanctus of Schubert's A♭ Mass, could suggest the pantheistic joy of the 'Vision of Dame Kind'. One should also note the curious start, with its first melodic figure sounding like an end rather than a beginning.[1] Conversely, the finale, having been written first, was creatively speaking a beginning rather than an ending. (Benedict's memoir speaks of his father as 'always conscious of beginning and end within a circle'.) Commentators – sympathetic ones, for who in the longer term writes about Rubbra except his sympathisers?[2] – have found weaknesses in the finale (Saxton finds it lacking in 'the sense of inevitability which makes the other three preceding movements so striking'), unmotivated shifts of tempo and direction, which can alternatively be viewed as interesting and having something of 'the unmediated directness with which one thing follows another in a dream' – or (to follow Payne's account of the mystical moment) with which the 'other condition' suddenly takes hold, unbidden. Such alleged weaknesses were thought to reflect the fact that the work was written 'in the wrong order', but whereas the finale of the First Symphony came into existence before Rubbra was aware he would be writing a symphony, here he composed the finale knowing what its context would be. Certainly it must be hard to write a piece to round off and sum up a larger one when the rest of the larger piece has yet to be written, but that could be all the more reason to take the greatest pains over ensuring within its bounds a strict sense of logic and causality.

The word 'inevitable' and its derivatives have been used fourteen times in this book, always as a term of praise, but there are fine distinctions here. In art, a sense of 'inevitability' is a function and duty of the creator; what seems to lack inevitability may, while not by that token any more avoidable, be taken as a sign of outside intervention, of what the insurance companies euphemistically call 'an act of God'. As remarked, mysticism is among other things a one-to-one relationship with Him (or It), and when He or It jogs one's elbow, God knows where one's pen will not stray to.

Be that as it may, at the outset it is as if Rubbra already wanted the sense, recalled from the end of the previous symphony, that 'full circle is made' – a strange starting-point, one might think, for a major work. No good composer is going to base half an hour of music on a total lack of progression, on total stasis (the term itself has acquired respectability, certainly since the mature output of Pierre Boulez), but so clear a signal at the outset could be saying something. It is a signal that has to do with form, an aspect Payne's list covers, a shade summarily, with 'fluctuating momentum and a basically episodic formality'.

In the Sixth Symphony's slow movement the frequent absence of sharp rhythms and fixed key, positively enhancing the music rather than seeming to mar it, could point us towards that 'ecstasy' and 'abdication of the will' mentioned in Musil's encapsulation of the 'other condition' or Koestler's 'inward unfolding of a kind of oceanic feeling and its slow ebbing-away'.[3] And in so quiet a movement there is clearly less place for Payne's 'melody which is forthright, positive and rhythmical', so that we may certainly regard it as 'unmetrical and ambiguous in tonality and modality'. That may seem a strange thing to say of music so far removed from discord of any kind, and yet the constant flux of the harmony makes it hard to assign any given passage to a key. Webern said of the early atonal music, 'We felt there was a tonality there but did not know which it was', and here Rubbra creates in his own totally different way a similar feeling.

His Leopardi quotation, speaking of the far horizon cut off by a low hedge, is beautiful and was clearly of huge importance to him, but does not in itself offer much of a clue, save for the idea of a deliberately chosen limitation of vision; the implied question could be, 'Why look into the distance when what you're looking for is in the here and now, modest though it may be?' Its title, however, is 'L' infinito', and the often-quoted opening continues with the less-often-quoted lines 'But as I sit and gaze, my thought conceives / Interminable vastnesses of space / Beyond it, and unearthly silences, / And profoundest calm.'

The music has, rather than 'lavish and varied harmony', a kind of 'holy poverty', a directed asceticism; as court reports used to say, it seems 'of no fixed address and without visible means of support'. Payne argued strongly that in *Song of the Soul* 'the harmony, with its ambiguous tonal and modal character, is a vital aspect of the total generic concept, contributing in a high degree to the elusive, mystical feeling of the work', and the same goes for this movement, even if it does not quite approach, as does *Song of the Soul*, the 'ecstatically detached' world of certain religious pieces by Messiaen.

For the slow movement of the Sixth Symphony to count as a classic example of Rubbra's mysticism in music, Payne's criteria need to be shown to apply, without the question-begging involved if one transfers Leopardi's sentiments directly to the music. Certainly the opening, with its wandering clarinet happy to go wherever the horns call it, and its echo of the *Dominic* Mass's 'Christe eleison', seems to tell of total detachment from the everyday world and obedience to some other, after which come the two great moments when the clarinet suddenly dives into its warm bath of cello sound; they are prime examples of 'sudden illumination'. The insistent summons towards the end could be a reminder that 'direct contact with the divine' is direct contact with something tremendous and awe-inspiring; any idea of the mystic sitting quietly with a Buddha-like smile, enjoying the company of Bruckner's 'dear God', may be very wide of the mark indeed. (A similar feeling of awe bordering on terror underlies certain numinous moments in Schubert, in both his religious and his secular music.)

As a final pointer to the nature of Rubbra's relationship with mysticism, one might recall his comment on the 'great musical mystic' Skryabin, whose reputation declined sharply with the post-1918 revulsion against over-ambitious, pseudo-spiritual theorising, but whose 'strength of purely musical thought' deserved to be reassessed once the inter-war period had danced, and then limped, its way towards world catastrophe.

An alternative view of the Sixth Symphony opens up when one realises the source of its E–F–A–B kernel – the initials of Rubbra himself, his first son Francis, his wife Antoinette and his other son Benedict. Rubbra settled the Payne–Ottaway argument by saying both were right about 'E–F–A–B', but passed over its function as an acrostic. Musically speaking, even Schumann could have been no more explicit, and the complex of names, notes and life points to concern for those his conduct had caught up in an inextricable tangle of emotions and actions. Hence the profundity of this slow movement, an exemplification of the new level Rubbra's music attained during his long and deep relationship with Antoinette. The quotations from the symphony in the Violin Concerto, two years after the final breakdown of the marriage and at a time when he had already composed another, could point in the same direction. It could also be more than coincidence that the passage from the

1948 *Missa Sancti Dominici* reproduced five years later in the slow movement's 'follow-my-leader' fifths and single notes set the words 'Christ have mercy on us'.

The Sixth Symphony stands at the mid-point of a sixty-year career lasting from the early 1920s to the early 1980s. The first half of Rubbra's creative life was a steady ascent, both musical and spiritual; the second deepened his insight, while bringing unexpected developments.

CHAPTER 8

The Seventh Symphony

Viewing Rubbra's involvement with the symphony as a lifelong journey, one might wonder where there was for him to go after the peak achieved in the Fifth and Sixth. In neither work had he 'entirely solved the finale problem' (to use a cliché favoured by commentators aiming to keep their elders and betters in their place); he had found, rather, his own more reflective way to round off a major work, and that would be his cue for action when he again reached the later stages of a symphony. One might for that matter have wondered where there was for Beethoven to go after the same number of symphonies – and go Rubbra certainly would, for a tireless composer never rests on his laurels: to such a man, writing music is too natural an activity ever to cease, and life and death for their part present constant new problems demanding fresh thought. As he said in a BBC talk on The Symphony, 'it is this very questioning at every step that moulds one's own idiom'.

Rubbra's mind continued to run on the symphony, another following only two years after the Sixth, during which time he wrote seven other works, some very brief, some of medium length, such as the *Ode to the Queen* (Op. 83) commissioned by the BBC for the Coronation celebrations, or two further recorder works, the *Fantasia on a Theme of Machaut* and *Cantata Pastorale*. In the latter he used as basis a melodic motif he had heard played by an Indian musician, and it was the only piece in which he was 'influenced ... by the exterior exoticisms of mode and rhythm' found in Indian music (*BCI*). Its obviously exotic features are the interval of the augmented second, B–A♭, between its second and third notes, and the brief shakes and trills over some of the melody. The intrinsic qualities of Indian music were, however, a powerful influence on the Piano Concerto written at about the same time. In 1955 he also produced *Two Sonnets* for medium voice, viola and piano, Op. 86, to 'intense'[1] texts by William Alabaster (1568–1640), who had after an eventful career become Dean of St Paul's – Rubbra commented that he 'had the unusual distinction of being persecuted by the Protestants when a Protestant, and by the Catholics when a Catholic'. The *Sonnets* were dedicated to Antoinette.

Rubbra meanwhile added a further trio of Tenebrae Nocturns to the set begun four years earlier, dedicating it to the Catholic priest, music critic and broadcaster Alec Robertson; the first set (which bears no dedication) waited until the same year for its première by the Orpington and Bromley Choir under

Audrey Langford at a concert in the Wigmore Hall. Judas the Traitor is the centre-piece of this trio's texts, and a sign of Rubbra's undiminished respect for tradition is found in the second, which makes incessant use of the interval of the augmented fourth/diminished fifth, that is to say the tritone, looked on by early church musicians as 'the devil in music' (*diabolus in musica*). The piece departs from the set's prevalent homophony, opening with a gaunt unison line to which a counterpointing second part is soon added. The final three Nocturns would not be written for a further six years; in that sustained preoccupation with Passiontide the *Sinfonia Sacra*, composed fifteen years later, found its roots.

But the major work from the time between the Sixth and Seventh symphonies, to yet another BBC commission, was a Piano Concerto, Op. 85 (in view of Op. 30 his second, though not so entitled). Denis Matthews was its first soloist, with Sir Malcolm Sargent once again conducting the BBC Symphony Orchestra, on 21 March 1956. Rubbra prefaced the score with a quotation from the *Inferno*: when in Book III Dante and Virgil, as yet only at Hell's vestibule rather than its punishment circles, come upon the 'opportunists', Virgil's comment is 'Non ragioniam di lor, ma guarda e passa' (Let us not speak of them, but look and pass on). In 1956 Rubbra had yet to feel the full impact of the musical profession's latest consignment of opportunists (see Chapter 9) and the quotation was to that extent prophetic. Whilst composing the concerto he heard performances by the great sarod player Ali Akbar Khan, and the work's dedication is 'To A.A.K. in homage'. (What Dr Alfred A. Kalmus made of that, should he have come across it, is anyone's guess!)

If there was ever a piece to fill the well-meaning music-lover with despair over words about music, while profoundly thanking his Maker for its existence, it must be Rubbra's Piano Concerto. With few of his works are his own comments quite so unhelpful, speaking of technical tricks that helped the composition process but can hardly enlighten the listener. They were conscientiously reproduced and commented on by Grover, but what one hears is fascinating at a far deeper, intuitive level. The concerto is by some way one of his simplest major works in terms of harmony, making much of its broken-chord opening and rarely deviating into anything the analyst could call 'chromatic'; it is as if he turned aside from the preoccupations of the day to rediscover simple things enjoyed earlier in life (which even included the sound and 'feel' of the piano). The first movement's structure is mercurial and, despite some superficial similarities to sonata form, hard to categorise. Rubbra gave it the title 'Corymbus', a biological term to do with the length of stalks growing upward to form a flower-head, and related that to a procedure whereby his ideas, when repeated, were added to. That happens not with immediate repetition but through the expansion of whole returning sections, and (as Grover convincingly demonstrated) the 'additions' are then enormous – a 'first subject' section lasting ten bars the first time round spreads to twenty-five the second, with a second subject expanded even more, from twenty to sixty-eight.[2] Such massive recomposition needs to impress by its own musical weight (and since this is Rubbra it of course does!) rather than by perceptible reference to what has gone before. What one hears is in effect a quotation followed by new material. Order does in a sense, a very quirky sense, prevail; the first movement is a *locus classicus* for Rubbra's impulsive changes of direction and sudden transitions. Indeed it is yet another – and in some ways among the best – of his 'single arcs of sound, with a long growth towards a climax point and then a relaxation of tension'. Its wealth of small but original ideas would deserve a study to itself; a memorable one just over three and a half minutes in offers us rippling piano figuration against a bell-like descending figure on the wind and harp, a counterpart to the 'happy birds' in the Sixth Symphony's first movement, and a foretaste of the 'starlight' music in the Seventh Symphony's a couple of years on. There is something of the 'Vision of Dame Kind' in these hints of joy from the natural world. It would take unusual and unusually sensitive antennae to detect anything oriental in the sound of this music. As, yet again, the movement 'makes full circle', it does so very concisely, and creates not the obvious 'O' shape but rather a 'Q' shape, for after the 'gradual return to the slow and reflective opening' a strongly contrasted and memorable quiet codetta makes strait the way for the slow movement, which Rubbra called a 'Dialogue'.

The work at times gives more the impression of a 'true' piano concerto, with its implications of strife and mutual emulation, than did the *Sinfonia Concertante*; Donald Mitchell's comment at the time that it was 'a piano concerto without a piano' seems hard to justify. Any concerto movement (except those of Chopin, who was more given to divine monologue with the orchestra smiling in the background) is likely to be either a dialogue or a confrontation; the latter is the more dramatic alternative, but what Rubbra, departing from his usual anti-adjectival stance, called the 'philosophical and at times impassioned discourse' of soloist and orchestra can be as rewarding in its quieter way. His slow movement has things in common with the most famous example of an ultra-impassioned discourse or dialogue, the corresponding movement in Beethoven's Fourth Piano Concerto, though that is really a unique case of confrontation which, through dialogue, changes into reconciliation. Grover usefully summarised the similarities and differences: the two movements have in common an opening with the orchestra stating its position in unharmonised octaves, and the piano responding with a 'harmonised' melody. (In the Rubbra the harmony is limited, as in the second Nocturn, to one counterpointing part.) And at the end of both, a hushed orchestral passage seems convinced and repentant. But the differences are greater – Beethoven confined his orchestra to the strings, hardly allowed piano and orchestra to be heard at the same time, and certainly never let them share any melodic ideas, whereas Rubbra uses the whole orchestra and lets it mix freely, in both the latter respects, with the piano. There lies the crucial distinction between dialogue and confrontation. The obvious issue is lines moving through wide intervals (the orchestra at the start) against conjunct movement (the piano's response). Some such dialogue has already occurred in the first respective entries of piano and strings in the first movement, indeed it is found throughout Rubbra's extended works. 'Philosophical discourse' must take place at a deeper level, and what Rubbra was referring to, in purely musical terms, is still open to analysis.

The finale, Danza alla Rondo, is for much of its length a rare example of The Bizarre Rubbra; nowhere else does he come so close to the relatively strident, ebullient world of a Prokofiev, but, above all, Bartók's Third Piano Concerto seems to be in the background. One of that composer's very last works, it was beginning to become familiar in Europe during the middle 1950s, its relative mellowness a surprise after his first two exceptionally percussive essays in the genre. There was already something of it in Rubbra's slow movement, and both concertos refer there to Beethoven; Bartók vividly recalls the 'Heiliger Dankgesang' in the late A minor String Quartet.

The Rondo's opening orchestral colours are garish; Rubbra treats himself to his most highly spiced percussion section, with celesta, glockenspiel, xylophone, castanets, tambourine, side drum and bass drum, though he uses them so sparingly that only one player is called for. There is even an optional organ part for a few bars. At the start the timpani, rather than doing their normal Cassandra job with steady beats, show off with a rhythm the piano immediately picks up. It spells out the alternating notes of the interval of the third, a call associated in life with babies, cats, cuckoos, and in recent times public-service vehicles on urgent errands. The second of Schönberg's otherwise eminently dissonant *Three Piano Pieces*, Op. 11, makes play with such undulating thirds, as a tantalising suggestion of a D minor tonality which never materialises, and in Rubbra's Rondo the 'first episode' also does so, first wishing them on a high solo trumpet,[3] though the piano immediately seizes on the idea.

A high clarinet brays disrespectfully, the xylophone enjoys one of its rare outings, and there is a well-judged intervention by the castanets (had Rubbra's Spanish ancestor mislaid his return ticket?). In colour terms, the nearest precedent for such music would be the opening of Ravel's concerto.

This driving finale has variety and a compelling train of thought, with memorable changes of mood and tempo such as the 'second episode', some two minutes in, where the Sixth Symphony's easy-going Allegretto seems to be in Rubbra's mind. That symphony's 'happy birds' found successors in the concerto's opening movement, and from time to time in the finale Rubbra's joyous bells are also strongly in evidence; he marked a steady triple-time section after the biggest orchestral climax 'trionfale', and at its peak it takes on a distinct touch of Elgarian 'nobility' for a bar or two. (This is where the optional organ pedal holds a long F♯ before moving down the scale to a low D: the scale means that the passage could not be 'covered' by someone unfamiliar with the organ who simply held down with his foot a single note, perhaps marked as a reminder!)[4]

From here the finale proceeds to the piano's one cadenza in the work. This, in view of its leisurely look at various ideas that have been important earlier, he headed 'retrospettiva'. Not quite an old-style showpiece for the soloist's virtuosity, it still reminds us what a feeling for the piano Rubbra had. Bit by bit he steers us magisterially back to the music with which the concerto opened, a calm G minor chord and its juxtaposed minor mediant (B♭ minor), so once again 'full circle' seems at hand; but he rouses himself from his reverie, with the help of those ever-ready timpani, to add a quite skittish coda, mostly quiet but with some surprising sudden *forte*s. The final fizzle is distinctly Bartókian in the most engaging way.

The Piano Concerto seems a one-off in Rubbra's output: Hans Sachs's words about Walther's trial song to the assembled Mastersingers could apply: 'It sounded so old, yet it was so new.' All in all, one might say it suggests a stage in life – not everyone's but some people's – which near the start of *Molloy*'s second half Samuel Beckett sums up in the words 'In such surroundings slipped away my last moments of peace and happiness.' The next concerto, for violin, and before that the next symphony, will offer glimpses of a changed inner world.

For the City of Birmingham Symphony Orchestra's 1956–7 and 1957–8 seasons three composers had major works commissioned with funds from the Feeney Trust. Michael Tippett produced his colossally difficult Piano Concerto, whose designated soloist declared it unplayable, whereupon the young John

Ogdon stepped confidently in to prove him wrong; Sir Arthur Bliss's commission was his *Meditations on a Theme of John Blow*, and Rubbra's a further symphony, his Op. 88. He had various other works in hand at the time, Rubbra said that for him a deadline inhibited the flow of ideas rather than helping it, and the orchestra agreed not to insist on a date for delivery. Once embarked on the symphony he took nine months, with many interruptions, but the impressive finale was completed in only three weeks. The orchestra's chief conductor Andrzej Panufnik was in charge of the Symphony's première on 1 October 1957, and Rubbra dedicated the work to the orchestra.

He talked about his Seventh Symphony for BBC Radio's *Music Magazine* on 23 March 1958, and began by saying that the more symphonies he wrote, the harder it became:

> the problems get progressively more difficult, unless one is content to repeat oneself – a thing that no self-respecting artist will consciously do ... My aim has always been to make each symphony inhabit, as far as possible, a distinct world of its own ... I don't start a symphony until I'm fully aware of the distinctiveness of the originating idea that comes to me ... In the new work I've re-lived my ideas in terms of orchestral colouring rather than clothed them in merely appropriate colours ... The listener should find in the new symphony that the melodic texture, which is still there as a natural part of my thinking, is 'spotlighted' in ways more various than have been usual in my previous symphonies.

Both the Seventh and Eighth symphonies, like the First, end with a slow movement, a sizeable scherzo intervening. Here the opening movement falls into two sections (Lento e molto espressivo, 3/2, C major, followed by Allegro moderato), a brief coda then recalling main ideas from the first. At the start, the distant horns that were so magical in the slow movement of the Sixth Symphony make their presence felt again, to more elegiac effect – 'the basic note-pattern of the first movement consists of two upward semitones and a falling fifth. Heard at the outset in the interweaving colour of two horns its presence is felt in the whole of the introduction'.

At the start the two-semitone-plus-fifth fragment (Ex. 40) is given out over a tremolo deep in the bass on the tonic of the key, C, with the sound of the harp as accompanying colour. This is the nearest Rubbra ever comes to a 'Brucknerian' beginning where shape slowly emerges from mystery. Reviewing *Veni Creator Spiritus* in *The Musical Times* in 1966, Andrew Porter wrote of a 'sometimes Brucknerian splendour' and detected at times 'the full, gentle

Ex. 40 Symphony no. 7, first movement

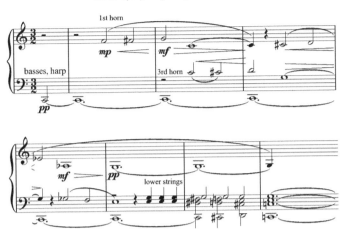

surge of Bruckner's *piano* writing for similar forces', but though the two composers share an overriding religious faith and a passion for counterpoint, a
great Brucknerian build-up is very much a matter of harmony, an unparalleled
command of the nooks and crannies in the 'cycle of fifths', which Rubbra felt
had had its day.

The immediate answering and warmer idea for the divided lower strings
(Ex. 40) could be a reminder, as in the slow movement of the preceding symphony, of a texture near the start of Schubert's 'Great' C Major. The fragment
of chromatic scale in the middle parts is like the one just heard from the horns.
This not-very-complex 'complex' is repeated and developed at slightly greater
length each time, in the way recently familiar from the Piano Concerto, and
with other instruments taking a prominent role – first the oboe, in a dialogue
with the horn that calls to mind Mahler's loneliness, then the upper strings.
It all offers one of the more easily followed ways to start an extended piece,
and what fascinates is the compelling and inevitable-seeming way in which
'material' opens up and blossoms to form melody. Harmony is less crucial
here, the opening C pedal continuing for a while. Rubbra has already begun to
be interested 'more by intervals than by keys', though he did not set that down
as his new guiding principle until the next symphony. There are more of the
impressive string-section 'cloudscapes' found in the work's two predecessors.

The semitone-plus-semitone figure is ubiquitous in this movement (Grover
detected no fewer than ninety appearances of it), and yet it is not one of the
movement's 'themes' – rather a component that can appear in innumerable
guises. Two minutes in, during the third statement of the opening complex,

the first violins lend their weight to the argument or plea, introducing an new-ish idea related to it (similar rhythm and semitones, the falling interval now widened to a sixth); this is a distinct reminiscence of the figure – Ex. 36 – that dominated the previous symphony's scherzo. Rubbra's characteristic quiet drum-beats are there in the background. The string version of the melody emphasises something mentioned by the composer but less obvious at the outset because of overlapping entries – the fact that the seminal idea not only rises through the fragment of chromatic scale, but then falls to give yet another version of a favourite Rubbra idea, semitone plus fifth. The wind instruments spin the line a little further on those terms, and finally the violins come up with one more strong variant of the original idea, which a little later than usual (something over three minutes in) gets the Allegro 'main body of the move-ment' under way without caesura of any kind and with the pulse remaining unchanged.

Until almost the end of the movement Rubbra dances, now sedately, now with a sense of awesome things on his mind. If there is an echo here, it would be of the quieter Tchaikovsky, for example the music at the corresponding point in the first movement of that composer's Fourth Symphony. Ex. 41 shows the most prominent and frequently repeated idea, and the unfailing double upbeat continues a pervading rhythm that has crept in with the drum-beats. Hence the sense of inevitability and yet improvisation at this point. Within Rubbra's output, a near relative is the corresponding section in the first move-ment of the 1952 Viola Concerto. In his radio talk Rubbra pointed out that the 'temporary damping-down' of the introduction theme's power made its subse-quent appearances all the more dramatic – by his standards a rare divagation into subjective comment! He went on to say that 'the whole movement closely follows classical sonata form'; after a central intensive process of development, themes are recapitulated in the order (but not necessarily the mood) in which they were first heard, justifying Saxton's nomination of this as one of Rubbra's two 'most classically modelled' symphonies, along with the Third. So one may fairly expect a second subject, or second-subject group; given the prevailing

Ex. 41 Symphony no. 7, first movement, bar 35 (fig. 3)

sense of continuity, one might have a problem choosing between various new melodic ideas heard from four minutes onward. In that sense the exposition has a Mozartean fullness. Fortunately Rubbra has done our work for us, since his talk nominated an oboe melody. It begins (Ex. 42) at bar 99 after a powerful climax dominated by drum-beats, and first quotes the work's opening (compare Ex. 40), which is by classical standards a strange way for a second, contrasting subject to behave. It also comes remarkably late in the section, but its twinkling arpeggiated accompaniment for the violins and violas[5] makes it a genuine onward step, and a most memorable one; here is another example of Rubbra's 'Dame Kind' euphoria, already met in the 'magic birds' sections of the preceding symphony's first movement. Though quite brief, and shorter still when recapitulated, it is a high point. Rubbra's further comment that even the bass accompanying his second subject embodies more than hints of the introductory music is, at this remove, hard to follow. The striking dance in the first movement of the 1956 *Cantata Pastorale* is in the background, and this is also the one passage in Rubbra that could remind a Franz-Schmidt-lover of the hedonistic music (for example, the First Symphony) written by that composer during his early years. A little of Schmidt's music (Carnival Music and Intermezzo from *Notre Dame*, Fourth Symphony) had been heard here during the 1930s, while Rubbra was a critic, BBC performances being conducted by Clarence Raybould and then by Schmidt's pupil and great interpreter Oswald Kabasta, but he never wrote about Schmidt, whose First Symphony has at times a comparably controlled euphoria.

Ex. 42 Symphony no. 7, first movement, 'second subject' – oboe theme at bar 99 (fig. 10)

What is less 'classically modelled' about the main section of this movement is its rhythmic unity. For a main symphonic movement to be 'monorhythmic', as distinct from monothematic (which, as we have just seen, this one is not), must be an extreme rarity. It is amazing to hear the variety Rubbra can achieve as he elaborates the dance rhythm of the main section's opening. The music passes through many moods, from monkishly determined to playful. The development section at first feel its way, then gains confidence in a long assertive paragraph for the upper strings which brings the first climax. The music quietens and for a while Payne's 'ephemeral' sounds – harp, but also celesta – dominate the accompaniment. Along with the harp, the stringed instruments playing pizzicato are also prominent in this first of Rubbra's symphonic movements whose ideas 'have been re-lived in terms of orchestral colour'.

The start of the recapitulation is hardly identifiable as such by the listener, crashing in amid the uproar of another big climax. True to his nature, Rubbra repeats very little literally, and when he does so the change is towards the dark and threatening; the extraordinary plucked-sound accompaniment to the next statement of the theme is a striking example. After another drum-dominated climax reproducing the one in the exposition, the twinkling 'second-subject' passage has only a brief lease of life – all part of this movement's gradual movement back towards darkness. Where in the 'exposition' there was a further short but strong idea on the violins to round off the section, Rubbra now moves straight to the 'codetta', the music reverting for its final minute to the initial slow tempo. First comes a remembrance of the strings' 'comfort and warmth' figure, which has taken on a new gravity, and then their secondary idea from two minutes in. It all makes a most effective ending, though for once the ensuing movement is not being set up.

In that movement, a scherzo (Vivace e leggiero, 9/8, D minor ending in C major), Rubbra is at his most spirited, and his most prodigal in the way that gave Dittersdorf trouble over Mozart. The initial dotted rhythm derives, according to Rubbra's talk, from one 'heard in isolation just before the coda of the first movement', though before that it has formed part of his 'second subject' (Ex. 42*); purely as a rhythm it is (probably by coincidence rather than design) also the one heard at the start of the scherzo in Beethoven's 'Choral' Symphony, with which it shares its key of D minor. It is so impressive and persistent that it must surely have stuck in a mind as receptive as Dittersdorf's! Apart from the idea Rubbra mentioned, two from previous scherzos combine in the main theme (Ex. 43) – the rising upbeat figure in 9/8 from the Second Symphony, and the constant mixture of triple and duple time found in the Sixth. Indeed, the asymmetric time-signatures 5/8 and 7/8 appear frequently, so that the music is full of cross-rhythms. Again as in the corresponding movement of the Second Symphony, sections in 2/4 also contradict the basic 9/8 measure; the end of Ex. 43 shows how the same rhythm fits into the two different time-signatures.

Ex. 43 Symphony no. 7, second movement: scherzo opening,
and inversion with different time-signature in 'Elizabethan' Trio I (bar 154, fig. 44)

This scherzo is also unusually rich in points of colour, one of the strangest coming when the cor anglais and first bassoon in octaves share a melody in a way that can mislead the score-less listener into believing he is hearing a saxophone. (That instrument is nowhere used in the symphony, nor in any other of Rubbra's.) Vaughan Williams had used the saxophone memorably in his 1931 'Masque for Dancing', *Job*, to characterise Satan, and would give it a comparably seductive tune in the Trio of his post-war Sixth Symphony's Scherzo. The melody at this point in Rubbra's Seventh Symphony is full of gawky-sounding five- or seven-quaver bars. There are well-timed brief entries for a number of percussion instruments, including the new 'treat' from the Sixth Symphony's scherzo and Piano Concerto, the xylophone, and also, notably, the side drum. In view of the possible Bartók reference immediately after the first side-drum passage, it may be worth recalling that the 'Intermezzo Interrotto' from the Bartók Concerto for Orchestra begins and ends with striking solos for that instrument.

Rubbra said (and marked in his score) that his scherzo had two trios, 'one bright ... almost like an Elizabethan dance ... and one sombre, but only because it's a very much slowed-down version of the opening theme'. (The section with the 'saxophone tune' must have struck him as too short to rate as a trio.) His 'trios' come quite a long way in, and without that pointer one might have trouble identifying them; the first could be taken for just one more in the incessant flow of apparently new ideas. This 'Elizabethan dance' is a little like the sort of pastiche Peter Warlock so effectively wrote in his *Capriol Suite*.[6]

A passage for paired wind instruments about four and a half minutes in offers a new version of Sir Donald Tovey's 'Great Bassoon Joke', and these bars with their constant movement in parallel thirds could make one wonder whether Rubbra had been listening to another movement, 'Play of the Couples', in Bartók's Concerto for Orchestra, which was his most often-heard work during the years after his death in 1945.

As for the quite short 'second trio', ushered in by the always-impressive sound of a gong, it acts rather as a weighty coda that changes the direction of the entire work. Its opening is a possible further echo of Tchaikovsky, whose 'Pathétique' Symphony introduces its final section with a gong-stroke like a summons to the Hereafter. Here it begins the process of setting up the finale; a brief final assertion of the pushy dotted rhythm takes the music to the very brink. It is easy to see how the composer's apostles could value this scherzo, with its bewildering 'flight of ideas',[7] above the one in the Fifth Symphony. Its constant rhythmic jinking deceives the ear rather as an outstanding rugby fly-half will trick and feint his way past the opposition, and it must count as Rubbra's most powerfully impressive scherzo so far – the Holst of 'Mercury the Winged Messenger' raised to a higher power, and the most daunting exemplification of the demonic Rubbra. Here is a mid-1950s version of Mephistopheles' 'wish to upset, that brings good about'.[8] Certainly Rubbra's stated aim 'to achieve continual bright contrasts' is brilliantly achieved. This is one of his greatest movements; he himself was aware of its 'stature' (though with typical modesty he meant merely its ten-minute length) and said it had deterred him from following the usual pattern of slow movement and finale: 'a slow Passacaglia and Fugue [would be] a more appropriate ending'.

Rubbra committed himself to the extent of calling this finale 'meditative throughout', but otherwise offered no hint of any emotional background beyond a conventional reference to 'impassioned climaxes'. It is a Passacaglia and Fugue (Lento, 8/8, C minor, which at the very end turns, as little more than a *tierce de Picardie*, to C major), and to a half-way sensitive listener a steady outpouring of something construable as profound emotion, as well as being an outstanding example of sustained thought. At almost fourteen minutes it is the second-longest movement in any Rubbra symphony, only the finale of the First being longer. Banfield's Finzi biography suggests that it was a memorial tribute to Rubbra's contemporary, greatest friend and composer-colleague, who had recently died, aged only fifty-six. That, if correct, would throw light on the gong-stroke near the end of the previous movement and answer the question 'Where next from the previous two symphonies?' with 'The world is too much with us'. A glimpse of eternity is no insurance against harrowing developments in 'real life'. Between the timelessness of the Sixth and the willed optimism at the end of the Eighth, with its evocation of Teilhard de Chardin, the Seventh and Eighth symphonies could tell of a renewed and agitated coming-to-terms with the demands of life and death.

The passacaglia finale is built on a three-section repeating paragraph (Ex. 44),[9] which, as Rubbra said, 'is never forgotten during the whole course of the movement – indeed it wouldn't have been a Passacaglia *had* I forgotten it'. Its third figure (*), with a falling triplet followed by a wide rising interval, is irresistibly reminiscent of the most memorable motif from the Shepherd's gloomy air in the third act of Wagner's *Tristan and Isolde*. In his 1953 lecture with the strictures on Schönberg Rubbra made it clear that he traced music's atonal disintegration back to Wagner and his ethos: 'I admit the giant stature of Wagner as a musician, but for me he's the most secular of all composers and the bogus religiosity of Parsifal only serves to underline his teeming portrayal, however idealised, of human ardours and passion, divorced from any qualities that stem from a humble acceptance of man as a being dependent upon God.' That 'giant stature' was manifest above all in Wagner's uncanny ability to find briefest musical ideas which in some inexplicable way impress themselves on one for ever as correlates of things in the 'secular' world; without it, his enormous apparatus of leitmotifs would have been an intellectual monstrosity, and it impressed itself deeply enough on Rubbra to occasion at least a couple of significant musical quotations.

Ex. 44 Symphony no. 7, third movement: Passacaglia theme

The figure in the Seventh Symphony's finale is also slightly reminiscent of the fugue subject in that of the *Sinfonia Concertante*. The cor anglais, so evocative in the Wagner, has two important statements of the crucial figure in Rubbra's later finale. As in *Tristan*, the feeling is as if a drama had passed its catastrophic crisis and the story must now move ineluctably towards its ending. The same prelude would be differently conjured up a year later in another passacaglia, *Pezzo Ostinato* for harp (see p. 151). That piece's extreme monothematicism would not have done for a symphonic finale, which given its function required more variety and a progression towards a climax for both itself and the work as a whole.

Two other features of this passacaglia theme should be mentioned. Its first and third figures are played only by the lower strings (cellos and basses, the violas being added in the third). A sense of recitative is created, especially at *, and one may well recall the double bass passages that turn the course of the finale in Beethoven's 'Choral' Symphony, as if already singing the words heard later from the baritone soloist, 'Oh friends, not these sounds, Let us tune our voices to something more agreeable.' The theme even reaches its final note[10] on A, which does not belong in C minor, but was the dominant on which that Beethoven bass line ended, leading into his movement's tonic, D major. The other feature, most unusually, is that the middle figure of the three is harmonised, by a line for the bassoons. Rubbra, like Beethoven at the first variation on his 'joy' theme, here rises above 'the great bassoon joke', but yet again a classical model is for Rubbra, as for all great composers before him, merely a starting-point – not a quotation, but a sign of a well-stocked mind.

A movement as vast as this finale presents composer and listener alike with the greatest challenges, which Rubbra exacerbates, declining to follow his great predecessors in treating a passacaglia as a set of variations. Saxton points, as an obvious model ignored, to that supreme symphonic passacaglia, the finale of Brahms's Fourth Symphony. Rubbra's finale he rightly calls 'not a set of variations, but ... continuously flowing, without fixed sections', something that applies even down to the way in which Rubbra overlaps the appearances of his basic paragraph, one arising seamlessly out of the end of the preceding one. Nor does the theme stay in the bass; its three segments are split among different parts of the orchestra in different registers. The web of counterpoint around the theme makes it often play much the role of the chorale melody in one type of Bach chorale prelude; one's attention is diverted so that the theme becomes a pervading flavour rather than a rigid frame.

When Rubbra returned to the passacaglia five years later in another recorder work for Carl Dolmetsch, the Passacaglia on Josquin's *Plusieurs regrets*, Op. 113, he cast it in a clear, if free, variation-form. The symphonic finale's abhorrence of any obvious matrix, be it variations or sonata, clearly carries the danger that the combination of a constantly repeated formula and continuous flux could make one feel 'But we've been here already, he's repeating himself!' The need for the composer to balance that danger against the chance of driving home his point, precisely by using the rhetoric inherent in such repetition, was mentioned when the Fourth Symphony's opening movement was discussed, and the same problem and opportunity are here solved and exploited with unfailing structural sense. From time to time the basic paragraph resurfaces from the contrapuntal whirlpool, and the 'Tristan' idea tends to stand out whenever it appears. A very detailed account of how Rubbra avoids monotony in all this was provided by Grover.

The mood changes subtly after eight statements of the passacaglia paragraph. Rather than the constant slow surge and heave met so far, we find a version of the basic theme which comes over as purer melody, with the oboe accompanied by stiller, repeated chords on the strings. This is peace of a sort, and the texture gradually thins down to a delicate fabric of high solo instruments, with the timpani quietly tapping out an accompaniment. Despite one further threatening surge of the theme, the music is calmer and more purely elegiac than in the opening minutes, with the harp and celesta adding their delicate voices now and then.

In a remarkable further clearing of the air, single woodwind instruments lead off the slow dance of the concluding fugue in 6/8, with the triply divided beat recalling the measure in the opening movement's main section. The necessary period of mourning is definitively over and it is time to give thanks for what was there.[11] In the fugue subject (Ex. 45) the intervals of the 'Tristan' idea (Ex. 44*) are well to the fore; indeed its second, third, fourth and fifth notes follow its shape at a different pitch, though with the significant difference that the original minor sixth becomes a major sixth, to curiously reassuring effect. In his Oxford Bach lectures Rubbra loved to point out connections of that kind between preludes and fugues.

Ex. 45 Symphony no. 7, third movement: Fugue theme

At the very end he yet again achieves an effortless change of mood; the first two figures only from the passacaglia theme quietly round off this great outburst of sustained feeling. The desolate Tristanesque third element, so prevalent all along, is suddenly a thing of the past. Mahler at the end of his Sixth Symphony conveys existential terror through the simple use of a minor chord not preceded, as it has been throughout the work, by the major; it is as if a lighthouse beam that had gone from light to dark to light, throughout a lifetime, now finally stayed dark.[12] Rubbra's equally simple omission of his theme's dark element has the opposite but equally sublime effect. All in all, the symphony marks a progression from *Sehnsucht* through frenzy and despair, to reconciliation.

The English musical climate would change dramatically over the eight years before Rubbra began to work on a further symphony, for a game of 'catch-up' was under way. It is tempting to think of William Glock's appointment to be the BBC's new Controller, Music, as the turning-point (he took up the post in the middle of 1959, and the next chapter deals with the consequences of that), but on closer examination it proves less simple. The full implications of the 'Glock Doctrine of Creative Unbalance' took time to become apparent, and in the short term all seemed well.

The twenty-three years between the composition of Rubbra's First Symphony and his Seventh also gave rise to thirty-seven non-symphonic works; the eight years between symphonies nos. 7 and 8 gave rise to forty-two. Liturgical pieces from 1957–8 were *In Honorem Mariae Matris Dei*, for soprano and contralto soloists, children's choir, mixed voices and orchestra (Op. 97) and a *Missa a tre* (Op. 98, 1958), commissioned by the Catholic Church Music Association with the limited resources and abilities of smaller choirs in mind. It followed a pattern provided four centuries earlier by the Catholic William Byrd in his very concise Three-Part Mass, but came out all the shorter (less than ten minutes) since Rubbra did not set the text of the Credo. This is his most inward-looking Mass. The sharpened fourth/diminished fifth of the scale, already mentioned in connection with his attitude to 'mediaevalism', was clearly at the forefront of his mind, and the music uses it resourcefully at critical moments. The diminished fifth (A♭) heard near the start later turns, by some theologically justifiable symbolism,[13] into the tonic note of the closing Agnus Dei, whereupon the latter key's equivalent note, the identical-sounding though differently labelled sharpened fourth (D), is used in a comparably striking way. The procession from 'Lord have mercy' to 'Lamb of God who taketh away the sins of the world, Grant us Peace' could scarcely be better represented than by this passage from an initial key to the one as far as possible away; the faith that reconciles the two abides in the prominent notes they share. For all its simplicity, these tritones' constant recurrence throughout the *Missa a tre* creates a curious and slightly disturbed feeling; in view of the stage in Rubbra's life at which it was composed, it is not unthinkable that somewhere at the back of his mind was the mediaeval view of the tritone as manifesting the devil in music. Its use would have been an effective, purely private way to transmute guilt into beauty, while not unsettling the Catholic Church Music Association and its congregations. Those notes also protrude within the diatonic texture, rather as they would were they one of the constituent notes in the scale underlying an Indian raga. But as there are also plenty of 'perfect' fourths and fifths in the Mass the analogy can not be pushed too far. For that matter, Rubbra pointed out in his lecture 'The Contemporary Composer – Tradition and Environment' that the opening theme of Bartók's *Music for Strings, Percussion and Celesta* divides its octave exactly in half rather than using the relationship tonic–fifth (dominant); it is unlikely that when he used those tritones Bartók had any 'suggestion diabolique' in mind.

The Sanctus also makes a slightly disturbing effect with its drastic juxtaposition of seemingly incompatible triads; not every composer has seen this part of the Mass in the same way, but the Sanctus has its origins in an awe-inspiring song of praise to the Deity delivered by the Heavenly Host in the Book of Revelation. For this short and basically very simple movement Rubbra gave each of the three parts a different key-signature, following a practice adopted by Holst in his 1925 *Terzetto* for flute, oboe and viola. The idea of 'polytonality' was in the air between the wars, Darius Milhaud being prominent among those who worked with it,[14] but neither Holst nor Rubbra tried to create a genuine and puzzling sense of being in more than one key at once – and certainly not to do what Milhaud and his fellow composers also loved to do, 'épater le bourgeois'. The multiple key signatures were for the most part an aid to performers, who did not have to read constant 'accidentals' when playing or singing this naturally chromatic music. The effect achieved is one of strangeness, but not of disorientation or confusion.

Rubbra returned to children's voices in 1969 for a *Missa Brevis* with organ. *Pezzo Ostinato* for solo harp is another work from 1958; Rubbra dedicated it to the ethnomusicologist and former BBC Opera Organiser Peter Crossley-Holland, much of whose non-BBC work was done as near as possible to forbidden places such as Nepal, and Rubbra said the piece was one of three which most clearly reflected long-standing influences from 'orientalising' thought (Kuanglin Pao, Madame Blavatsky's book, but also the *Indian Love-Lyrics* of Amy Woodforde-Finden, familiar from the time when he accompanied his mother). The other two pieces he had in mind were the first movement of the 1955–6 Piano Concerto and the 1930s opera *Bee-bee-bei*, later retitled *The Shadow*.

Also from 1958 was a short three-movement Oboe Sonata Op. 100, dedicated to Evelyn Rothwell and first performed by her and the composer in the Arts Council Drawing Room, London, on 17 October that year. Both *Pezzo Ostinato* and the Oboe Sonata are of interest in the context of Rubbra's larger output; the Sonata's slow second movement, 'Elegy', and fleet finale are minor gems. The Elegy is pervaded by an upbeat figure of five repeated notes (an incomplete triplet group, then a complete one), followed by a three-note figure (initially a scale fragment) on the downbeat. Crucial here is the playing-off of a note against its sharpened version, with the unsharpened one always having the last word, as if in some musical representation of regret. Oboe and piano copy each other's moves for a while, then we come to another of the passages where Rubbra, for all his emphasis on counterpoint, proves himself in the simplest way a master of harmony and its magic. Here there is a paradisal euphony reminiscent of the Sixth Symphony's slow movement, but also a strange feeling as if someone else, perhaps Gerald Finzi with his limpid diatonicism, were speaking through Rubbra. The analyst in Grover led him to say of this passage that 'the harmonies produced by the entire piano part and the oboe are not up to the standards of the rest of the section'; it could, of course, be a matter of accommodation to someone else's norms and standards, namely Finzi's. If the finale of the Seventh were indeed a major tribute to a great friend, this piece could show Rubbra anxious to complement it with a more intimate recollection. The music develops into one of his bell-like passages, with the typical scales first gentle on the oboe, the piano moving in contrary motion to it (a reminder of the Symphony's 'slow ostinato' scales), then reappearing with unexpected forcefulness as the piano takes over. This latter point marks the start (and almost the end!) of what must be Rubbra's shortest 'middle section'; its new lively melody dies away within seconds, as if the Elegy's emotions reasserted themselves to cut the party short. The brief remainder of the movement is not a reprise of what was heard earlier; it is more of a glance back, and a good deal more static (one almost dares to say 'exhausted'). But here, yet again, Rubbra is also thinking forward to 'what comes next'. A great deal is said in this Elegy's four and a half minutes.

The finale's extremely flowing piano-writing (Presto) could be a faint persisting trace of Debussy, whom Rubbra so admired. Here the bells are not 'downward-drifting and disembodied', but surrounded by a whirling haze of figuration, a reminder of the composer's pianistic ability, as of the comparably headlong music in the scherzo of his Cello Sonata twelve years earlier. One or two snatches of vigorous English-sounding melody could also make one think back to the forthright 'second section' tunes in that sonata's opening movement. The oboe is finally drawn into the vortex, and after so much quietude the ending is upbeat.

Pezzo Ostinato could scarcely be more different. Rubbra wrote it after going to a concert by Ali Akbar Khan, who eight years earlier had been the dedicatee of his Piano Concerto, and its extreme slowness of development, indeed the absence of it in any true sense, could be thought similar to that in an Indian raga. In his 1972 book *Contemporary British Music* Francis Routh wrote that 'the music revolves, with ametrical rhythms, round raga-like material, like an Indian improvisation'. In a raga, however, the static opening minutes are normally just the start of something far larger and more varied, which often culminates in frantic activity. It is all the same true (as Routh also pointed out) that the harp's pedals, once fixed, never change during the piece, any more than does the pitch to which a sarod's strings are tuned for any particular raga. Like the finale of the Seventh Symphony, *Pezzo Ostinato* is a passacaglia of peculiarly sombre character, pervaded by a fragment of scale that ascends from the second to the fifth. (Curiously, a very similar figure appears more than once in the slow movement of Alan Rawsthorne's 1949 Cello Sonata.) Monothematicism is carried to an absolute extreme, not one bar failing to echo in one way or another the two alternative versions of the scale fragment – *au naturel*, and with the seventh of the scale tagged on. Though at eight minutes' duration it is not quite a miniature, *Pezzo Ostinato* is still a cameo, a document of meditative stillness; a performer who has recorded it, Danielle Perrett, comments in her CD note that it did something not yet fashionable in the late 1950s, which would become highly trendy half a century later. (It did so without the infuriating flipness and idiot-child air flaunted by much 'minimal music'.)

During the summer of 1959 Rubbra completed a Violin Concerto (Op. 103) begun the previous year. It was first performed on 17 February 1960 by Endre Wolf with the BBC Symphony Orchestra under its Chief Conductor of the time, Rudolf Schwarz. To compare this work with, say, the one commissioned by the Cheltenham Festival a couple of years later from Alexander Goehr (b. 1932) is to become aware of the immense gap that had opened up between the ends of the English musical spectrum (something discussed more fully in the next chapter). There are symphonic echoes, not of the fairly recent Seventh but of the more distant Sixth. Immediate reminiscences of the first subject in that work's opening movement (main section) are followed later by a lyrical, decorative passage with rising and falling scales and a certain amount of twittering from the soloist, like a memory of the 'happy birds' in the same movement. It comes as welcome if temporary relief from predominantly sombre music where drum-beats have hardly let up since the start; the concerto (which unlike those for viola and for piano has no slow introduction) feels like a route-march, with repetitive beats of some kind rarely absent, whether on the drums or on other instruments. For all the differences in idiom, there may to the associative ear be a curious resemblance to a range of openings in Viennese classical music, from Beethoven's Violin Concerto, through Bruckner's

First Symphony and Mahler's Sixth to the grim march as the Israelites set off for the wilderness at the end of the second act of Schönberg's *Moses und Aron*. We have seen how frequent such beats are in Rubbra's music, but their presence from the outset is unique in his work and some kind of mood-indicator. Another figure heard a good deal is almost identical with the 'goodbye-to-all-that' idea at the very opening of No. 6 (Ex. 35), with falling fifth and U-turning minor second. There is a difference, for here the note in the middle of the figure (the tonic) is not repeated as in the symphony, but the similarity is still striking.

The solo violin part is eminently lyrical and *cantabile*, with just a little use of the instrument's ability to spin a filigree web of figuration. After a broadcast of the second performance Cyril Scott wrote to Rubbra, 'What a knowledge of the violin you have!' Even apart from its specific quotations, the concerto often feels like a throwback to the time before the Seventh Symphony, with who knows what memories in play? Its first movement is a sizeable piece, from which, for all its range of moods, the relentless beats are hardly ever absent in one form or another, like an unforgiving conscience or a heart beating feverishly. Rubbra manages to reconcile the sombre opening and the idyll, as if a man finally came to see whole someone (indeed, a violinist!) who meant so much to him. After almost a quarter of an hour the movement goes into a brief, un-virtuosic cadenza, after which it does not so much end as give way abruptly to a slow movement which Rubbra subtitled 'Poema'.

Here again there are echoes of the Sixth Symphony and its opening, evoked in who knows what spirit? The background drum-beats are felt from time to time, especially in the later stages. The brooding opening tutti, like the *Missa a tre* from a year earlier and the 1954–5 second set of Nocturns, is a further passage pervaded by Judas's uneasy tritones. The late 1950s were the time when, as Rubbra was to say apropos his next symphony, he 'gradually became aware of the dramatic and expressive values inherent in intervals' (see p. 165); different ones prevail at different points in the movement – tritone, fifth, fourth, and, in a luscious passage for the soloist, thirds, appearing as simultaneous sounds as often as they do as melody.

The initial gloom persists for almost a fifth of the movement, until the solo violin enters in C major, bringing comfort in one more of Rubbra's magical instant changes of mood. Later the solo line has a series of dialogues with wind instruments – first his favourite, the oboe; then the horns, which move slowly in parallel fifths as they so memorably did at the outset of the Sixth Symphony's slow movement; and later still with the cor anglais and flute. A climactic surge of threatening repeated notes on the brass shortly before the end recalls the 'stern summons' that broke into the Sixth Symphony's slow movement at a similar point; all this wealth of allusion is lightly touched on in passing, with even the 'moving string cloudscapes' of the two middle symphonies briefly recalled. The late summons is, for once, not a case of Rubbra's hinting at things to come, for the mood in the finale will be distinctly different. The ending itself is peaceful. This movement, too, combines great variety with a cumulative seriousness.

At the start of the finale, marked 'Allegro giocoso', Rubbra's 'Spanish ancestor' could yet again be making himself felt. Or maybe it is simply the composer's mind running back to a turning point both in terms of public success and for its associations with Antoinette: the Second Violin Sonata. The 'jocosity' proves patchy at best; Sir Donald Tovey's expression, apropos Hindemith, 'the lean athletic style' could apply as it strides resolutely out. Ronald Stevenson (*ERC*) saw this movement as a 'peasant's dance', in which 'the harmonic aesthetic is based on the open fifth, bridging the medieval age and our own', and though nothing else about the concerto points to the middle ages, the perception about fifths is in line with Rubbra's confession that intervals had begun to be of overriding interest. If the Fifth Symphony's scherzo lacked 'pungent peasantries', this music could fill a long-felt want; maybe it's best to leave it that if some of the Violin Concerto's finale is 'giocose', one would be curious to see its composer admitting to grumpiness!

The first movement ended abruptly, but the end of the entire work is positively brutal. The present-day phrase 'going pear-shaped' would suit, for the music first withers on the branch, then collapses as if lopped off. ('It was all going so well, then ...') Where the foreshortened finale of the Fifth Symphony hinted at a choice of life-styles, this drastic abbreviation could speak of disaster and surrender. Stevenson compared the sliding-up-and-down passages for the violin just before the end, and the ensuing short silence, to 'a momentary glimpse of the Angel of Death' – a daring association, but sometimes hermeneutics can tell one more than intervallic analysis. The crisis immediately follows the very last Sixth-Symphony allusion (to between bars 60 and 70 of the first movement): something was certainly dying in Rubbra's life around then. The note for a recording of the concerto spoke of its 'ending in the highest of spirits' – were that so, they must be those of the condemned man at his hearty breakfast.

Concertos, more than works in any other musical genre, put the composer uniquely 'on show', even if they are for an instrument he does not himself play. The arc formed by the three Rubbra composed between 1952 and 1959 suggest a complex pattern of inner reaction to developments in life. There is apprehension in the 1952 one for viola; almost a sense of being 'in denial' in the Piano Concerto from 1955–6, with memories vividly evoked – anything rather than having to confront the reality of the present – and an admission of defeat, however gracious, in the 1959 Violin Concerto.

Vocal music from the early 1960s included *Lauda Sion* (Op. 110, 1960), for double choir with soprano and baritone soloists,

> an outstanding example of a symphonic structure applied to an unaccompanied choral work; a rondo structure gives the work strength and cohesion ... Rubbra never surpassed this major work of grandeur and dignity; the mood of the text, which is an all-embracing poem of great power by St. Thomas Aquinas, is entirely integrated with the thematic material; and the growth and development of each run parallel. The polyphonic writing is masterly, and considerably more original than the use of a triadic idiom sometimes implies. The counterpoint is in places a chordal counterpoint; for instance, at the words 'Sub utraque specie' the canon between two 3-part chords results in a harmonic saturation, which is a unique characteristic of Rubbra's style. This recalls the opening of *Song of the Soul*. The motet marks a summit of achievement; its successor will probably not come until the 9th Symphony.[15]

Lauda Sion's melodies carry one away, the fullness of its double-choir harmonies bathes the senses in euphony, and its structure takes one through a range of moods. Not least among those are two finely retrospective quiet restatements of its vigorous opening, one of which starts a gradual winding-down of the intensity, the other initiating a further spurt, with an episode that dances as if responding to Yeats's 'Come from the holy fire, perne in a gyre'.[16]

Subsequent choral works were, in 1961, the *Cantata di Camera*, Op. 111, for tenor, mixed voices and ensemble, and a final three Nocturns for the set Op. 72, written for the Cork Festival, performed there on 19 May 1962, and dedicated to Denys Darlow and the Tilford Bach Choir. As in the second three, Judas the Traitor is invoked a good deal in the texts, and the middle piece departs from the prevailing homophony, with a curious slinking unison line that could well depict him 'on his way to betray me', though at the opening it is in fact set to Jesus' 'Could you not watch one hour with me?' (Una hora non potuistis vigilare mecum). The final 'The Elders of the people consulted together' (Seniores populi consilium fecerunt) has the highest concentration of parallel triads in the entire cycle, something possibly pertinent to Elsie Payne's examination of the mystical qualities in Rubbra's music, though one could equally take it as a late homage to Vaughan Williams and his master Holst, in whom such passages occur very often.

The Jade Mountain, a set of five songs for soprano and harp, Op. 116, dates from 1962. In classical Chinese culture, mountains were sacred for their association with deities and immortality, and ones modelled in jade doubly so. The final song, 'Farewell to a Japanese Buddhist Priest Bound Homeward', is a sign of Rubbra's ever-growing interest in comparative religion; it is examined in the next chapter, for its relationship to the Eighth Symphony. A comparable stillness is met again in the middle movement of the Third String Quartet, Op. 112, from 1963. That work was preceded by two other essays in solo-string-writing, a set of variations for violin on 'on a Phrygian[17] theme' (Op. 105), and for viola *Meditations on a Byzantine Hymn*, based on part of a melody quoted in a volume of the Oxford University Press *History of Music in Sound*, whose editor was an Oxford colleague and Byzantine scholar, Egon Wellesz. The *Variations on a Phrygian Theme* have already been mentioned apropos their variation-technique and the finale of the Third Symphony. The *Meditations* were composed for an American violist active on the London orchestral scene, Maurice Loban. Though not the most famous, he is recalled in glowing terms by those familiar with his playing.[18] Loban gave the first performance of the *Meditations* on 20 December 1962 in a recital for the BBC Home Service. Such recitals took place mostly in the morning and were not prestigious engagements; a new work by Birtwistle, Maxwell Davies or Goehr would hardly have been tucked away like that.

The *Meditations* have something of the nature of a set of variations, but with the greater freedom their title implies; they would be less suitable than the cello Improvisation or the organ Meditation as a first introduction to Rubbra's thinking, in view of their greater length, which means that references between similar ideas are, if not fewer, then certainly farther between.

Rubbra later recomposed the *Meditations* for two violas and both versions were published, as Op. 117 and 117a. Should one wonder how a work for one melody instrument can lend itself to transcription for two of the same, the answer is that Rubbra used a range of devices, the simplest being the redistribution of the work's countless double-stops between the two violas; a constant sense of dialogue is created by the passage of the original material from one viola to the other. He also spelled out harmonies that had been left implicit, partly through making implied 'pedal-notes' actual, but also with genuinely contrapuntal second lines, doing in his modest way what Busoni's great piano transcription did to Bach's violin Chaconne. The most striking passage in what is altogether a striking and transforming transcription comes just before the final reprise of the 'theme', in a stately measure a little reminiscent of the 'Elizabethan dance' trio in the Seventh Symphony's scherzo five years earlier. Here the second viola has an additional line that takes the piece, exceptionally, into full three-part harmony; the effect is grandiose. In the 'coda' Rubbra's recomposition changes what was a reminiscence into a climax, just as he has already changed a solo piece into a powerful chamber-music work.

In the Third String Quartet (Op. 112, 1963),[19] an important product of Rubbra's 'late-middle period', certain Beethoven quartet-textures are reflected. The very opening suggests the influence of the 'Heiliger Dankgesang' slow movement of the late A minor quartet op. 132. Near the end of the 'first movement' (in fact the work runs continuously, with sustained notes joining what would have been its separate movements), the shape of the Eighth Symphony's main finale theme (see Ex. 51 on p. 171) is distinctly hinted at, and some two-thirds of the way through, towards the end of the slow 'middle movement', we find a distinct pre-echo of the 'ticking clock' passages that will figure in Rubbra symphonies from No. 8 onward. The freely associating commentator might even wonder, from the 'clucking' main subject of the lively and engagingly brief finale, whether Rubbra at any point during his many years living in the country kept chickens; and, sure enough, Banfield's Finzi biography unearthed the fact that as his non-combatant work during the 1939–40 'phoney war', before being called up for military service, he worked part-time at a poultry farm. Five years later, in the first of the *Four Creature Songs*, op. 134, 'The Mother Hen', Rubbra found a more obvious reason for a brief sound-picture of the bird.[20] These chickens for a time turn into fighting-cocks, but the quartet has a most unexpected peaceful ending.

CHAPTER 9

The Tide Turns: The Eighth Symphony

To go by the *Sunday Times*'s 'Portrait Gallery' piece, Rubbra cut no less striking a figure in the late 1950s than he had thirty years earlier, with his beard 'now conferring on him, as on Kodály, the saintly look of an Apostle ... A smile is rarely absent from his face, which radiates good nature and a complete lack of malice.' Such the public persona. But Western music led a double life after the war, with those living the one seldom prepared to acknowledge the other's existence or even its right to exist. Rubbra began to be overshadowed as more attention was devoted to a new generation both Continental and British. There was, in particular, the 'Manchester School' of Richard Hall's former students at the Royal Manchester College of Music, with the composers Peter Maxwell Davies and Harrison Birtwistle, both eventually knighted, and Alexander Goehr, plus the pianist John Ogdon and trumpet-player and conductor Elgar Howarth. War had nipped in the bud the work of familiarising a fairly reluctant public with the newest music and methods from the Continent,[1] and it needed doing all over again. Most of it had to wait until the BBC's post-1959 'Glock regime', by which time the avant-garde had taken on so radical a face that 'traditionalist' composers such as Rubbra found themselves quite out of fashion. Twelve-tone technique was *de rigueur*, Webern's total spareness a fetish,[2] serialisation of duration, rhythm and tone-colour lumbered out of the test-tube or off the drawing-board like Frankenstein's monster, to remain a fad for a whole generation, and there were the newest experiments with electronic manipulation of sounds, 'graphic notation', 'music in space' or (as *musique concrète*) something Schönberg's prophetic joke in his 1911 *Harmonielehre* had described as 'wirklich Atonales' – material unrelated to the 'tone' or musical note as hitherto understood. Here was a wonderful new box of toys for the kiddies[3] – would-be composers, impresarios, media-men; an 'honest workman' like Rubbra, by then up to seven symphonies, seemed no longer of interest. If you weren't in the van you were in the cart, and his admirers from the 1960s onward had to put up with as much as had Schönberg's in the 1930s, with as little to show for it.

As early as 1955 Hugh Ottaway wrote prophetically in a *Musical Times* review of the Sixth Symphony, 'the conservatism of his position is becoming increasingly clear, and in this, no doubt, there are latent dangers'. In his 1963 interview with Murray Schafer (*BCI*) Rubbra said guardedly that recent developments in music had been unfortunate, not for himself but 'only in so far as fashions get in the way of performances of works that do not conform to fashion'. Asked by Schafer whether he was referring to his own work, he replied 'Possibly. I suppose my work is unfashionable today.' As for criticism and whether it affected him, 'Not fundamentally. At the moment perhaps, but I realize what I'm doing and what I have to do.' Benedict Rubbra takes the view that his father's 'awkwardness in dealing with the privileged … stifled some success' and was 'the root of neglect', so making it a personal rather than a musico-political matter. William Glock certainly counted by both his upbringing and his manner as 'privileged'; a former piano pupil of Schnabel who had played at the Proms just before the war, he loved and understood the great Viennese classics as did few others, and was also a forward-looking, adventurous figure capable nonetheless of underestimating some 'classic' contemporary composers. He adored Stravinsky, and had written so often about Bartók for *The Observer* that in 1945, after a warning, the editor sacked him, but Schönberg[4] he respected rather than liked. Even an apparent 'in-figure' such as Schönberg's pupil Roberto Gerhard, a Spaniard long settled in Cambridge, was, according to that composer's widow,[5] someone whose music Glock presented 'because he knew he ought to, not because he liked it'.

Caution is advisable over any picture of a totalitarian BBC plot to victimise composers such as Rubbra. I worked quite closely with Glock for a time, and suspect that he was simply indifferent to, or blissfully ignorant of, many composers who imagined him as terribly down on them; but then your composer is one of Nature's Leninists – 'Whoever is not with me is against me' – and neglect is neglect, whether it stems from ignorance or hostility. Like many people, Glock was at his best when enthusiasm was in play. Once he returned from a trip to Switzerland and dropped on my desk the programme of a performance of the *Elegy to poems by Lenau and Eichendorff* by Othmar Schoeck, to whom I had until then reacted with the classic British intellectual's 'Know it? I don't even *like* it!' William's rubric was 'I thought this a very beautiful piece, which we should do.' Do it we did, and it was as he said, with all its obsolescent virtues. That he never had any such epiphany with a Rubbra symphony was his loss as well as the British listening public's; there is, at most, an extant miniature score of the 1956 *Improvisation* for Violin and Orchestra, presumably sent to him for review in his periodical *The Score*, in which wrote his name, something one would hardly do if one thought the piece was rubbish. The *Cantata di Camera, Crucifixus pro nobis*, commissioned by a New York choir, had its first British performance in March 1962 at one of his pioneering mixed-programme Invitation Concerts, and there was even a Prom commission, *Veni Creator Spiritus* for mixed voices and brass, Op. 130, performed during the 1966 season. William's ghost might well ask, like Sachs reminding his 'enemy' Beckmesser that he worked on his shoes late into the night, 'I commissioned a piece from him. What sort of blacklisting is that?' He respected Rubbra as a master of choral music, even while programming ephemera such as Luigi Nono's *Ha venido: Canciones para Silvia*,[6] though also Messiaen's masterly *Cinq rechants*, whose choral techniques and rich sound have things in common with those in Rubbra's major *a cappella* works. The symphonies unfortunately seem not to have appealed, and Glock's memoirs suggest by omission that he attached no particular value to any personal contact with Rubbra. Nor did their shared enthusiasm for Bartók and Stravinsky earn Rubbra any brownie-points.

Despite rumours to the contrary, BBC Radio's vast music output, especially after the daytime Music Programme began in December 1964, was not and could not be monolithic. Glock and his senior managers had broad enough sympathies to allow the recruitment of a variety of minds, and individual producers remained free to include Rubbra's music in their programmes.[7] The critic and composer Anthony Payne was invited to write notes in 1971 for a complete broadcast cycle of the symphonies Rubbra had composed up to that point, which was still within Glock's time.[8] Rubbra was also still one of the 'readers' who were asked to evaluate unsolicited new scores and advise as to their suitability for broadcasting; he would have been chosen by a member of the 'old guard', Harry Croft-Jackson, but continued once the co-ordination of 'new music' was taken over in the early 1970s by Hans Keller, who is said to have rated him very highly as a reader, and certainly admired his music.[9]

The other contributory cause of a decline in Rubbra's prominence from 1960 onward could, in Yardley's view,[10] have been that the developments in his private life during the later 1950s left understandable conflicts of loyalty in the minds of many people influential on the English musical scene at that time. There would be much here for a biographer to sift and present; from the accounts of his post-war music in the preceding pages it seems that some watershed, not unlike that found in the music of 1934–6, was traversed in the middle 1950s (before the 'Glock revolution'), with the Piano Concerto on one slope and the Seventh Symphony and Violin Concerto on the other. Inner and outer conditions conspired to cast a shadow over his final quarter of a century, but his music stayed ever new, taking him into previously unexplored realms;

his later works offer at least as much as does the corpus of works written in 'happier times'. In the middle 1950s he still had five symphonies to go, and what symphonies they turned out to be!

Soon after *Lauda Sion* and *Crucifixus pro nobis*, with their Christian message, Rubbra's penchant for Buddhism was reflected in *The Jade Mountain*, whose final poem, 'Farewell to a Japanese Buddhist Priest Bound Homeward', begins 'You were foreordained to find the source', and speaks of 'tracing your way as in a dream', 'waning from the world' with 'the water and the moon … as calm as your faith'. The early 1960s saw the composition of a further work featuring the cello, a succinct and effective solo *Improvisation* (Op. 124, 1964), premièred of course by friend Pleeth; it was followed by the powerfully cumulative but lyrical *Discourse* for cello and harp (Op. 127, published in 1969), which uses material from a harp concerto, planned but never composed.[11] A performer of *Discourse*, the cellist Felicity Vincent,[12] finds in much of its *forte* harp-writing another embodiment of Rubbra's fascination with bells, here not drifting in from a distance but striking with great force close by.

Inscape (Op. 122) for chorus, strings and harp, followed in 1964–5; it sets pantheistic texts by a great Jesuit, Gerard Manley Hopkins, and its Christian theme fits the predominant pattern for the vocal music of Rubbra's final two decades, where no title points in the direction of mysticism. 'Inscape' was a word of Hopkins's own invention, and a letter to his fellow-poet Robert Bridges shows him equating it with 'design or pattern'. Hopkins' lasting freshness, other-worldliness and ability to provoke are confirmed by a striking source from the eminently worldly, no-nonsense 1950s, the literary prime of 'The Movement':

> I had another go at his poetry the other day, and confirmed my previous impressions of it of it as *going after the wrong thing*, trying to treat words as if they were music. They aren't, are they? … Outrider – aaaaagh; counterpointed rhythm – uuuuugh, and you can't *have* counterpointed *rhythm*.[13]

1965–6 saw the composition of two further significant choral works, a 'Suite in Five Movements', *In Die et Nocte Canticum*, for mixed voices and orchestra (Op. 129), and the *Advent Cantata* (*Natum Maria Virgine*) for baritone, mixed voices and orchestra (Op. 136). Elsie Payne's article on the non-liturgical choral music in *ERC* pointed out that the 1971–2 Ninth Symphony (*Sinfonia Sacra*) owes a great deal to them. Also from immediately before the Eighth Symphony was the BBC commission *Veni Creator Spiritus* (see pp. 163–4).

Though Rubbra never composed a Passion, the few years covering the composition of the *Advent Cantata* and *Sinfonia Sacra* saw him dwelling on the temporal extremes of the Saviour's time in the world. The cantata opens with a complex chord made up of two superimposed 'second-inversions' (6-4s), much the combination of sounds found thirteen years earlier at the start of *Song of the Soul* and commented on by Payne as contributing to that work's mystical character. There the chords are both in the major, immediately setting up a positive mood, however abstracted; the 6-4 chords in the *Cantata* are both in the minor, as they will be when met yet again, a decade later still, as the basis of the recorder piece *Fantasia on a Chord* (the six notes are there first heard in a different order which conceals the fact that they amount to two 6-4s). The pairing of minor chords in the *Cantata* and *Fantasia* makes for a distinctly severer atmosphere.

The *Cantata's* 'message' is of the hope and inspiration Advent offers to a soul bowed down by the weight of sin; the transition is typically instantaneous, driven home by a switch at the crucial point from English to a fifth-century Latin hymn. Payne found that the Latin text brings 'an air almost of fantasy, certainly a feeling of remoteness, timelessness'. The final section opens with an instrumental 'chorale' based on a melody from Bach's church cantata no. 27, *Wer weiß, wie nahe mir mein Ende?* (Who knows how near is mine end?, for the Sixteenth Sunday after Trinity, last before Advent). The final choral section again has English words. This music, especially the sizeable orchestral 'chorale' before the final vocal entries, is a pointer in the direction of the 1971–2 *Sinfonia Sacra*, for the same structural pattern is found with the 'conversation piece' interlude before the risen Jesus appears to his disciples on the road to Emmaus. The cantata's mixture of languages is another harbinger of the *Sinfonia Sacra*, while the running together of its contrasting sections takes us even further forward to the time of the final two symphonies.

Payne also commented interestingly on the *Cantata's* structure, saying that the 'adding of section to section to produce an extended form' had become increasingly a characteristic of Rubbra's style, 'significantly associated with the more contemplative and mystical as opposed to the dramatic and eventful part of his expression. To put it in human rather than musical terminology, this is the re-focusing of a single and static experience as opposed to an exciting and developing one'. The Tenth and Eleventh symphonies would show the mastery with which Rubbra combined 'added-section form' and the 'developing' one typical of the symphony and sonata.

Veni Creator Spiritus sets for mixed chorus and brass (four horns, two trumpets, two tenor trombones, bass trombone and tuba) the Latin hymn used by Mahler in the first part of his Eighth Symphony. That work was long known in Great Britain merely from its nickname 'The Symphony of a Thousand', but began to make its way here at a concert conducted by Jascha Horenstein at the Royal Albert Hall in 1959. A reviewer after Malcolm Arnold's première on 5 August 1966, possibly recalling the unbelievable *fortississimo* chord on which Horenstein had ended the Goethe-based second part of the symphony, welcomed the quietness of Rubbra's setting of *Veni Creator Spiritus*, and Grover quoted a letter to the work's second conductor, Charles Mackerras, in which Rubbra agreed that his piece came as 'a pleasant change from the usual "hearty" approach to that beautiful text'. Where Mahler seems to identify in his Part 1 with the mighty rushing Pentecostal wind of the Holy Ghost,[14] Rubbra moves steadily from almost longing invocation to acclamation at a respectful distance. Compared with *Lauda Sion, Veni Sancte Spiritus* could seem gaunt and ascetic; it is one of Rubbra's more impenetrable pieces, but monumentally impressive and well suited to the reverberant spaces of the Albert Hall. A hint at least of what its text meant to him may be found in the opening choral figure, which rises from the tonic to the fifth above, and then further up to the octave; not only does this make salient use of the interval he found so 'positive, affirmative, mysterious'; it also echoes, for example, the 'reaching out' figures in the slow movements of the Fifth Symphony and Second String Quartet. The idea reappears half-way through the piece.

Neglect takes as long to develop as its opposite, fame, and Rubbra was made a CBE in the 1960 New Year's Honours List.[15] It was, nevertheless, a crucial time. If any sign of reaction to the world's growing disregard is discernible in the Eighth Symphony (which would be surprising, given the subtitle 'Hommage to Teilhard de Chardin', the optimistic Roman Catholic philosopher), it could take the form of a puzzlement that made the composer cast about him, evoking one idea after another in a way that can at first hearing seem incoherent. The music took two full years, until 1968, to complete, and waited a further three for its première, at which Sir Charles Groves conducted the Royal Liverpool Philharmonic Orchestra.

During work on the Eighth, Rubbra found time to respond to a private commission (the printed copy carries the name of Walter J. Berry) for a violin sonata to be played by Peter Mountain and his pianist wife Angela Dale, who first performed it in 1968, likewise at the Cheltenham Festival. It is worth wondering which 'elitisms' or 'opinionists' might have caused it not to be heard in London until 1985, when Yossi Zivoni and Rosemarie Wright played it at a celebratory concert reflecting the fortieth anniversary of the founding of the Composers' Guild of Great Britain. Rubbra, like Lennox Berkeley, Alan Bush, Arnold Cooke and William Alwyn, had been a founder member,[16] and the programme contained pieces by all five composers, who were in or approaching their eighties. The three movements of this Third Violin Sonata (which, given the memory of Mr Bertram Ablethorpe, was in fact Rubbra's fourth) take a mere twelve minutes to play, and, unusually, very little of it could be described as slow. As ever, a lyrical view of the violin prevails, while the piano alternates between typically lively counterpoint and a quite massive chordal writing that could be yet another allotrope of Rubbra's beloved bells. It shows little if any connection with the symphony from the same time, and is an effective *pièce d'occasion.*

The Eighth Symphony, Rubbra's Op. 132, came out as his shortest up to the time of its composition, and would remain the shortest of the nine that he divided conventionally. (The Ninth and Eleventh are single-movement works, while the Tenth runs together its four movements.) In a *Listener* article in January 1971 he said that in a way the Eighth marked a turning-point in his symphonic journey, since in the ten years after the Seventh: 'I gradually became aware of the dramatic and expressive values inherent in intervals as such, and in the new Symphony the play of interval against interval, rather than of key against key, provides the motivating force behind the argument.' He disclosed another change of approach in the words, already quoted in Chapter 1, about his new way of composing straight into full score, so that 'the ideas arose spontaneously clothed in an appropriate colour'.

The first movement is indeed more colourful in its orchestration and more chromatic in its harmonies than any predecessor, and offers at first hearing an extreme example of the 'flight of ideas', by turns heavy and boisterous. One is tempted to wonder, given the dedicatee's thoughts on evolution, whether this could be Rubbra's 'Representation of Chaos' to match Haydn's at the start of *The Creation* – and if so, what version of a perfected universe he will be celebrating by the end. It is a reminder, however much maturer the technique, of the 'over-full, anxious mind hardly knowing what to do first' met at the earliest stage of his symphonic Odyssey, in the First Symphony's opening movement.

In the course of the Eighth Symphony progressive tonality takes us from C major to G major. At the outset (Moderato, 6/4, molto flessibile) we are immediately presented, if not with conflict, then at least with coexistence. The first minute introduces us to the piece's 'stage army' of figures, which will keep cropping up from all angles, sometimes in disguise, like the characters in a harlequinade. Sustained strings in high and low registers play the tonic and fifth of the key, spanning the texture like a line of pillars that holds up a church. So far we lack the third of the scale, that would complete the tonic triad and also tell us whether we were in major or minor (Ex. 46a). The first few bars' wealth of sound-complexes brings as an effective double first step, paired woodwind instruments playing a fourth apart, which spell out the notes of an augmented triad (Ex. 46b).[17] Both the (vertical) fourths and the (linear) major thirds that make up the spelled-out chord are going to be leading participants. Strange intrusive shapes loom up out of the mist, providing yet more notes of the chromatic scale, and soon there is a hint of a call to arms on muted trumpets (Ex. 46c), whose top line spells out an eerie figure splitting the octave neatly in half as it touches in the diminished fifth (see p. 136, also note 15 to Chapter 8, concerning the Locrian mode!). Where the beginning of the Seventh Symphony could make one think briefly of Bruckner, here there is a kinship with the long-drawn-out opening, pervaded by a drone that bespeaks nature's sleeping presence, in Mahler's First Symphony.

Ex. 46 Symphony no. 8, first movement: figures at opening, bars 8–10 and 15–17

A further idea is totally diatonic, though in its rhythm and outline it has grown out of those 'strange intrusive' and chromatic chords in the seventh and eighth bars; this melody has what one might rather freely call a 'yeoman' character.[18] It is first heard with its inversion running beneath it in the bass (Ex. 46d), one of the few occasions in Rubbra's music where an important theme is given out first time in both its original form and its inversion. (The two examples of inversion in his reminiscence for Grover use the two versions successively, in what musical terminology calls 'stretto'.) For the moment it is elbowed out of the way, but it is not to be denied in the long run, soon coming twice more (once in inversion), separated by obstructive thoughts from those trumpets. Amid all the colourful competing ideas this theme sustains the whole, as a steel mesh holds together a suspect wall; it will appear a dozen times in the course of the movement.

We find here yet another, rather different version of a Rubbra 'introduction passing so naturally into a faster main section that one hardly notices the change'[19] – which comes two and a half minutes in, after a forthright appearance of the 'yeoman' or 'creator' theme has offered the most Vaughan-Williams-like music in the work (one could almost be in his Fifth Symphony). The tempo hardly varies; the opening tonality is still firmly there, but now a woodwind line doubled at the lower third (Rubbra's mind turning to yet another interval, Ex. 47) seems like a second or at least new subject. It has to be said, though, that in this music any attempt to identify some allotrope of sonata form, however analytically justifiable,[20] is very little help in following the flow of sound. What matters is the constant interplay of the figures, so vividly characterised and flexible, plus Rubbra's genius for the sudden twist and turn and mood-transformation. His 'motet' texture unites church music's scrupulous attention to fine detail with a sense of drama which is not quite the traditional 'symphonic conflict' but rather something to remind us of Schiller's dictum that man is most human when at play. It may take time and repeated hearings before the listener can find his way confidently around so complex and improvisatory a movement (that was certainly so in my case), so a few landmarks should be pointed out.

Ex. 47 Symphony no. 8, first movement, bar 34

For a while the new line in thirds (Ex. 47) and the fourths figure (Ex. 46b) have their say; Ex. 47 with its way of working within the 'diabolical' interval of the diminished fifth (tritone) is slightly disturbing. Next, the earlier tritone from Ex. 46c seizes its chance to drive the music on to a climax over a drumming 'pedal-note' which is in fact two alternating notes, themselves a tritone apart (A♯, E). Were this movement any representation of chaos, the *diabolus in musica* could not complain of unfair treatment. Next, something like the slow-dance tempo of the preceding symphony's first movement, with still more versions of the tritone, prepares us for a vigorous, almost scherzo-like subsection. This appears twice, and in the interim the 'yeoman' figure makes an impressive though brief appearance, again both ways up. This, like everything around it, is transitory, and Ex. 46b soon reasserts itself: but Rubbra's mind, never given to literal repetition, here makes it outline a different vagrant chord, the diminished seventh (see note 16), whose notes lie closer together than those of the original augmented sixth. This is not the kind of change an innocent music-lover's mind will immediately register, but it does minutely alter the atmosphere from here to the end. The line in thirds (Ex. 47) comes to join in, and suddenly we are into the second 'scherzetto', which, like the first trio of the previous symphony's scherzo, has a slightly Elizabethan, *Capriol Suite* feeling to it. This lasts only seconds, but is so strongly characterised that one is bound to notice it. From here on, the yeoman theme gradually comes to dominate the competition, even putting on a false nose at one point to disguise itself as a figure from the 6/8 scherzetto. Finally it is declaimed in an impressive half-speed augmentation. This is certainly the climax of the movement, but a climax to an 'insubstantial pageant' that fades to leave us with the music of the opening, or at least the strings' lower half and the vagrant chord in its new version. These our actors were all shadows, and as in the first movement of the preceding symphony we are back where we started. The very last woodwind line goes to the least abrasive competitor, Ex. 47. It is fitting that after a movement so impulsive and redolent of uncertainty the composer should end up seemingly little further on. Once again 'full circle is made', but in a mood nearer puzzlement or frustration than fulfilment. If one took the 'yeoman' figure and the plethora of tritones as ideas pulling in opposite directions, one might feel this movement had more of a Gnostic than a Christian feeling (see note 7 to Chapter 8).

The search can only start all over again, and the 'scherzo', if that is the right word to classify the equally strange middle movement (Allegretto con brio, no key signature, i.e. A minor, ending in C major), offers for much of its six and a half minutes a wealth of no less awkwardly searching, astringent music that still refuses to settle into any pattern for long. Despite the change to a vigorously ongoing tempo, the foregoing restlessness and bewilderment are still clearly there, with cross-rhythm the rule rather than the exception. One idea after another is tried out, at times with a hint of the bitonality explored half a century earlier by Holst, at others with the music sitting obstinately on a pedal note (or indeed an entire complex chord) for bar after bar: man proposes, God disposes. The harmonic norm is like that in Bartók's Concerto for Orchestra, though also something of a throwback to the music of composers such as John Ireland – 'sweet and sour' (as it might be, ylang-ylang and juniper berries!). Roughly contemporary music by Lennox Berkeley and Alan Rawsthorne, mostly lighter in character, at times shows a similar tendency, bruising its consonances with a hint of dissonance; the feeling is not 'the end of European civilisation as we know it', more that of a mild hangover. If one bears in mind Rubbra's preoccupation with different intervals, it is of interest that here much of the music proceeds in consecutive thirds, which is one of the most euphonious ways to couple instruments.

The movement's main subject is divided between various instruments. (Ex. 48 shows its audible shape, and an immediate answering figure on the violas and divided violins which is going to grow into the melody of the 'trio' section.) After about a minute's development, with many thirds both simultaneous and successive, the slightest let-up in the tension leads to a Trio (3/8 × 2 = 3/4, Ex. 49), contrasting even though it is based on that figure from the opening (end of Ex. 48). It soon brings a hint of *Petrushka* to go with the one thirty years earlier in the *Sinfonia Concertante*; Rubbra did, after all, name Stravinsky as one of his four favourite composers. This trio section falls into two subsections separated by the briefest reappearance of the initial clomping dance.

Ex. 48 Symphony no. 8, second movement: schematic presentation of opening of scherzo

Ex. 49 Symphony no. 8, second movement, bar 75 (fig. 27+4)

The formula 'scherzo and trio', though not as irrelevant to this movement as was 'sonata form' to the first, is nonetheless subsidiary, for the crucial contrast is between the movement's beginning and end. To throw us further off the scent, when the 'trio' is repeated only the first of its two sections is heard, if in a fairly literal recapitulation. Rather than being followed by its companion 3/8 section, it has already been preceded by one in that tempo but with different content; all of which makes it quite hard to know just where one stands. The crucial thing is that two thirds of the way through the movement Rubbra offers a classic demonstration of his ability to turn on a sixpence,[21] instantly transforming the mood; at the same point as in the Seventh Symphony he changes course radically, a change that works itself out not only until the end of the scherzo but over the remainder of the work. The first trio's earlier part has had its fairly literal reprise; now, quite unobtrusively, the 'fade' seems 'to have happened', rather than happening. This is another, indeed a crowning example of Rubbra's interlinking of sections. Before one knows it, the music has calmed, the harmonic tension subsided, the rhythms are mollified, and we are in one of his classic passages with both rising and falling conjunct scales, of the kind he said stemmed from his early epiphany with distant bells.[22] In search of a technicality to explain it all, one could pick on the way Rubbra's interest suddenly switches to the interval of the sixth (Ex. 50). If the Sixth Symphony celebrated 'happy birds', this music in the Eighth could be consorting with the angels. It was all gently hinted at in that 'slightest let-up of the tension' just before the first trio. A little of the earlier unrest returns before the end, but a direction has been pointed out.

Ex. 50 Symphony no. 8, second movement, bar 229 (fig. 42+7)

That direction is followed with total commitment in the finale (Poco Lento, 3/2, no key signature), a meditation on a theme (Ex. 51a) that stresses intervals at the two ends of an octave (G–G'). First comes the rising major second between its lower note (the tonic of the key) and the supertonic, A, then the semitone rising to the upper octave from the leading-note, F♯, and finally the falling major second from supertonic down to the lower octave again. Those inner notes A and F♯ are a major sixth apart, an interval that inevitably comes to the fore as the idea is developed; in the course of the movement its compass in fact tends to shrink from an octave to a major sixth. We have already heard this happening in the scherzo; Ex. 51b shows the theme as it appears in the forty-third bar of the finale. Within the theme the sixth's upward surge suggests fervent aspiration, while the return to the lower octave then gives an in-built sense of 'making full circle'. Again there is immediate inversion, this time not simultaneous but at the distance of one beat. In this opening there is some of the ambiguity and harmonic tension that have marked nearly all the music since the start of the work, but now taken in hand, calmed and

Ex. 51 Symphony no. 8, third movement: opening and 'contracted' version of theme at bar 43

made beautiful. Of such is the Holy Grail of the deep musical analysts, 'unity in diversity'.

For a good deal of the movement, that is all Rubbra needs in order to generate one of his inimitable long, slow waves, constantly finding new ways to move on from his very concise idea. After the wealth of figures in the preceding movements, there is here an entrancing single-mindedness. The exposition of the main theme is not without its curious and discordant accompanying parts, and interesting things, striking enough to act as landmarks, happen in the accompaniment as the music unfolds; some two minutes in, there is the distinct ticking of a clock (tremolo violas doubled by the harp), through the interval of a minor third. The effect is quite like that evoked by Britten in the sixth and final song, 'Lines Written During a Sleepless Night', of his roughly contemporary Pushkin cycle *The Poet's Echo* (1965), but a passage near the end of the slow movement of Rubbra's 1963 Third String Quartet anticipates both the Britten and this symphony, doing so without recourse to pizzicato. If one looks far further back, there were those memorable passages with the harp in the finale of the Viola Concerto, while in the First String Quartet of 1933–4 the first half of a mostly elegiac slow movement has wistful phrases for the various instruments, accompanied by persistent upbeat chords, which with hindsight also appear to be forerunners of the ominous drum-beats found throughout Rubbra's symphonies. In the late ones these ticking sounds' ostinato function could make one think of the tolling bell in Ravel's 'Le Gibet', from the piano trilogy *Gaspard de la nuit*, though persistent bell-like sounds were nothing new, as witness the opening of Bach's[23] church cantata no. 53, the funereal *Schlage doch, gewünschte Stunde*, or Schubert's song *Das Zügeng-löcklein* (The Angelus). There was a not dissimilar moment a little way into the recapitulation of the Seventh Symphony's first movement (see p. 144), and something comparable will occur in the extremely sombre earliest stage of the next, choral symphony, with its meditation on the empty sepulchre after the Crucifixion.

In the second half of the movement a good deal changes – the octave gradually fills in, with a conjunct melody on the violins and later the violas. The clock returns with a more sinister sound, but the music is gradually moving into calm waters. It is if a sense of arrival rewarded constant aspiration and searching: that would indeed be one way to sum up Rubbra's achievement over a lifetime, which in this movement reaches one of its peaks. A very firm statement of a still more conjunct melody over another of Rubbra's really insistent drumming pedal points sets the seal on the change. He reserves some magic for the very end, when the high violins add a gently dancing staccato figure against the now fully matured main melody; it is as if night-time clouds finally parted to reveal a sky full of stars, such as Schubert evoked with the high repeated piano chords in his male-voice part-song *Nachthelle*. There is one last climax, then an almost-final hearing of the germ idea on solo cello and viola (with the harp just recalling the ticking clock), before the music comes to rest in its home key of G major. 'Home is where one starts from.'[24] The instrumental sounds just mentioned show what Rubbra had in mind when he wrote that 'the balancing of these colours was an important element in the overall formal scheme of the symphony'. They are no mere effects, but components of his original inspiration. At the very end the flute sings on high, and the celesta gently waves goodbye with the faintest recollection of the curious intervals from the start of the first movement (so long ago!), or for that matter of the very end of Mahler's *Das Lied von der Erde*. But this is no tragedy of loneliness like the Mahler *Abschied*, rather the recapturing, at the latest possible stage, of a sense of timeless peace last sensed in the Sixth Symphony's slow movement. The German word 'einsam' means 'lonely' but also 'solitary', and here, surely, Rubbra is at one, in solitude, with a universal rhythm.

In his chapter on Rubbra Routh summed up the Eighth Symphony's special virtues: 'the goals that he has set of breadth of phrase, melodic continuity, harmonic fluidity and structural strength, are achieved to a greater extent than in any previous symphony. The sequences are less exact, the sonorities are more original, while the expansive eloquence of the slow third movement is unsurpassed.' The comment about 'melodic continuity' is particularly apt, for that is what draws one on through all the music's bewildering changes of mood and matter.

The major name prominent in Rubbra's mature post-war thinking around music is that of another great Christian – the twentieth-century geologist, palaeontologist and Jesuit priest Teilhard de Chardin, to whom its subtitle does homage. A practical churchman and scholar rather than a mystic, he reached a synthesis between the scientific view of Creation as an evolutionary process and the religious view of it as part of a Divine plan: Jesus represented fulfilment, the 'Omega moment'.[25] Once converted to Roman Catholicism, Rubbra studied and accepted Teilhard's optimistic and positive reconciliation of biblical narrative with evolutionary theory, setting down his reactions in an introduction to the symphony (*The Listener*, 31 December 1970):

> His cosmic view of evolution gives, if one responds to it, a picture of a purpose, a oneness, that makes nonsense of any fundamental antago-nism or real separation between the world-view of science and that of Christianity. The energy which is responsible for life as a whole and for later self-consciousness has not ceased with the evolution to man but becomes concentrated in him, so that with the spiritual insights given by religion he can act as a spearhead for further evolutionary development ... It was not part of my intention, even if possible, to translate these ideas into music: but they meet, I hope, in a like optimism.

Rubbra allowed himself the uncharacteristically fanciful comment that the intensity generated in his finale by progressive contraction of intervals could be compared to the 'astronomical phenomenon of star contraction', but empha-sised that no such idea was in his mind as he wrote the music. If his 'hope' was fulfilled, it happened at a very late stage in one of his most enigmatic works. (Though looked at overall and in the right light, the Eighth is not enigmatic at all, but very simple, as simple as a day with a stormy morning and after-noon, a beautiful sunny evening and a peaceful starlit end. The Devil and Deity are in the detail!) What its balance of forces does, however, suggest is that any 'optimism' is private, rather than cosmic or related to a book reconciling science and religion. It comes to crown a movement that solves its problems almost as late as had that paragon among documents of spiritual struggle, the finale of Bruckner's Fourth Symphony.

To Yardley[26] the course of the Eighth Symphony 'portrays a pilgrimage, also hinted at in the choral suite *Inscape* of 1965 and the extraordinary final song of the *Jade Mountain*'. The stillness of that song was commented on above. But to avoid the classic words-and-music trap, one should rather seek the message in the music, and it is a far cry from the song's extreme asceticism to the encompassing warmth on which the strings end the symphony, for all the kinship detectable in the mysterious plucking of the harp. It punctuates the song, while near the end of the symphony it helps bring about the final transition into stillness. Quietist works such as *Pezzo Ostinato* and *The Jade Mountain* seem related in spirit to the sombre though temporally more distant *Sinfonia Sacra*, rather than to the Eighth, with its condensation of Rubbra's first three decades of symphonic thinking. It inhabits Rubbra's unique symphonic world, and its journey from upheaval to transfigured calm, which sits so well with the concept of divinely designed evolution out of chaos. It ranks among his greatest works.

Admiration for the 'progressive Christian' Teilhard led by the most natural of transitions to the subject-matter (it being for once valid to use that term about a symphony) of the work's successor, the *Sinfonia Sacra*. A quarter of a century earlier Rubbra had found that the six movements of the Latin Mass expressed the beliefs 'crystallized' in him after his conversion; the *Sinfonia Sacra*, for all his cultivation of Oriental thinking, would make the biblical message paramount, in a work he thought his most personal achievement.

Rubbra's final quarter of a century was a story of quiet determination to keep exploring, keep composing, and keep any skeletons firmly in the cupboard. The mixture of unremitting work and creativity continued, even as he had to come to terms with a decline in his performances. Those who met him in his last years, including composition pupils at London's Guildhall School of Music and Drama from 1961 onward, noticed that he seemed to sense the world's indifference and to be puzzled by it – Higginson writes, tantalisingly, that he 'obviously felt the hurt that had been inflicted on him but never mentioned it'.[27] His clairvoyant remark that 'to dismiss a work merely because it does not fit into the critics' category of what constitutes modernity is a fatal narrowing of vision' came as early as 1956, in his article 'Letter to a Young Composer'. The years after 1959 brought the lesson painfully home; the fatalities, unfortunately, were among composers rather than the bureaucrats and other 'professional opinionists' who did the narrowing. A slightly more kindly BBC attitude in the 1970s came rather late, while reserve on the part of the more general English musical Establishment has yet to disappear, though there are signs of a reviving interest.

Rubbra saw clearly what was happening in his later years; his lecture, 'The

Contemporary Composer – Tradition and Environment', undated but evidently from after the European Common Market came into existence (though not necessarily from after Britain joined in 1971) ends with the words

> National differences seem, in the newest music, to be quite absent; in their place is a common language, even though the language is uncommon! A supra-national environment – a sort of common marketry – is exercising its influence and ironing out local idiosyncrasies of thought. This is a great pity, and one welcomes the courage and tenacity of those composers, labelled by avant-garde critics as 'fringe composers', who sturdily give voice to their own traditions and environment even though it goes contrary to fashion to do so.[28]

That was written, in part, *pro domo*, but also *pro bono publico*.

The three symphonies composed during the 1970s are further essays in high-level musical thinking, and the decade and a half before Rubbra's death also saw the production of the *Sinfonietta* for strings, several important chamber works and many choral pieces. Inwardly, we have seen how the Seventh Symphony, over and above its existence as 'essence', seemed to reflect new questions and resolve problems both old and new – perhaps mortality as reflected in the loss of a dear friend. Something comparable appears in No. 8 – an atmosphere in which a new synthesis of religion and science could come about. Rubbra's own remarks on these symphonies were as guarded as ever, limiting themselves to musical aspects and giving nothing away. In the ensuing *Sinfonia Sacra* any still-unburnt boats would go up in flames; here was, beyond doubt, a fervently Christian composer.

CHAPTER 10

The Last Three Symphonies

The final decade and a half of Rubbra's composing career, after the completion of 'Hommage to Teilhard', saw the production of twenty-eight works
(Opp. 137–64), including the final three symphonies. In 1969 he completed
Discourse for cello and harp, discussed on p. 162, and one piece from 1970 was
a short (two-movement) but very intense Second Piano Trio (Op. 138) that
encapsulates decades of piano-trio writing between Brahms's string–piano
dualism and the bristling vitality of Fauré's late chamber music; Rubbra had
after all spent half a lifetime as a member of such an ensemble. Commissioned
by the Evesham Music Club for its twenty-first birthday, it received its first
performance there in 1970, with the Rubbra–Gruenberg–Pleeth Trio resurrected for one last time. The music's brooding intensity is a harbinger of things
in the *Sinfonia Sacra*, and near the end of the first movement a passage with
the strings in octaves against granite-like piano chords could suggest, like
moments in its predecessor, that Rubbra had listened with some interest to
Messiaen. The brief second movement is marked 'Allegretto scherzando', but
the game or joke is a fairly tight-lipped one tailing off into a middle section that
recaptures the intensity from the start of the work, with the main idea allowed
only a few seconds by way of 'repeated A-section'. The Trio closes as it began,
in deep thoughtfulness.

    During the mid-1960s, five years before he began work on the Eighth Sym-
phony, Rubbra saw a remarkable picture by Bramantino (*c.* 1455–1535) in which
the resurrected Saviour appeared, not in glory, but with all his wounds and
pain. One vastly impressive text familiar to many educated people in the 1930s
was D. H. Lawrence's powerful fantasy on the Resurrection, *The Man Who
Died*. It stands the story on its head, giving it a secular, well-nigh blasphemous
continuation that in some ways anticipates a best-selling 'invention' of the early
twenty-first century, *The Da Vinci Code*. The opening, with its description of
an agonising return to life, is a classic passage. Rubbra's publisher Bernard de
Nevers had long since suggested that he contribute to the English oratorio
tradition, and the idea of such a piece, which would take as subject the Resurrection and its aftermath, sprang from that encounter with Bramante's picture.
It was in fact de Nevers who originally compiled the libretto. Composition was
fitful, being interrupted by other work and in particular by Rubbra's labours on
the Teilhard de Chardin symphony. That allowed time for second thoughts: as

he wrote in 'Edmund Rubbra writes about his "Sinfonia Sacra"' (*The Listener*, 15 February 1973):

> I began to feel doubt as to the validity, in our time, of a large-scale oratorio, based on the familiar pattern of recitatives, arias and choruses. Would a pre-ordained scheme of that kind go against the present-day listener's expectation of a developmental arc leading him forward uninterruptedly from the stark impact of the Crucifixion to the joy and light of the Resurrection and the Ascension?

That is revealing; one would have thought a composer with Rubbra's constructive skill well able to form a pattern of recitatives, arias and choruses into a 'developmental arc', even into one leading *uninterruptedly* forward; Bach's Passions take those types of section as their formal basis with no lack of 'developmental' impetus. And the sudden worry over a listener's expectations is something new in a composer who 'knew what he had to do'. Perhaps it was really the inner symphonist who rebelled against the thought of devoting so much time and labour in order to conform to one of the 'familiar patterns' that had never interested him. The work eventually turned into a choral symphony with three vocal soloists, making reality of an idea first considered after the Fourth Symphony, and echoing the progression of 'Hommage to Teilhard' from dark opening to divine brightness.

The *Sinfonia Sacra* (Op. 140, completed in 1972) is a sequel to the Passions, subtitled 'The Resurrection' and covering the time between the Crucifixion and Jesus' reappearance to His disciples in Galilee immediately before the Ascension. Unsurprisingly, it has proved not just enigmatic but downright awkward for analysts accustomed to The Symphony As We Know It. It stands as successor, not only to Beethoven's final symphony, which calls for singers only in the finale, but to more recent works such as Mahler's Eighth (1906) and Havergal Brian's very first, the 'Gothic' Symphony from the 1920s. The text comes from the Bible and from Latin hymns; Payne mentions as one typical Rubbra fingerprint an 'adherence to the natural sound of both English and Latin words'. Its Anglo-German aspect also suggested to her a comparison with Britten's *War Requiem* from only few years earlier – and, refreshingly, she found Rubbra's symphony a good deal subtler than either the Britten or Tippett's *A Child of Our Time* (1939–41). In an ecumenical spirit commoner now than at the time of its composition, it also uses Lutheran chorale melodies to round off three of its four continuously running sections, with much the effect of the spirituals in *A Child of Our Time*. The second Latin hymn, 'Resurrexi' is set to a melody that begins very like Tippett's version of the spiritual 'Nobody knows the trouble I see'. A little later, in the choral fugue that continues the 'Resurrexi' subsection, the two composers' musical worlds come as near to each other as they ever did after the polymetric scherzo of the Second String Quartet. The hymns and chorales help to divide into sections a work which, unlike most oratorios, runs continuously. They also replace a good deal of text that Rubbra jettisoned.

The successive sections correspond in hardly any way to the movements of a symphony as normally conceived, but certainly make the work a 'developmental arc'. In the only recording so far the sections last respectively nine and a half, eight and a half, twelve, and fourteen minutes, which is no help, apart perhaps from the hint of a big finale, to anyone determined to persist with a comparison between its proportions and those within a traditional symphony. The *Sinfonia Sacra* was completed on Good Friday 1972. The same conductor and orchestra (Groves, Liverpool) gave the premières of nos. 8 and 9, the Ninth being first heard on 20 February 1973.

The detail of the text chosen by Rubbra bears examination. Much of it dwells on the sheer difficulty of belief, even for those who had been closest to Jesus. Once it seemed that He was gone, the disciples only gradually came to realise the fact of His resurrection, a miracle which indeed forms the vast, cosmic implausibility at the heart of a world religion. To accept it, one must make the greatest leap of faith. First the women at the empty sepulchre are told by the angels 'He is risen' (Matthew 28:6, Mark 16:6, Luke 24:6), but when they tell the disciples they meet with disbelief (Luke 24:11). Later Mary Magdalene sees Jesus in the flesh but mistakes him for the gardener (John 20:15); and in the final section we are reminded how on the road to Emmaus 'Jesus drew near, and went with them. But their eyes were holden that they should not know Him' (Luke 24:16). The closing texts are the disciples' last question to Jesus, about a return of the Kingdom of Israel, and His Ascension, followed by the angel's greeting to the 'men of Galilee' (Acts 1:4–11). An easy-going believer might happily remain ignorant of such background, as of the fact that each Latin hymn is associated in the liturgy with the appropriate stage of the story,[1] but Rubbra had to come to terms with it all and, after whatever unspoken struggle, find music to match his total belief in the biblical narrative. The conscientious listener is hardly to be blamed if he, too, makes hard work of following this symphony's journey from A to O.

Payne stressed the closeness with which Rubbra adhered to the model of Bach; there is also a possible parallel with another work strongly influenced by Bach's Passions, and yet, like the Rubbra, totally different – Franz Schmidt's crowning achievement, the apocalyptic oratorio *The Book with Seven Seals* (1935–7). The 'evangelist' in Rubbra's symphonic Passion is not a tenor, as in Bach and Schmidt, but a mezzo-soprano or contralto: women, and in particular Mary Magdalene, play an important part in the events narrated. At the première the Evangelist was sung by one of the greatest deep voices in modern times, that of Norma Procter. There are three lengthy narrations in the second, third and fourth parts of the symphony, written in the kind of accompanied monody one finds as 'arioso' in Bach's Passions, 'recitativo accompagnato' in Mozart's operas, and in spiritual works such as Schubert's *Lazarus*. Pickard (see note 1) has drawn attention to, and closely examined, the care and artifice Rubbra devoted to organising the motives and figures in the *Sinfonia Sacra*'s narrations. The style found in all three of them in no way helps one distinguish between the work's sections in terms of any traditional division into movements.

The work plunges straight into drama, with a sombre orchestral Prelude; Rubbra prefaced the score with the biblical words 'There was darkness over all the earth until the ninth hour.' There follow Jesus' black sayings from the Cross – 'Eli, Eli, Lama Sabachthani' (which the chorus quietly translates – 'My God, My God, why hast Thou forsaken me?') and 'It is finished; Father, into Thy hands I commend my spirit.' The solo and choral passages are separated by a continuation of the sombre orchestral music; no work could possibly open more in the spirit of *De Profundis*. As Jesus gives up the ghost, a very loud orchestral outburst with heavy timpani beats renders for us the earthquake and rending of the veil of the Temple. After a further orchestral meditation we come to the Latin hymn-text *Crux Fidelis*, and then to Johannes Crüger's chorale melody (one of those prominent in Bach's Passions) 'Ach, Lieber Jesu, was hast Du gesündet?', here set to the words 'Almighty Lord, we pray Thee, teach us always / That Thy will shall be done on earth as in Heaven.' At the pace set by Rubbra, all of that takes up the first ten minutes of the work, which is long for an introduction but viable for a first movement.

However, as if to dispel thoughts of having just heard any such thing, the opening Evangelist narrative follows the chorale melody without a break. The harp is prominent during this narration, about Jesus' burial and the two women's visit to the sepulchre; something very like the clock-ticking of the Eighth Symphony returns at the appearance of the 'two men in shining garments' who tell them 'He is not here, but is risen.' There is as yet no sense of triumph at 'and the third day rise again' – that is reserved for the moment a little later when, after the disciples have failed to believe the women's report, the choir enters with the second Latin text (not in this case a hymn), 'Resurrexi'. This section, with its faint similarity to music by Tippett, develops a genuine joy and marks a new stage in what has so far been an extremely sombre work. Here there is no chorale tune.

The next narrative, reverting to the stately tempo present almost unbrokenly since the outset, faithfully sets to music some quite pernickety detail: which of the disciples, Peter and John, ran faster and arrived at the sepulchre first, and the precise disposition of Christ's discarded clothes. Next comes the moving incident of Mary Magdalene's belated recognition of Jesus, and His 'Noli me tangere' – 'Touch me not, for I am not yet ascended to my Father.' Her 'Rabboni, Master' after He has hailed her in His true voice could have prompted a powerful emotional outburst if set by a differently inclined composer, but here it is marked by the briefest possible outcry – a fourth rising from an already high note, a falling octave, a rising third. From his first songs onward, Rubbra, unlike Tippett, was rarely one for melisma, rather for concise and syntactically faithful word-setting. The narrative's sedate progress continues through Jesus' 'I ascend unto my Father and your Father; and to my God, and your God.' The third hymn develops smoothly out of this; where 'Resurrexi' communicated a true feeling of joy, here, in 'Regina Coeli, laetare' (whose designated addressee is, naturally, the Blessed Virgin, not the mundane if aspiring Magdalene!) there is rather serenity as the mostly conjunct melody proceeds to its climax. After its 'Alleluia' has died away, the next of the chorales (a melody by the seventeenth-century German musician Melchior Teschner) is delivered, proving to have a comparably conjunct melody.

The narrative continues, quite unexpectedly, in speaking voice; after such continuity, the sudden absence of music takes one aback, and according to Higginson Rubbra later found this passage 'awkward and made excuses for its presence'. The break lasts about half a minute, spanning one of Rubbra's subtle but decisive changes of mood; it is as if the weather changed from deepest winter to a hesitant, early spring. Throughout his symphonies he has often made such changes, and instantaneously; here, however, the totally contrasting spoken interlude emphasises the distance between the place where he was (among the disciples still unaware that the risen Jesus is with them) and the one where he now is, on the road to Emmaus with Jesus and the same men, who are now his future apostles. Such a context demands no clever composer's tricks, but rather the sheer alienation effect that can result from silence and the speaking voice. Nor does singing resume straight away, for the longest orchestral interlude in the work follows. It introduces a steady triple time previously little heard, and is mostly dominated by the wind instruments, though the strings take over for two impressive climaxes. This interlude was marked by the composer 'Conversation piece'.

Finally Jesus, about to ascend into heaven, tells the disciples of their imminent 'baptism by the Holy Ghost', in preparation for lives of apostolic mission. Here the baritone soloist, silent since Jesus' appearance to Mary Magdalene, plays an important role, with one choral interjection for the disciples' 'Lord, wilt Thou at this time restore the Kingdom to Israel?' As the 'cloud receives Him out of their sight' the music tactfully but unmistakably describes Jesus vanishing from view. The final hymn, 'Viri Galilaei', grows inevitably out of that stillness and rises to a very powerful climax; this is Rubbra's consummate 'Alleluia' among so many! He even allows himself the luxury of a set of tubular bells, one of the very few times in his entire output when he resorts to the 'real thing' rather than offering one of his countless imitations. (Another comes before the interlude near the end of the *Advent Cantata.*) A long path led from the 'downward-drifting disembodied' bell-sounds experienced by the boy Rubbra at 'nine or ten', to these bells with which the seventy-year-old composer marked the Saviour's Ascent into Heaven. The concluding chorale is associated with the Passion text 'O Haupt voll Blut und Wunden', and is by a major German composer from a century before Bach's time, Hans Leo Hassler. It offers a final reminder that for all its concluding joy the *Sinfonia Sacra* is a reflection on a dark and sacred mystery. As the Gewandhaus in Bach's city of Leipzig reminds concert-goers over its podium, 'Res Severa Verum Gaudium' – true joy lies in difficult things. Even the triumphant final major chord is coloured for some of its duration by a flattened seventh in an inner part, final sign of the mixture of pain and joy in the Passion and Ascension story.

Leaving aside the academic question, 'in what sense is this a symphony?',[2] the work's overpoweringly even pace and almost uniformly sombre nature are likely to reserve it to true devotees (something that has equally been felt about the outer acts of Wagner's *Parsifal*!). Here the Deity is undoubtedly in the detail, and any listener's reaction may stand or fall by the amount he finds to interest him in the many minutes of accompanied narration. According to his own son, Rubbra looked on it as his most personal achievement; but did not Richard Strauss, according to Neville Cardus in his autobiography, deliver the equally contentious judgment that *Die Frau ohne Schatten* was, 'mein Meisterwerk'? Though Rubbra was an intensely private man, anyone who lays bare his inmost workings for others to hear is by that token a public man too – so one could call the *Sinfonia Sacra* the most private work of a private public man. It also ushered in a new and final phase of his creative career.

The Tenth and Eleventh symphonies followed over the next four years. Composition took longer as Rubbra's health deteriorated, but further sizeable or at least fascinating works included a Fourth String Quartet, a short *Duo* for cor anglais and piano that shares some of the Second Piano Trio's intensity and Faurean echoes, the *Mass in Honour of St Teresa of Avila* plus a short companion piece for choir and organ, *St Teresa's Bookmark*, and finally a *Sinfonietta* for large string orchestra.

About the time of the *Sinfonia Sacra*'s first performance the Arts Council of Great Britain commissioned from Rubbra a work to be played by the Northern Sinfonia chamber orchestra based in Newcastle upon Tyne. In a note for its first recording he told how after writing for the very considerable orchestra he had just been using he already had thoughts of something for smaller forces. The symphony that ensued (*Transformations* for harp being the sole piece of note in the interim) is the only one of his eleven so minimally scored, with a single flute, two each of the other woodwind (the almost obligatory cor anglais is here doubled by the second oboist) and two horns, without trumpets, trombones or the small percussion section he originally envisaged. Rubbra wrote this Tenth Symphony (Op. 145) in 1974, subtitling it 'Sinfonia da Camera' and dedicating it to Sir Arthur Bliss; it received its first performance under Rudolf Schwarz on 8 January 1975.

Formally, the Tenth follows the example of the *Sinfonia Sacra* in running its movements together. They are separated (Rubbra's note) only by 'brief interruptions of sound that, far from breaking the thread of thought, are so placed as to lead the listener to expect a change of mood and pace'. What the preceding symphony had achieved through the speaking voice is in this case brought about by 'the gap between sounds'. The composer here provided chapter and verse for the motto that had been apparent in his symphonies from the outset – 'What next?' He was, however, as aware as anyone of an important principle in serious art, summarised by Hans Keller as the delayed over-fulfilment of expectation, and used the first major break rather as Elliott Carter had in his 1951 First String Quartet; the music resumes much as it was – line and pulse continue, accompaniment becomes a shade more dance-like – and only gradually changes character in keeping with a new movement. The caesura at the end of that one is minimal, whereas there are quite distinct breaks before the ensuing slow movement and brief very slow coda.

The Tenth Symphony treats sonata form, too, in an unusual way. Accounts of Rubbra such as Truscott's in *ERC* have done justice to his unconventional and original approach in the matter of sonata form and its basic elements. One fascinating variant found since Schubert's time effectively expands it to take in not a single movement but the entirety of a work; successive 'movements' run one into the next without a break of the traditional kind, to make up the successive sections that would be found in single-movement sonata form (exposition, development, recapitulation, coda). This idea is hinted at as early as Schubert's 1822 'Wanderer' Fantasy for piano, where the first of the four continuously running sections takes us to the end of the development, breaking off to accommodate free variations on a melody from his 1816 song 'Der Wanderer' and then a scherzo which further develops ideas from the opening. The 'recapitulation', a very free one in fugal style, comes with the finale, which conforms to the sonata-form pattern at least, or most, by confining itself to the home key from which the expository first movement had moved away. (It is based, moreover, on the hammering rhythm that has been prevalent throughout the work.) A worthy successor eighty years later was Schönberg's First Chamber Symphony.

It may be some time before the listener to such a work becomes aware of this additional subtlety; that will depend partly on the clarity with which any particular performer makes clear sonata form's three inherent contrasts – those of themes and of keys, and that between exposition and development (taking the latter terms to mean ways of handling material, not the sections in which they by tradition predominate). A crucial factor in determining the listener's awareness of the special 'one-in-four' variant of sonata form is the degree to which the composer gives each section the requisite 'feel' associated with its function within the overall design. In considering the Fifth Symphony's opening movement, it was pointed out that Rubbra, like Schubert, is apt to let 'development' spill over backwards into his 'exposition' and continue into his 'recapitulation'. Two centuries before him, the two sections had grown out of a very mild degree of contrast inherent in binary (two-section) dance forms, with a principle of 'developing variation' then driving the form to great heights. Exposition section and development section reached a point where they were sharply contrasted, above all in Beethoven's sonata forms, but the distinction between them began to be eroded, notably in Schubert's extended instrumental pieces.

The whole question of sonata form in Rubbra is thus at some slight risk of becoming academic, but one must respect his clearly stated intention in works such as the Fourth, Seventh and Tenth symphonies. Certainly the latter's 'recapitulatory' slow third movement lets us hear again, in some order or other, important material from the ones before it.

The work opens somewhere near the key of A major (Lento e Liberamente, 4/4, ♩ = 42 circa); the score is prefaced by the instruction 'The basic tempo of the work fluctuates between 42 and 52, whether these refer to a quaver, a crotchet or a dotted crotchet. Between these extremes the music should move very freely.' At the start the sound of the cello is well to the fore, first in a single solo phrase (a rising fragment of scale that is developed throughout the symphony), and soon in a heartfelt melody for the whole section, which takes the line up and then down (Ex. 52: the 'turning point', marked ⌐, is particularly important later, recurring several times). Once this figure is in one's head, or held on paper in one's hand, it is astonishing how often and in what varied guises it will be found to reappear. Not for nothing had Rubbra made himself so totally at home in Bach's world of ever-generative ideas. But, as is so often the case with his naturally contrapuntal mind, the 'accompaniments' matter as much as the 'melodies'. They are pervaded by his ever-present rising and falling lines and so, yet again, by reflections of that bell-experience as a nine-year-old. His bell figures tend mostly to descend, but a peal of bells can also rise, as these lines do, at times like incense rather than bells. The brief but telling pauses in the course of the initial paragraph (three are marked * in Ex. 52) are of some importance, as precursors of the strategic silences between the work's main sections.

Ex. 52 Symphony no. 10, first movement

It will have become clear by now that Rubbra's symphonies are often peopled by a certain 'stage army' of ideas, or marked by a set of fingerprints, including drum-beats. In this work there are no drums to beat, but pizzicato bass notes do duty for them after the music breaks off for the first time, just under a minute in (sixth bar of Ex. 52). They do what the drum-beats have often done, furthering the propulsion of the music and its gathering into waves, several of them, separated by brief pauses or very concise interjections, mostly from the wind principals. Forty years on from the First Symphony, this music shows a continuity not far removed from that behind Rubbra's very first 1935 movement with its triple wave, which found a home as the symphony's finale. To maintain the tension and musical interest over several minutes, he uses every resource his orchestra offers – a little blaring brass, some dramatic string tremolo, and even, near the end of the section, a hammering accompaniment figure that could put one in mind of Bruckner working up to one of his great climaxes. This movement's single-mindedness recalls the granite-like blocks found in the pre-war symphonies rather than the clarified essences in Nos. 5–8 (if one excepts No. 7's monolithic, elegiac finale).

Grover accounted convincingly for all the detail of Rubbra's engineering, with its long-drawn-out first subject wave and 'second subject group' (about two and half minutes in), which is not so very different from what has gone before but grows into a powerful further wave debouching into the beginnings of a development. Ex. 52 ⌐ returns just before the end of this 'exposition' movement; it was not uncommon for the composers of the First Viennese School to quote their main subject briefly by way of codetta to the exposition.

After the first real break, it is the nature of the accompaniment that suggests a new movement (Scherzando ma grazioso, ♪. = ♩. ma poco meno mosso), rather than any immediate change in pulse or variation of line. Nothing in the metronome markings suggests the quicker tempo of a scherzo, indeed this section starts with a slightly slower pulse than the one just ended, still within the set range. Ex. 53 shows the opening idea, also the quicker, caressing duplet figure in the strings that helps give the dance its momentum. Both will return in innumerable guises. Before too long we realise where we are – in the company of dancing bells. To quote Saxton, this 'radiant dance' is 'not only a development of supreme technical quality, but also takes us into the world of the dance as celebration, a feature of earlier English music and an aspect of musical expression dear to Holst and Tippett'. Somewhere in the background there is also the discreet ghost of Jan Sibelius – the more rarefied Sibelius met in very late works such as the incidental music for *The Tempest*.

Rejoicing has rarely been a simple matter with Rubbra, and though unlike his earlier dancing scherzos this one neither begins with a memorably folksy tune nor proceeds to 'de-construct' it, there are complexities and complications. As in the Fourth Symphony's 'waltz interlude', the section, again based

Ex. 53 Symphony no. 10, second movement, bar 76

on rising and falling conjunct lines, manages despite its mere four minute-length to fit in what seems a 'Trio' section of slightly greater urgency, with a worried-sounding melody in the middle of the texture. It has its say for less than a minute and is then elbowed aside by broader music reasserting the mood from the close of the first movement. (Ex. 52 ⌐ yet again!) The next pause follows immediately; where the first one seemed a mere interruption, we here find a distinct caesura, the music resuming in a very different mood for a Lento slow movement.

As the equivalent of a recapitulation (A Tempo I, ♩ = 42 ma molto rubato) this could be described as free to the point of unrecognisability; Grover settled for 'an almost wholly new synthesis of the original subject matter' and found its effect 'for all intents and purposes new', while Rubbra's own note for the Bournemouth Sinfonietta's recording of the work called it 'inward in charac-ter' and spoke of its starting with a rescored version (cor anglais in contrast to cellos, Ex. 54) of music heard in the first section, but developing it at greater length. For something that is supposed to be a reprise, this cor anglais line is likely to strike the listener as remarkably different and strange (compare Ex. 52). Rubbra wrote elsewhere that the cor anglais was 'an instrument I love', and Truscott (*ERC*) noted that in very slow tempi he could make both the

Ex. 54 Symphony no. 10, third movement, bar 175

double-reed instruments, oboe and cor anglais, sound totally different, almost as if one had never heard them before. The Second, Third and Eighth symphonies are the only ones not to use the cor anglais.

The immediately prominent feature is that the preceding section's relative euphoria becomes a thing of the past. Here is the latest of Rubbra's instantaneous film-fade transitions, and we seem to be back with the moodiness of the opening, whence he has to do it all over again. During the 'development at greater length' of the initial ideas first the oboe and then the flute are dominant, taking us into the higher registers, where a more ongoing feeling, as in a slow dance, tries to banish the melancholy that has set in again. It succeeds, not by establishing itself but by giving way to a more settled and leisurely movement, into which a solo violin suddenly introduces some remembrance of things past. Passages for high solo violin in Rubbra's symphonies are few and far between, but usually of some significance (Second Symphony first movement, Sixth Symphony second movement; there is also a beautiful and striking one in the prelude that opens the *Sinfonia Concertante*'s finale). Given the feminine associations of the intolerably insistent story-telling violin in Rimsky-Korsakov's *Sheherazade*, and the equally unbearable, nagging 'life's-partner' violin in Strauss's *Ein Heldenleben*, the associations would have been unmistakable to Rubbra's well-stocked mind – but his manifestation of the 'eternal feminine' is kept brief and totally consolatory, rather like the appearance of the dead wife in the first act of Pfitzner's *Palestrina*. The solo violin balances, at the opposite end of the texture, the solo cello sound from the very start of the symphony. The first viola's response proves some kind of final turning-point; the slow dance reasserts itself and there is a brief but intense radiance on the high strings (Saxton: 'a controlled ecstasy – the greatest moment in the work'). This brings yet another appearance of Ex. 52⌐ to match the one near the end of the scherzo. Since we are technically in a recapitulation, it is formally appropriate for that movement also to be remembered, but this motive also seems to sum up in its own right the passion behind Rubbra's late symphonic music.

Such music can hardly fail to appeal to anyone who nurses a fierce loyalty to the best products of the English tradition in the pre-Manchester-School mid-twentieth century. The finest moments in the work of Michael Tippett are not dissimilar; Rubbra has a clearer aural concept of perfection, Tippett a more outlandish if at times imperfectly realised 'vision'.

After this hardly recognisable recapitulation the last of the minimal breaks introduces the final five very slow bars (Molto adagio), which undoubtedly feel like a coda – not the kind of 'second development' such a section had tended to turn into with Beethoven's 'Eroica', but a true afterthought, as in the earlier stages of sonata form. Once again almost the last word is given to the double-reed sound, here that of the oboe, whose sustained melody is something of a mystery; it sounds like a quotation, but not of anything heard earlier in the work; the nearest approach to it would be the opening of the Fifth Symphony. Here is one of the last of Rubbra's Mozartean 'new ideas' at the end of a move-ment. A very typical Rubbra line, it makes play with the interval of a tritone which has been prominent at various points in the symphony, notably during the cor anglais melody that opened the slow movement. It also contributed to the 'worried' quality of the scherzo's brief trio. The work closes, as it began, in A major.

By the early 1970s seventy-odd was no great age for a Western European, but with life's flame burning more gently and steadily it could nonetheless be the time to take stock. Nothing about the Tenth Symphony apart from its mod-est length and orchestral forces makes it anything but a major work typical of its composer, showing him well into a final period of retrospection and sum-ming-up. It runs the gamut from deeply serious reflectiveness to a touch, or rather more than a touch, of the joy and dancing found in the music written in the prime of life, to end in serenity rather than affirmation. Memory is a great solace, powerful enough to prompt an ageing composer to at least a wry, irresistible smile. Once again the lover of Hans Pfitzner's music may detect a kinship with the creator of the burned-out but fulfilled Palestrina in the final act of that great opera,[3] sitting in meditation at his chamber organ while out-side in the street his son mixes with the Roman populace as it hails the 'sav-iour of church music' – 'Evviva Palestrina!' The scale of Rubbra's symphonic achievement over half a century could make one inclined to follow suit with 'Evviva Rubbra!' It was not given to him to 'save' English music, but he added most memorably to it.

Nor was the saga yet complete. With time and illness bearing down on him, Rubbra composed less during the middle 1970s, the most important work being the Fourth String Quartet from 1976–7. At last the BBC again found it thinkable to acknowledge his stature with a further commission. Glock's suc-cessor as Controller, Music was Robert Ponsonby, who for all his determina-tion to prove a worthy heir in encouraging the 'new and valuable' proved less draconian over the Pontius Pilate question, 'What *is* new and valuable?' He 'lifted the ban', such as it was in view of *Veni Creator Spiritus*, by including that piece in the 1976 Proms, and followed through by commissioning a symphony for 1980. Another followed for an event marking the Corporation's sixtieth birthday in 1982, a suitable accolade and amends to one of the country's most senior composers. Rubbra obliged with a choral *Introit*, whose first performance was given by the BBC Singers under John Poole.

Since Rubbra's death, a few years after that welcome volte-face, his 'posthumous career' with BBC music has been exiguous. For the 2001 centenary the Henry Wood Promenade Concerts' director Nicholas Kenyon did a modicum of the right thing with a performance of the Fourth Symphony, as did Radio 3's Head of Music Production John Evans with five programmes in the series *Composer of the Week*. There was then a break before a broadcast of the eleven symphonies (on CD, and, somewhat unimaginatively, all in the Hickox versions), spread over a fortnight in 2006.

An important work from just before the time Rubbra began work on the BBC's symphony was the last of his four string quartets (1975–7). First performed by the veteran Amici Quartet, it was dedicated to a fellow-composer, indeed another master of both the symphony and the string quartet, Robert Simpson, who remained a loyal ally during the lean years. A BBC veteran long before Glock was thought of, he was totally sceptical about most aspects of the new regime, but stayed on to do further valuable work, as if acting out a much-quoted maxim of Glock's Cambridge mentor Edward Dent, 'There is no strength in absence.' He had only a very short time to go to the Corporation's retirement age of sixty when he resigned over the issue of the proposed abolition of the BBC Scottish Symphony Orchestra. As we shall see, the orchestral strike that resulted from the controversy almost caused the postponement of the Eleventh Symphony's première.

The Fourth Quartet is by some way the shortest of the four, at barely a quarter of an hour, and though it does not quite round off Rubbra's output of chamber music (there would still be the *Fantasia on a Chord*, for recorder and harpsichord (1977), and the *Duo* for cor anglais and piano from 1980), it sums up his contribution to the string quartet genre. This final quartet was commissioned by an American, Sally Tarshish, who asked him to write a work in memory of her husband Bennett; the printed score contains both an introductory 'In Memoriam' and a dedication over the first page, to the two different admirers. Tarshish had got to know Rubbra well, and as writer and broadcaster done all he could to propagate his work, but he died when still in his thirties, in 1972. There is often something specially touching about the spectacle of a young enthusiast entering the lists with fresh energy on behalf of an elderly creator who may perhaps have begun to wonder whether the world still cares – and

Rubbra for his part must have cherished the memory of his young friend, for, as Charles Koechlin said in his beautiful book on his fellow-composer Fauré,

> As death approaches, man turns with increasing tenderness towards the memories of childhood, or to the youth actually existing around him; visions of freshness, adolescence, charm, and – in the case of a fine artist – purity crowd upon him … The inspiration, even the writing … [is] likewise purified – reduced to essentials, with an ever-increasing self-confidence.[4]

'Reduction to essentials' is very apparent in this compact string quartet, as in the preceding and ensuing symphonies; perhaps the most essential quality of all in Rubbra's music is its sense of improvisation, which is most clearly felt in the first of the quartet's two seven-minute movements. On a superficial level it divides, like so much else of his, into slow introduction and quick main section, but a separation into sections Ia and Ib leaves the initial slow and quicker music as equal components of Ia. As so often, the quicker part of Ia seems to dance, in however sedate and subdued a way, with a very rapid succession of character-changes, Rubbra's inimitable command of the 'instant fade' remaining undiminished over forty years. His separation of styles between the various genres was, however, as scrupulously realistic and practical as that of any other major composer, and in other respects there is less musical 'overlap' with the ensuing symphony than with music from far earlier, such as the third movement of the 1950-vintage Second String Quartet (see pp. 116–17). After a sombre start, the later stages of the first movement offer a sizeable dose of another Rubbra essential, bells and rejoicing: it sets in about five minutes into the music, pausing briefly before the section Rubbra marked Ib (Allegretto scherzando). As Pickard points out in his notes for a recording, the distinction between the two parts is largely one of texture, Ib feeling lighter. Every resource of quartet technique is invoked to make the celebration convincing and exhilarating.

Where the Seventh Symphony's 'commemorative' finale moved from remembrance to celebration, in the commemorative Fourth Quartet things happen in the opposite order: the second movement is truly elegiac, and constantly inventive in forming new versions of its opening idea. That is simplicity itself; a rising minor third followed by a major third from the same first note, with a stress on the last note of the four. Pickard finds here an allusion to the opening of Beethoven's C♯ minor String Quartet, Op. 131, and certainly an early variant of the idea makes it literally quote the four-note motive from the opening of the Beethoven. But one should not make too much of this; Beethoven's movement is a genuine fugue that would have been worthy of a place in Bach's '48', Rubbra's, like so much of his music, simply uses fugal technique. The constant reinvention of the opening idea leads to a strong and more positive-sounding climax, with again a trace at least of the steadily moving scales that go with Rubbra's bell-mode; after that, the light has altered, the atmosphere eased, and the ending justifies Rubbra's marking for the final bars – 'con dignità e calmo'.

In 1976, as Rubbra was working on a piece for recorder and harpsichord intended for a pupil's tenth wedding anniversary, he was approached by his old patron Carl Dolmetsch with yet another commission. He adapted the 'work in progress', adding a part for viola da gamba, and it had its première in 1978 at the Dolmetsch Ensemble's annual Wigmore Hall concert. The *Fantasia on a Chord* (Op. 154) opens a door just wide enough to admit one proto-penultimate Rubbra–Schönberg comparison. In the third of his 1909 *Five Orchestral Pieces* (Op. 16) Schönberg had written 'variations on a chord', the variations being at first only in the scoring of an otherwise-unchanged complex sonority, though in the course of the piece a good deal more than that happened. Rubbra's *Fantasia* likewise takes a complex chord as basis, though he weaves his typical sinuous lines above it, obtaining a remarkable fullness of sound from a mere three instruments.

Work on the newest symphony (Op. 153) began in 1977 but went slowly. He had great difficulty getting it right, something he with characteristic circumspection put down initially to the fact that 'like most things I compose I like to keep the original idea in abeyance for quite a considerable time in order to digest it … It was a long time before I got to work on it, and then I completed it in 1979.' (The published score gives its period of composition as July 1977 – February 1979, curiously dating the whole thing 8.6.79.) In July 1979 he had a stroke, which he felt had been partly caused by the strain of completing the symphony, and once one knows of that it is tempting to put the delay down partly to failing health. It is, however, also thinkable that he was slowed down by the obligation, of which he must have been acutely aware, to make what was probably his last symphonic statement all-embracing and authoritative. A Verdi at the end of his life could discover a heavenly vein of comedy for Falstaff and his raffish ways; Rubbra needed to round off what he had already achieved – or to believe he had, even if what he in fact delivered was wondrously loose and open-ended. The symphony eventually had its first performance at the Promenade Concert on 20 August of the fraught 1980 season, the time of reorganisation when BBC Scotland responded to a call for swingeing economies by offering up its Symphony Orchestra; central management's acceptance of the idea provoked the only strike in the history of the Proms. The first few were cancelled, questions were asked in Parliament, but by mid-August it was settled after a fashion, and Nicholas Cleobury conducted the première with the BBC Northern Symphony Orchestra, as it still was, before its imminent redesignation as the BBC Philharmonic. Rubbra dedicated the work to Colette Yardley, soon to become his wife. He was not well enough to attend the concert, which despite a shortage of rehearsal time connected with the strike elicited cordial reviews.

The Eleventh came out as his shortest symphony, the première taking less than a quarter of an hour. Rubbra composed it to run continuously, and one can no longer even speak with any confidence, as one could in the case of the Tenth, of distinct movements conflated, rather of a genuinely seamless tissue of ideas alternating often at great speed to make up his most mercurial symphonic composition. Grover found it virtually unidentifiable as a 'symphony' and suggested that it should have been called 'Improvisation' – which, as we shall see, was how its composer felt listeners heard it. To go by switches of subject matter, tempo and character, it could be said to fall into anything from five to eight sections,[5] and on a more immediate level about twenty subsections, some lasting a minute or more, some only a few seconds. On first hearing it I felt it resembled a kaleidoscope, and later came across the composer's words in his Radio 3 talk before the première, 'transferring the elements all the time, like a kaleidoscope, that is to say shaking them up'. Payne's 'fluctuating momentum and a basically episodic formality' here proves to have been prophetic.

The main theme (Ex. 55) at the very quiet opening (Andante moderato, 4/4, ♩ = 60–62 circa, C major) is a chain of falling and rising fifths, Rubbra's favourite interval, to which as we have seen he attributed almost mystical qualities. The fall and rise of these fifths could be a reminder of times past, for

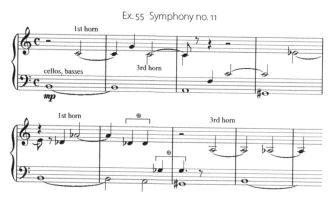

Ex. 55 Symphony no. 11

thirty years earlier the post-war Cello Sonata had been pervaded by the same interval falling and rising, and the constant changing landscapes that soon go by, irretrievable once glimpsed, may take us back to the sonata's scherzo, where there was a similar though much quicker procession. As in the Seventh Symphony,[6] the horn dominates the opening, but to different effect. The initial line, divided between the first and third horns, develops into a paragraph spanning a full minute, a generous allowance in a work that is to last only a quarter of an hour; such stability is not to last! The theme comes as a series of short phrases; each ends on a rising or falling third, but there is development, since on their first appearance the fifths are pure interval, each note being heard only once, while at their second the later note of each fifth is repeated to inaugurate the next one (Ex. 55*). That produces something more recognisably melody, and also turns before long into a very useful rocking accompaniment figure, up and down. It is all offset by a conjunct line in the bass; the symbiosis of these two ways of moving – through wide intervals and close ones – is for the most part the substance of the work.

As the first oboe picks up the fifths, the aspiring violin line in the slow movement of the Fifth Symphony and one or two successors like *Veni Creator Spiritus* seems to signal approval. The strings have been biding their time, now they emerge with their own singing paragraph of melody. (Ex. 56 shows its opening, the most recognisable feature as it recurs.) This begins to be a characteristic Rubbra wave, developing for about a minute and a half, and some characteristic Rubbra drum-beats underline the feeling of a first climax. For a moment the fifths even become simultaneous – shades of the 'Schönberg twelve-tone technique' Rubbra detected in the parallel sixths at the end of the Bach F♯ major fugue, but also of the magical horn-fifths in the Sixth Symphony's slow movement. Another minute on and the tempo picks up a little more; something over four minutes in it has been just possible to make out the general outlines of an introduction and miniature first movement. As things begin to calm down, there is the most striking statement so far of the line of fifths (six up, four down, and so on, in the rocking version), which dies away, giving place to a much simplified line, likewise up-and-down but this time conjunct, for an instrument rarely met in Rubbra's music, the celesta (it was first 'featured' in the scherzo of the Sixth Symphony, and later at the end of the Eighth), doubled by the flutes and a clarinet.

Ex. 56 Symphony no. 11, bar 27

Rubbra's very tactful touches of unusual orchestral colour are successive landmarks punctuating the symphony; the celesta is followed by a gong, a xylophone and eventually a harp (though that instrument in fact doubles the very first note of the work, in the bass), all used with great economy (one is again reminded of Brahms and his Fourth-Symphony triangle). Grover detected in three passages during this symphony 'a strangely visionary quality', this one with the celesta being the first. If it marks a 'development', we now also have the makings of a slow movement.

Soon after the celesta tune the interval of the fourth (the fifth's inversion or complement) comes to the fore, purely as colour: mediaeval music was for a long time dominated by a form called organum, in which the voices moved in parallel fourths or fifths, and that is how Rubbra uses the fourths here.[7] The next subsection of the pseudo-slow-movement seems to be turning into another drum-beat-laden wave, with more appearances of Ex. 56 and, about seven minutes in, another quite significant, persistent idea coming into play, a three-repeated-note figure on the brass that by its nature is bound to be a shade menacing. The second movement of Vaughan Williams's 1947 Sixth Symphony had made enormously effective use of this motif; something similar threatened the first movement of Rubbra's Seventh and formed part of the passacaglia theme in the Eighth. With a sudden acceleration (to $\flat = 92$, 'molto mosso') marked by an intervention from the xylophone, we are offered what one can only call, paradoxically, a march in three-time developing into a quicker, restless passage. This offers the triangle its three brief moments and could take us back to the 'North African' variation in the finale of the Third Symphony. Is this composer drowning, that his past life should flash by at such a rate? Or enjoying the pleasures of recollection, surveying his achievement (without the bombast and self-congratulation of Strauss in *Ein Heldenleben*)? Or, third alternative, going over in particular the eventful period since the Fifth and Sixth symphonies and the break-up with Antoinette? Samuel Beckett's tramps in *Waiting for Godot* ask the classic question, 'What do we do now we're happy?' – and some such question has been heard to underlie the symphonic music that followed the glorious, almost impossible musical idyll of those two magical middle works. The reminders of the Fifth Symphony and of the opening quiet horns in the Sixth justify some such speculation about the Eleventh.

Be that as it may, we are clearly into something like a scherzo in triple time. The pace quickens, though over the next minute it becomes very hard to say what the tempo really is – quicker, slower, a few seconds of almost frantic movement, and immediately another big slowing-down, with three strange offbeat strokes on the xylophone.

The ever-baleful sound of the gong marks something of a watershed. Less than ten minutes in, we have already had, in effect, three 'movements' – no wonder that after the première the critic Peter Stadlen recorded his disbelief on realising that the entire work had lasted a mere quarter of an hour, so much had happened. With things occurring this fast it is not too surprising that the 'creative indecision' of the Eighth Symphony's first movement at times appears to have set in again. A fascinating aspect of the rapid succession of subsections is that each is detectable only some time after it has begun. (Rubbra said of the work: 'the listener views it as a huge improvisation'.) The pattern is that after a trifling change still reconcilable with the preceding character something genuinely surprising and new makes us realise we have in fact moved on. Rubbra was always a master of transition and still is here; in fact this melting of the boundaries, though hinted at in the 'interrelated meditations' that made up the finale of the Viola Concerto, takes further the previous symphony's way of changing character some time after a 'movement pause'. Here there are neither pauses nor, on the whole, clear lines of demarcation; the moment with the gong is the nearest we come to one.

In this new section a triple-time theme unfolds on the oboe (Adagio calmo e sereno, Ex. 57). Rubbra in his radio interview described it as 'newish', and Grover found this the one element of the symphony that could be called a melody. As at the end of Tchaikovsky's 'Pathétique' Symphony, the gong moves the music into a quite new area, as different as death from life. All the foregoing improvisation has been a prime example of Payne's 're-focusing of a single and static experience'; this is the first passage to make its way like a quite normal tune, and the first where the opposition of fifths and conjunct movement is not of the essence. The melody is soon tested by strange growling lower-register sounds (cellos playing *sul ponticello*), and, in Grover's second visionary passage, by the menacing three-note figure. It just about holds its own, Cerberus eventually being pacified with the help of some tubular bells, and as the

Ex. 57 Symphony no. 11, bar 175

admirable melody reasserts itself in the middle register the high violins offer a filigree of twinkling movement. This is like a memory of the happiest moments in the middle symphonies. Two minutes further on, at Grover's final 'visionary point', we re-meet the final member of the 'stage army', the harp or harp-like plucked notes like a ticking clock. In the past they have suggested, first, loneliness, and then the mysterious radiance of the two men in shining garments at Christ's sepulchre. Paradoxically, in this 'posthumous' world they trigger off the liveliest music in the whole work, which soon dances in an almost Holstian way. For thirty-three bars (out of a total of 284) the time-signatures constantly fluctuate between seven and five in a bar, which would upset most classical dancers but is scarcely noticeable to a listener. The fifths and the idea of conjunct movement are by now on level terms, indeed the upper strings seem to be winning with what could be a faint echo (though no more) of the ecstatic descending bell-like lines found near the end of many previous Rubbra works. It all culminates in what seems the symphony's actual climax, C major with a cymbal clash.

From here on it should be plain sailing (or contented lumbering) towards a happy end, a goal achieved – what Harold Truscott (*ERC*) called 'that philosophical and tranquil frame of mind that one finds in the late music of composers who live to a ripe age'. So one does, but not perhaps here; by now we know Rubbra well enough to have learned that his way is different. In Büchner's and Berg's *Wozzeck* the Captain asks his anti-hero batman 'What am I supposed to do with the few minutes you save by shaving me so frantically?'; Rubbra, after his almost frantic dance, owes himself another minute's music and must decide what to do with it. In a final change of mood and pace, drastic though the outcome is the opposite, he is into the calm waters that have up till now receded, as if tormenting Tantalus, each time they hove into view. His point is made with disconcerting succinctness. Parallel triads for the horns and then the strings spell out for one last time the start of the last section's 'melody' (Ex. 56). Such 'close harmony' is rare in an almost invariably contrapuntal composer like Rubbra, and when these basic chords are heard it is usually to great effect, as with the simultaneous triads in different keys that immediately conveyed *Song of the Soul*'s religious character. Here, as there, they are in the least stable inversion, with the fourth at the bottom (6-4), but this time they are not 'bottomless', being underpinned by a line for the double bass. This briefest glimpse of a world of pure euphony shows Rubbra in his late seventies still looking ahead; he would go memorably further into that world in the 1982 *Sinfonietta*.

The horns, which spoke the first word, are denied the last by a final interjection, first on the trumpet and then on clarinet and harp, whose juxtaposition of falling and rising fifth could put a Franz-Schmidt-lover in mind of the trumpet tune (made up of the fifth's inversion, the fourth, both rising and falling) at the beginning and end of his valedictory Fourth Symphony. How strange that two major symphonists should by sheer coincidence bow out on similar figures! Rather than triumphing, or even soothing with a touch of a 'philosophical, tranquil frame of mind', Rubbra's coda is over so quickly that it could almost be called perfunctory, provisional, as if he meant it to be just the introduction to something more substantial, but finally left it at that. Unlike the Fifth Symphony's abbreviated finale or the brief Adagio at the end of the Tenth, this abrupt ending has a touch of pathos: it is not a case of 'leave them wanting more'. Flowing straight on, it leaves open as many questions as it answers (even ending not on the most direct, 'root-position' version of its final chord, but in 'first inversion', i.e. with the third, not the tonic, at the bottom). Rubbra's First Symphony began 'in medias res'; his final one ends there.

So ambiguous an ending to his symphonic odyssey reminds us of something spotted by Mellers thirty-five years before – that Rubbra's was a dual nature, in the world yet not of it. By that token the Eleventh Symphony could be said to have two alternative endings – a practical one leading up to the final minute with cymbal clash and 'the C major of this life',[8] and a contemplative one, which he happens to place second. In the Sixth Symphony, too, he had a choice of endings but whereas there it was indeed a choice – he had to settle for one or the other – here the miniature time-scale allows him both. Considerations of relative weight are uppermost in the mind of even an 'improvisatory' composer not given to graphing things out in advance.

The above catalogue of events can have given little idea what the Eleventh actually sounds and 'feels' like; for that, the only recourse is to a recording, since a sedulous analysis of its interval structure (*pace* Grover and the other Old Believers) is not going to help either. The all-pervading fifths here are in fact a good deal more audible to the untutored ear than many 'dominant intervals' elsewhere in Rubbra; Stephen Banfield's 1983 review in *Music and Letters* took their sheer profusion amiss, saying it left 'not much else to latch on to', and to that extent made the work disappointing. But they contribute only a little to a grasp of what this highly compressed music 'has to say', over and above its existence as essence. Its ideas are constantly renewed and transformed, and as a 'flight of ideas' the Eleventh is comparable only to a work such as the Third Symphony of Charles Ives – not the hysterical overloaded Ives haunted by his father's simultaneous marching brass bands, but the inward-looking Ives who never settled anywhere for long, finding the moment adequately beautiful. And perhaps, outlandish as it may seem, with the free expressionist world of a Schönberg work such as *Erwartung*, only the language there is atonal and things develop at an even quicker pace.

Rubbra's comments on his two final symphonies differed interestingly: the Tenth 'says all I want to say', this one 'is a culmination of all my symphonies compressed into one movement'. Grover begged to differ: the Tenth 'represents the culmination for the very reasons that the Eleventh *is* a problem', and it 'has a well-defined structure that is not, however, in any way rigid or inflexible, and in this respect it is a worthy successor to – indeed, a culmination of – all of those earlier movements in which the same freer tendencies were manifested'. Though hard to gainsay, that crucially ignores Rubbra's indefinite article; the Eleventh was not 'the culmination', implying exclusiveness and comprehensiveness, but 'a culmination', one possible way in which things about his other symphonies could be carried further.

It is easy to fall into cliché-thinking about aged composers; one so wants to see them in a safe haven, where nothing can any longer threaten their mellow wisdom and serenity, and it may be sad to watch a man whose music so often suggested confidence, joy and contented detachment from the world's ever-increasing madness now seem, with so little time left, to cast about in search of something final. But a continuing search ('this very questioning at every step') is part of the creative temperament as of the religious, and to a believer such as Rubbra the only 'final thing' must be God, who is by definition unattainable save in exceptional moments of insight. To say it yet again, transcendence is a glimpse, not a state; an old Buddhist saying runs 'Before enlightenment, draw water and hew wood; after enlightenment, draw water and hew wood.' In this outwardly cryptic and confusing last symphonic document Rubbra enhances the value of his precious final minute by reminding us of its cost: it is the pearl of great price, to gain which a man 'must sell even all he has' (and draw water and hew wood!). The Eleventh is a maverick, and, like most mavericks, totally fascinating. Much as one admires, respects and treasures all his symphonies, one could love this one almost more than any.

Rubbra did not formally look on the Eleventh as his farewell to the symphony, as witness the few bars of sketches for a Twelfth. Just as Ulysses eventually reached home to enjoy (one hopes) a rich and richly deserved old age, Rubbra lived and worked for six more years. Composition was more difficult after his stroke; a planned cello piece for Rohan de Saram and an ex-Oxford pupil, the pianist Michael Hill, never materialised,[9] but a handful of works completed between 1980 and 1986 manifest still-new qualities and views of life. It is almost as if the completion of his symphonic cycle set him free to look in new directions, or very old ones.

Initially, a *Duo* for cor anglais and piano (Op. 156) presented the old Rubbra virtues of serious concise statement, but in the equally concise *Mass in Honour of St Teresa of Avila* (Op. 157) something surprising appeared, to continue in the *Sinfonietta*: a late luxuriance of harmony and texture. St Teresa (1515–82), an important sixteenth-century spiritual figure, was the mentor of John of the Cross. She interested Lennox Berkeley, whose 1947 setting of four of her mystical poems became one of his most deservedly successful works. The Mass was intended to celebrate the 400th anniversary of the saint's death, due in 1982; it was completed on 18 January 1981. Like the *Missa a tre*, it came out all the shorter since the Credo text was left to be intoned. Notable for its soaring conjunct lines and vagrant harmonies, the Mass offers not the slightest hint of post-Vatican-II reformism. Where the 1948 *Missa Sancti Dominici* was a direct and concise summons to worship, with perhaps a little of the spirit later reflected by that Council, here there is burgeoning melody and chromatically tinged shot-silk harmony. In its Benedictus Grover detected a late appearance of 'mirror images' (if inexact ones) which in their way of presenting lines both ways up at once reflected for one last time Rubbra's childhood experience with the snow. Though such music could hardly have been foreseen by Pius X, it answers that great spiritual leader's wish for profundity and dignity, and one could wish to see Britain's major Roman institutions deviate now and then from their loyalty to Palestrina and give such extraordinary music a hearing. Other short choral pieces included the companion *Bookmark* for voices and organ (op. 159), *How Shall my Tongue Express?* (Op. 155), the *Introit* (Op. 162) for the BBC Singers, and a setting of the first and last verses of the 122nd Psalm (Op. 164), considered below.

The commission for the 1980 *Duo* from the Dutch oboist Peter Bree must have been particularly welcome, given Rubbra's love of the cor anglais. According to Grover, a newspaper story at the time of its first performance reported Bree's embarrassment on finding that he could not afford the commissioning fee promised to Rubbra. (The Arts Council came to the rescue.) This further short work vividly presents one side of Rubbra's late musical personality. Starting one of those 'mystical six-four chords', which is contradicted, like most of the opening harmonies, by a bass note on the piano that makes it into a dissonance, it at first confines the piano to a chordal, accompanying role, by turns firm and gentle. Finally the pianist is allowed to spin a melodic line against the one for the cor anglais. A rhythm of two short notes followed by a long one could be a reminder of a favourite composer, Schubert, who used it time and again, never more memorably than in the great song 'Der Tod und das Mädchen' (Death and the Maiden) and the equally great string quartet based on it. Against all that, the cor anglais spins a comparably austere line. The feeling is monumental (Martin Anderson notes 'the stark formality of some ceremonial event') rather as at the start of the Second Piano Trio ten years earlier. Things flow a little more as the piece proceeds, softening for a while into a Faurean lyricism, last echo of a composer touched on so many decades before in the Second Violin Sonata and *Four Easy Pieces* for violin; there is a flowing triplet movement in the accompaniment. In the later stages the up-and-down fifths that were prominent in Rubbra's last symphony reappear, more or less taking over and persisting into a short, touching passage for the cor anglais on its own. That leads to a calm but firm ending with at the very end one more statement of the 'Death-and-the Maiden' rhythm. In little more than five minutes this adds up to an impressive piece with the air of a 'Tombeau' or memorial; it may or may not be relevant that Antoinette died not so long before the *Duo* was composed. The middle movement of the 1958 sonata for another well-loved double-reed instrument, the oboe, had been entitled 'Elegy'; this *Duo*, a still sterner piece, offers no such clue, but if it were indeed a memorial to Antoinette, then Freudians could find an interesting case of defensive substitution in the fact that it is for Rubbra's favourite instrument, not hers.

The remaining element in this late flowering was a couple of piano pieces – an *Invention on the name of Haydn* (Op. 160, written as a contribution to the 250th-anniversary celebrations in 1982), and for Michael Hill a *Fantasy Fugue* (Op. 161, 1981), which Rubbra meant to complement with a prelude. A remarkable document of his very last years, it shows a Busoni-like mixture of studiousness and daring; in a note for its Wigmore Hall première, Rubbra described it as 'free and seemingly improvisational'; a very prompt 'liberty' comes as the 'fugal answer' (i.e. the second entry of the subject) alters the rhythm of the later part of his theme, by which time we have reached bar 6! Rubbra also stressed, however, that even in its contrasting sections the fugue 'utilizes all the minutiae of the subject-matter', something which, he said, would probably be for a dedicatee a reminder of 'all those detailed lectures that gave me in preparing them hitherto unrealised insights into the structural and musical possibilities of each subject'. Its often strikingly resonant piano-writing turns to advantage the leap of an octave forming part of the subject (shades of his comment about 'twelve-tone technique' when Bach transformed a melodic sixth into a succession of harmonic ones!), while its later stages hint in a gaunt, enigmatic way at his beloved bells, quite suddenly offering further distinct reminiscences of Rubbra's early musical idol Debussy. In a late essay, *On revient toujours*, Schönberg tried to explain the nostalgia that led him to compose, for one last time, in a long-outmoded style, as if taking a ride in a horse-drawn 'fiacre'. Rubbra went less far, yet here he undoubtedly returned to things long gone but not forgotten.

The idea of a cello sonata for Hill and Rohan de Saram came to nothing, but the *Fantasy Fugue* took on a further lease of life in Rubbra's final orchestral venture, a *Sinfonietta* for large string orchestra (Op. 163) begun in 1982 to a commission from the symphony orchestra in New York State's capital city, Albany. Its first movement, originally entitled 'Nocturne', was ready by 1983, but Rubbra then hit a major blockage, until he realised that its 'intervallic structure' was related to that of the *Fantasy Fugue*. His solution to the problem of completing the work was to transcribe the fugue. (Grover suggested, as a second but unspoken reason, that he may simply have been afraid he would not be granted time to compose a new second movement, an idea he found confirmed by the 'Deo gratias' appended as postscript to the completed score.) As Michael Hill pointed out in the Wigmore Hall programme, he thus created, in effect, a Prelude and Fugue. Hill also recorded Rubbra's unease at having 're-used' the fugue without reference to its dedicatee; as with the original recipient of the *Fantasia on a Chord*, he was reassured that no offence had been taken. The orchestra's chief conductor Julius Hegyi conducted the work's first two performances, at a Friday concert on 5 December 1986 in the neighbouring town of Troy, and the following Saturday in Albany itself. Rubbra dedicated the work to Adrian Yardley and his half-brother Julian.

The first movement plunges us straight away into a world of string-sound that can only be described with a word rather seldom applicable to Rubbra – luscious. Together with the *St Teresa Mass* it suggests that some Epicurean or sybaritic Falstaff was, after all, waiting in the wings. Stringed instruments had been a vital part of Rubbra's life in one way and another; in the *Sinfonietta* one senses his love of their sound and his profound understanding of them, to which Cyril Scott had paid tribute after hearing the Violin Concerto. The movement is the very last example, and a major one, of a Rubbra piece that simply takes one with it like an improvisation. From an opening that for the briefest moment puts one in mind of Bach's 'Air on the G String' Rubbra spins a texture of full, floating chords in the upper register against a repeating bass line; a masterly final example of his command of ostinato, it consists of a falling scale made up of two four-note halves that often don't really fit each other but fit the music above them wonderfully. Given Rubbra's turn of mind, they must be expected to migrate promptly into the upper parts and become overt melody. The magic of contrary motion, so well understood by Beethoven, immediately weaves its spell. Many of the upper-register chords are the 6-4s singled out long before by Elsie Payne in her exposé of Rubbra's mystical side. The conjunct four-note figures seem totally dominant; about a minute in, we hear one in a middle part with its successive notes emphasised and separated by pauses, giving the first of the piece's bell effects. A minute or so later there is a real shock and stimulus when the conjunct movement is suddenly interrupted by a succession of rising fourths. We could almost be back with the pervasive rising fifths of the Eleventh Symphony. This is a striking variation of the melodic line, but the music immediately falls back into its previous gait, pressing on to a climax and a sustained loud chord. The more intimate voices of a solo quartet, briefly deepening the mood, are soon swallowed up.

In this latter part of the movement one may well feel a kinship with Richard Strauss's *Metamorphosen* – there is even a repeated figure with a group of six notes very like one of the later ideas in the Strauss – but no funereal Beethoven quotation comes to spell out the message: Rubbra is happy with his own fugue. The many twists and turns of this movement can be coldly analysed and lamely described, but when heard they are warmth itself, thanks to the suppleness of an unfailing aural imagination.

In Rubbra's inventive transcription the Fugue emerges as for the most part slightly softer than the original, with many half-lights; one or two effects do, however, considerably strengthen points in the music where the version for piano was gentler. For occasional intensification he uses a device absent from the first movement, tremolo. The transcription is not absolutely literal, for there is one striking modification: at the very end, what was originally a single quiet chord emerges as a sustained sound against which isolated pizzicato notes offer the final example of Rubbra's enigmatic 'clock-ticking'.[10] He seems to say, 'Now, time really is up'; if Grover's supposition was correct, he could afford to say it at the end, hence the addition.

Albany made the most of its distinguished commission, which was not the only English commission by the orchestra of the time; a George Lloyd symphony, his Eleventh, was performed later in the same season. The city's music critic Scott Cantrell published an enthusiastic review of the *Sinfonietta* after attending the rehearsals, in time to persuade his fellow-citizens to go and hear 'their' piece. Nor was this mere small-town-American good-nature, for Rub-bra had produced something fit to stand alongside his best, and, in its beauty of string-orchestral sound, alongside classics in the genre by Dvořák, Tchai-kovsky, Elgar, Schönberg, Vaughan Williams, Barber, Strauss and Tippett. Like Schönberg's *Verklärte Nacht* and Barber's *Adagio* it is, at least in part, a tran-scription, but in spirit it comes nearest to *Metamorphosen*, for both works are profoundly valedictory. Strauss wrote the elegy for twenty-three solo strings as he mourned the war-time destruction of his beloved Munich Opera House; Rubbra had no such 'city of desolation' before him, but who can say what he found within? In any case, one should not forget that for all the good humour of the late wind pieces and the divine serenity of the *Four Last Songs* Strauss had, like any other man, to reconcile himself at some point or other to his own imminent mortality, without the balm of Eichendorff and Hermann Hesse to soothe his 'existential Angst'. By the early 1980s that, for all the Church's reas-surances, was Rubbra's position too, and part of his response was to recreate the beauty of an older tradition of string-orchestral writing. *On revient toujo-urs.*

The *Sinfonietta* had an almost immediate hearing in Great Britain, for the local radio station in Albany made a recording available, which was duly broad-cast on BBC Radio 3 as a pendant to a cycle of the symphonies compiled by Rubbra's ex-pupil Robert Layton.

The last work Rubbra completed was a setting of the 122nd Psalm (Op. 164, 1985) for mixed chorus, commissioned by St Andrew's Cathedral, Aberdeen, to mark the 200th anniversary of the installation of the first American bishop (Bishop Seabury) within the Episcopalian Church's See of Aberdeen. Sir Hubert Parry had set the same psalm, and Rubbra's piece was intended as a foil to it.[11] The verses of the euphoric psalm selected for setting were the ones that refer directly to the building – the first, most suitably, 'I was glad when they said unto me, Let us go into the house of the Lord', and the ninth and last, 'Because of the house of the Lord thy God I will seek thy good.' The piece was conducted by the cathedral's organist and choirmaster Andrew Morrison.

Only a few weeks after completing *Psalm 122* Rubbra had another stroke, and he died a few weeks later, on St Valentine's Day 1986. Colette survived him by four years, dying in 1990. Thirty years earlier, his greatest friend had said of him, 'from the word go everything he has ever written has been Rubbra',[12] and it remained so to the end. With his death English music lost a figure of unique integrity and stature. A naïve young Oxford graduate half a century ago was not, after all, so wide of the mark in writing 'only when historical perspective has got the picture suitably out of focus and nobody cares whether a work was written in 1903 or 1953 will it be possible for the doubters to decide whether Dr Rubbra's Sixth Symphony is the finest symphony and the most inspired music of the twentieth century' (see pp. 208–8); the crucial thing is the music's sheer quality, its ideas, the personality it communicates, the world of search and discovery that opens up to us when we hear it. Rubbra's journey from his first symphony to his last was one such as many of us make in the course of a lifetime; its uniqueness comes from the fact that at every stage it announces itself through unforgettably inventive and attractive music. That is something to survive all fluctuations of taste: may its time come again, and soon.

Rubbra on the Fourth Symphony (1942)

This is the text of Rubbra's spoken introduction before the BBC Home Service broadcast of the première of his Fourth Symphony, Henry Wood Promenade Concerts, London, 14 August 1942.

There's no programme attached to my Fourth Symphony; that is, it does not *consciously* illustrate subjective states, or seek to convey to the listener anything appertaining to the surrounding objective world. The listener may, if he wishes, translate the images of this symphonic world into those of the world of his everyday experience, and say, 'Here the music is triumphant; there it is apprehensive; somewhere else it is carefree', but to do so is, as it were, to bypass the centre of the music. The symphony is in the philosophical sense of the word a musical essence, rounded, complete and independent. In other words, it forms its own world; it is subject to its own laws and volition, and not in any sense illustrative of, or a commentary upon, the phenomena of everyday life.

Now a word as to the structure of the work. It consists of three movements (or four, if one considers the slow introduction to the finale as a slow movement, as in many respects it is), two big fifteen-minute movements sandwiching a five-minute intermezzo. This intermezzo, which is in waltz-time, takes the place of a scherzo, and is a very subdued and delicate one. This movement is designed to give mental relief and refreshment between two movements full of tension.

The Rubbra Sixth: Some Reflections (1955)

This article by the author originally appeared in Isis *(Oxford), 23 February 1955.*

Youthful music critics who know enough to be able to follow complex patterns but not enough to have been disenchanted of the chimera of originality tend to be tolerant in their discussion of present-day musical production; within limits, the nastier a noise the more likely they are to hail it as good, as 'modern' music, but the enlightened junior Beckmesser can take most things from Vaughan Williams to Searle, Henze and the latest Stravinsky. One kind of music, however, one just *does not write* nowadays – it uses the diatonic scale, goes through a series of intelligible modulations from one key to another and resolves most of its dissonances. So that when Dr. Rubbra produces, in his Sixth Symphony, a work displaying all these characteristics and it is hailed, by those our critic respects, as a fine, even a great work, the latter is in considerable perturbation. His magnanimity has let him down – surely he has made his definition of legitimacy pretty inclusive: why can't people play the game?

Let us be fair; our critic is not just being over-sophisticated, blasé, sensation-seeking or snobbish; he has found, over a period of years, that it is at least workable to regard music as a criticism of life, related to its time; moreover, certain tendencies, scientific, philosophical and particularly psychological, in the life of the present century have given him a modern world-picture, and he can relate to it anything from Vaughan Williams to Berg, and even on good days to Skalkottas. Dr. Rubbra's Sixth Symphony he cannot so relate, except by regarding it as completely out of date and *fade* in a way that even he realises would be naïve and jejune. In fact he has to reconsider his admittedly tolerant views of what modern music should be, by trying to work out what this particular piece of modern music is trying to do.

Arthur Koestler has compared the novelist, and this could be said of any creative artist, to a man sitting with his feet in a bucket of hot water (inspiration), in front of an open window (the world he has to deal with). One way to handle the window is to shut it completely, to concentrate on the inner workings: Koestler regards this as a dangerous thing to do – 'the perfect novel presupposes a totally open window – the author should have an all-embracing knowledge of the essential currents and facts ... of his time ... for use by implication.' This idea has a great attraction for our critic, who is concerned more than anything else with the relationship of Art and Life. But Koestler, as a good materialist, regards the closed window as a thing that can lead only to ivory towers and hot-houses: here Dr. Rubbra would certainly join issue with him. This is the source of all our critic's bewilderment. He finds Dr. Rubbra 'behind the times', not omitting to bear in mind that Bach was similarly behind his times when he produced some of the world's greatest music. Koestler has more accurately posited a position of being *outside* the times. Dr. Rubbra presents us with a timeless experience, so naturally he presents it to us in a timeless medium: his symphony is situated far out at the Yogi end of the spectrum, and you might as well talk about colour to a man blind since birth as play mystical music to the average bright young man brought up on Mozart and Wagner. Our critic's system of values is quite upset when he is confronted by music that resolutely ignores everything contemporary in favour of something eternal, music that gives no hint of recognition to the modern trends and discoveries, in all fields, that affect his views. It seems to him, in particular, that twentieth-century music in its emancipated treatment of dissonance provides a parallel to the uncovering by psychoanalysis of the blacker secrets of the human subconscious. There is a definite distorting-mirror quality about some modern music, as if, to use Jungian terms, the Shadow were speaking instead of the normal personality. An obsession with the details of *how* things work at the expense of *why* they work seems to him (at times) to be part and parcel of a general decadence that comes as a stage, perhaps a penultimate stage, in a materialistic decline of Western civilisation that set in during the seventeenth century or perhaps even earlier.

As far as music is concerned, the rot set in with Josquin, with the fatal discovery of Musica Reservata, the means of expressing the passions in sound. The mediaeval equation of pure constructional music-making and (religious) ritual, as found in the earlier church music, survived and reached its climax during the succeeding years alongside the expressive approach of the madrigal; for a time the two even use the same technique and sound remarkably similar – this is why there is considerable justification for the view that in music there is no Renaissance, only an overlap of a hundred years between Mediaeval and Baroque. Now, in the disintegration and chaos resulting from the Wagnerian working-out of the line that started with Josquin, we meet composers who are trying to get back to the mediaeval feel for pure, ritual music – Stravinsky is the leader here, and he has explicitly stated that we ask the impossible of music when we ask it to express feelings and emotions. This is obviously nonsense – the question is not whether expression is possible but whether it is inevitable or even *desirable*. On this point the century is irremediably divided; the dodecaphonists, handling a neurasthenically over-charged idiom that arose from the breaking down of Wagnerian expressiveness, are opposed at the other extreme by Stravinsky with his ritual neo-mediaevalism. The latter has had the clear sight to go back to before the great divide about 1500 whereas Hindemith has made an uneasy compromise with the High Baroque.

Musical mysticism as such is only describable as 'mediaeval' insofar as mysticism was the foundation of mediaeval art-music – its expression can be quite 'contemporary', as in the late quartets of Beethoven. Only when historical perspective has got the picture suitably out of focus and nobody cares whether a work was written in 1903 or 1953 will it be possible for the doubters to decide whether Dr. Rubbra's Sixth Symphony is the finest symphony and the most inspired music of the twentieth century or a highly accomplished essay in an outmoded manner – an isolated peak or a relic.

It is quite conceivable that there is no great music being written any more. 'Great men are an institution, like prisons or the army; once it is there, someone has to be put in it', observes Robert Musil; our one-way materialistic decadence is so far advanced in building (over the malodorous cesspool of the collective unconscious) chromium-plated palaces for rationalist bureaucrats that perhaps the history books of the future will record Stravinsky as the last great composer. Or might they choose Dr. Rubbra?

Notes

INTRODUCTION Rubbra in the Third Millenium?

1 Ralph Scott Grover, *The Music of Edmund Rubbra* (Aldershot, 1993).

2 Ronald Stevenson set a welcome precedent in his article on the concerted works in the symposium *Edmund Rubbra, Composer* (Rickmansworth, 1970), edited by Lewis Foreman with contributions from all the most knowledgeable people writing on Rubbra during his later years – it is referred to in the course of this study as *ERC*.

3 The late *Mass in Honour of St Teresa of Avila* is on the same high level but should stand rather as a splendid example of a luxuriant final style.

4 Notes for the Endymion Ensemble CD of the trios and the music for oboe and cor anglais. 'Essence' was an important word for Rubbra, as will emerge in the course of this book.

5 Interview with Murray Schafer in *British Composers in Interview* (London, 1963), referred to as *BCI*.

6 Lecture delivered in Birmingham, 4 April 1949.

7 'In the crisis of culture we are experiencing, it is only from islands of spiritual concentration that a new cultural and spiritual purification can break out at all.' Joseph Cardinal Ratzinger, later Pope Benedict XVI, 'In the presence of the Angels' (1994), in *A New Song for the Lord* (Oxford, 1995).

8 'Edmund Rubbra Writes about his Eighth Symphony', *The Listener*, 31 December 1970. Compare Paul Hindemith in his *Craft of Musical Composition*, 2 vols. (London, 1941–2): 'Is not an immense mastery of the medium needed to translate into tones what the heart dictates?'

CHAPTER 1 General Features

1 Note by Robert Saxton and Adrian Yardley for a CD recording of *A Tribute*.

2 In *British Composers in Interview* he included Bach among his favourite composers ('at his best' – standards must be maintained!), along with Monteverdi, Stravinsky and Shostakovich, but not Beethoven nor, surprisingly, Brahms. An untitled 1953 lecture expressed his admiration for a 'diverse group of modern composers with the common denominator of being integrated artists with vision and the means to objectify that vision: Debussy, Bartók, Stravinsky, Sibelius, Vaughan Williams, Holst and Carl Nielsen'.

3 Research at Vienna University has meanwhile shown how general such 'flickering' is in following music (see Hellmut Petsche, 'Die flirrende Welt der Aufmerksamkeit: Zur Neurophysiologie kognitiver Prozesse ('The scintillating

world of attention: Neurophysiological aspects of cognitive processes'), *EEG EMG*, Vienna March 1995.

[4] For an exposé of a historic time-lag between Europe and Britain, see Hugh Wood, 'English Music', in *European Music in the Twentieth Century*, ed. Howard Hartog, rev. edn (Harmondsworth, 1961).

[5] Hugh Ottoway, 'Rubbra at 75', *The Listener*, 3 June 1976.

[6] Cesare Pavese, *This Business of Living* [*Il mestiere di vivere*], trans. A. E. Murch (London, 1961).

[7] BBC Home Service *Music Magazine*, 1952, reprinted in BBC book with the same title (London, 1953).

[8] Schönberg's preferred term was 'method of composing with twelve tones'.

[9] Sol Babitz, 'Stravinsky's Symphony in C (1940)', *Musical Quarterly*, vol. 27 (1941).

[10] Perhaps the finest example of such preparation of a new movement in music before Rubbra's day is to be found in a work he must have played many times, Brahms's B major Piano Trio, between the scherzo and slow movement. John Daverio (*Robert Schumann*, New York/Oxford 1997) has pointed out a similar 'preparation' at the end of the first movement of Schumann's 'Spring' Symphony.

[11] Mendelssohn's way of sliding one casually into a recapitulation without its being in any way signalled in advance or marked off is an artistic feature on a comparable level.

[12] Compare: 'almost like a film emphasising turmoil by suddenly cutting to and from quiet country vistas' (Lewis Foreman, note for CD of Second Violin Sonata).

[13] For example, nobody in their right mind held the nineteenth-century Australian cricketer F. R. Spofforth, hero of the England–Australia match that gave rise to 'The Ashes', to be a bad man, yet he has gone down in history as 'the demon bowler'. The ancient Greek word 'daimon' meant 'a guardian spirit'; its negative connotations came later, from the Fathers of the Church.

[14] 'A Composer's Problems', *Music Magazine* (1953), pp. 42–5.

[15] 'Edmund Rubbra writes about his Eighth Symphony'.

[16] 'Edmund Rubbra writes about his Eighth Symphony'.

[17] Stephen Banfield, first biographer of Rubbra's great friend Gerald Finzi, points out in *Gerald Finzi, An English Composer* (London, 1997) that at the Royal College of Music in the 1920s everyone studied orchestration with Gordon Jacob. Two decades later Dr Jacob achieved nationwide fame with his arrangements heard weekly during the BBC's greatest war-time comedy programme, *ITMA*.

CHAPTER 2 The Early Years

[1] In *ERC*. Memories of the time after his early twenties are based on tapes recorded for Grover near the end of Rubbra's life and used in *Edmund Rubbra, The Man and his Music*.

[2] Compulsory primary education dated from 1870, and a minimum school-leaving age was first set in 1902, under the same Act of Parliament that made secondary

education compulsory. The age was raised from thirteen to fourteen in 1918, four years after Rubbra left school; as early as a 1919 report into juvenile delinquency there were plans to raise it further, though what with one thing and another it was not actually raised to fifteen until 1 April 1947, by a Labour government making law the war-time Education Act of a Conservative politician, R. A. Butler. The current school-leaving age, 16, dates from 1972. Kettering Road School has meanwhile been transformed into a Northamptonshire Music Centre, with a room named after Rubbra.

3 In many important paintings by the most religious of German nineteenth-century painters, Caspar David Friedrich, there is a comparable distribution of light, with the foreground in deep shadow within which one can only gradually make out detail, and a steady progression towards a distant light at the top of the picture, which has a clear symbolic message.

4 There are several Mozart piano sonatas in C major, and with an already excellent piano technique Rubbra would not necessarily have had to confine himself to the famous 'easy sonata', K545, though at the time that probably came nearest to people's idea of Mozart. The one K330 has the most substantial musical content.

5 Article on Holst, undated.

6 My own family followed a similar pattern of a gradually less tenable vegetarianism and pacifism.

7 Early in the third millennium there was still a German school near Richmond Bridge.

8 My Jewish father, not even a Communist but merely a Fabian Socialist, seriously thought of moving himself, his wife and a young family to Russia during the 1930s, at the height of Stalin's anti-Jewish paranoia, but was dissuaded by no less a figure than the Russian ambassador in London, Mr. Maisky. (And, though I was not yet of an age to register it, presumably by his own wife.)

9 Cyril Scott's *The Philosophy of Modernism* referred to a more recent poet familiar to Rubbra, Francis Thompson, as 'a new, but nevertheless reincarnated Crashaw'.

10 A still earlier one, written for an amateur violinist in Northampton named Bertram Ablethorpe and performed by Rubbra and a violinist with the honoured musical name of Skeaping, was disowned but survived. Rubbra in his middle seventies was even 'unsure of the value' of the one now known as No. 1, so that he kept it unpublished (*ERC*, in Harold Truscott's chapter on the chamber music).

11 A remark quoted by the veteran critic Frank Howes.

12 Jacobson also recorded Rubbra's passion for the more percussive piano music of Béla Bartók, then and subsequently a favourite composer. In the 1920s Bartók, a man of infinite sensibility but famous at the time mostly for his piano piece *Allegro barbaro*, would become very impatient when aspiring pianist after aspiring pianist visited him and insisted on playing it, rather than one of his other pieces. His typical comment on a performance of his music (passed on by the pianist Andor Foldes) was 'It is too Bartókian!'

[13] 'Conjunct': in music, moving mostly or solely through the smallest intervals (minor and major second) and thus tending to have a smooth effect. The opposite, 'disjunct' is less used.

CHAPTER 3 The First Four Symphonies

[1] Christopher Marlowe, *Doctor Faustus*.

[2] Rubbra's note for a recording of the Farnaby piece documents Kalmus's criterion, familiar to anyone who worked for or was published by him, 'less costly to produce'.

[3] 'Hermeneutics: The art or science of interpretation, esp. of Scripture. Commonly distinguished from *exegesis* or practical exposition' (*Oxford English Dictionary*). In the case of a musical work it means correlation of events or moods/emotions from the extra-musical world with ideas in the sound of the music.

[4] 'The British Composer and the Symphony'.

[5] 'Edmund Rubbra, Now 70, Looks at his Eight Symphonies', *The Listener*, 27 May 1971.

[6] Compare 'It is not really surprising that the "introduction" figure is left out of the recapitulation: one has heard little else for several minutes.' The work in question is Schubert's 'Unfinished' Symphony. Leo Black, *Franz Schubert: Music and Belief* (Woodbridge, 2003).

[7] 'Linear Counterpoint' and 'Linear Counterpoint: Linear Polyphony' (both 1931), in Arnold Schönberg, *Style and Idea*, expanded version (London, 1975).

[8] 'Attach' rather than 'Attack'.

[9] A crucial difference between musical and poetic rondo form is that in the latter the recurring idea or refrain comes at the end of each strophe, whereas in a musical rondo the recurring idea sets the whole thing going. That was pointed out by Schönberg in a so-far-unpublished essay.

[10] A *tierce de Picardie* is a major third placed where the music has led one to expect the minor. It was a convention going back to the days when the human ear was so sensitive to overtones that a minor chord at the end would feel like a dissonance and therefore not like an ending.

[11] Diana McVeagh, *Finzi: His Life and Music* (Woodbridge, 2005).

[12] William Fleming and Abraham Veinus, *Understanding Music* (New York, 1958). A comparable problem arises if a piece in ternary (A–B–A) form is held to have a 'programme', see my critique in *Franz Schubert: Music and Belief* of Edward Cone's exegesis of Schubert's sixth *Moment musical*.

[13] In fact he apologised to Piper, who was famous for his dark pictures, when he was due to paint Windsor Castle: 'It looks as if we're in for a fine day!' (Bevis Hillier, book review in *The Spectator*, 2 December 2006).

[14] 'Edmund Rubbra, Now 70, Looks at his Eight Symphonies'. *New Grove*, 1980 edition, defines the dominant seventh as 'a chord consisting of a major triad built on the fifth scale degree, with an added minor 7th ... Its strongest tendency is to

resolve to the tonic: its root is the same as the 5th of the tonic, its 7th tends to resolve to the 3rd of the tonic, and its 3rd – the leading note of the tonality – tends strongly to resolve upward to the root of the tonic.'

15 This type of cadence is suitably known in American terminology as a 'deceptive close' (from the German, *Trugschluss*); the resolution is onto some harmony other than the tonic, which makes it one of the more useful ways to create surprise. (Hans Keller put it in a more complex way in *Music, Closed Societies and Football*: 'the feeling of meaningful inhibition, of a purposive accumulation of tension instead of its expected, anticipated relaxation'.)

16 He clearly had great respect for Casella, mentioning his orchestration of the Chaconne from Bach's D minor Violin Partita in a Third Programme broadcast, *Thoughts on Transcription*, 30 August 1971.

17 A seventh equivalent to a sixth may seem an anomaly, but (for example) the interval C–B♭ (a minor seventh), at least in the equal temperament used on the piano, sounds identical with C–A♯ (an augmented sixth). As *New Grove* puts it: 'German sixth: the augmented sixth chord that has both a major 3rd and a doubly augmented 4th or perfect 5th in addition to an augmented sixth above the flattened submediant.'

18 Again there is a Schubertian parallel, the extraordinary 'hole' and unconnected harmonies in the middle of his important 1816 song 'Geheimnis'. See Black, *Franz Schubert: Music and Belief*, pp. 58–9.

19 Vernon Handley recorded the work during Rubbra's lifetime and gave this movement little more breathing space than had the composer; the later recording under Hickox gives it a good deal more, his tempo coming nearest to Rubbra's published metronome marking. During the eight years between première and publication the composer could have had second thoughts about the ideal tempo for this 'very delicate' intermezzo; in the note for his recording of the *Fantasy Fugue* the pianist Michael Hill tells how Rubbra reconsidered the tempo of the Prelude in his *Prelude and Fugue on a Theme of Cyril Scott*.

20 There were, of course, many other ways of making a several-movement work into a coherent whole, which had been made use of since the time of Haydn and Mozart.

21 McVeagh, *Finzi: His Life and Music*.

CHAPTER 4 The Fifth Symphony

1 Gary Higginson, 'Edmund Rubbra: Teacher & Guide – As I Knew Him' (April 1998), MusicWeb: Classical Music on the Web <http://www.musicweb-international.com/classrev/2000/mar00/higginson.htm>), accessed 13 June 2007.

2 As already mentioned, he appeared again at the Proms on 10 August 1943, as soloist in the first performance of his 1934 *Sinfonia Concertante*.

3 Benjamin Britten did 'post-war service' of at times a fairly harrowing nature, and fifteen years later, at a rehearsal for a Schubert broadcast with Peter Pears, he enquired of his producer (myself) from which NAAFI had the BBC acquired this

piano (a nine-foot Steinway). It was his way of establishing the pecking order rather than a serious comment on the instrument in question.

4 He also taught me harmony and counterpoint, his supervision of my exercises again showing the stringency of his musical thinking and his acute ear; though extremely gentle and rarely what the present-day world calls 'judgmental', he was far less permissive than my previous tutor Bernard Naylor (himself no mean composer) and would regularly red-pencil one or other passage, asking as the most purely rhetorical of questions, 'Did you *really* hear that in your head?'

5 T. S. Eliot's reader's report on early Philip Larkin poems submitted to Faber & Faber said, 'Mr. Larkin can often make words do what he wants them to do.'

6 Richard Strauss is reputed to have told Franz Schmidt, apropos his second opera *Fredigundis*, 'I'd have made four operas out of that', and Schmidt himself commented that the score had material for three symphonies.

7 McVeagh, *Finzi: His Life and Music.*

8 Cormac Rigby, *The Lord Be with You* (Oxford, 2002).

9 Personal communication.

CHAPTER 5 A Question of Mysticism - I

1 In his reply to a questionnaire from the psychologist Julius Bahle, quoted in Willi Reich, *Schoenberg: A Critical Biography* (Harlow, 1971).

2 Evelyn Underhill, *The Essentials of Mysticism* (London, 1920). Ferdinand Hiller said that Schubert 'really only did music, and lived by the way'.

3 Auden sets out these categories in his extensive introduction to *The Protestant Mystics*, ed. Anne Fremantle, 2nd edition (New York and London, 1965). The Pentecostal vision of Agape appears in a poem vividly set by Schubert in his Friedrich Schlegel song 'Im Walde', D708 (1821), bringing together the Pentecostal idea of a 'mighty rushing wind' and that of creativity, for which Schlegel's shorthand is 'der Gedanke' (the thought, idea, or, to follow St John's Gospel, The Logos or Word). Classic instances of the Vision of Eros are Dante's Beatrice, Petrarch's Laura, and, as a dire warning, Verlaine's Mathilde, where the sexual element was insubordinate enough to lead him into a brief and catastrophic marriage. Buddhist mysticism is rich in the Vision of Dame Kind.

4 Arthur Koestler, *The Act of Creation* (London, 1962).

5 Koestler, *The Act of Creation.*

6 Rather curiously, but further bearing out the idea of a slight affinity between Schönberg and Rubbra, the fascinating scoring at the start of scene 2 in the first act of *Moses und Aron* also matches Payne's description.

7 Hans Keller, 'Why this piece is about *Billy Budd*', *The Listener*, 28 September 1972, reprinted in *Essays on Music* (Cambridge, 1994).

8 Joseph Ratzinger, 'Sing Artistically for the Lord', in *A New Song for the Lord* (London, 1990/New York 1996).

9 Arthur Schopenhauer, *Die Welt als Wille und Vorstellung*, Book 3, 36.

CHAPTER 6 The Sixth Symphony

1 McVeagh, *Finzi: His Life and Music.*

2 Quoted by Grover, from *Musical Opinion.*

3 Walton is on record as saying similar things.

4 Graham Greene, a fellow Catholic convert, two years younger than Rubbra, made the narrator of his novel *The End of the Affair* say 'So much of a novelist's work ... takes place in the unconscious: in those depths the last word is written before the first word appears on paper. We remember the details of our story, we do not invent them.'

5 'It is precisely the test of true creativity that the artist steps out of the esoteric circle and knows how to form his or her intuition in such a way that the others – the many – may perceive what the artist has perceived.' Ratzinger, 'Sing Artistically for the Lord'.

6 Joseph Ratzinger, *The Feast of Faith* (San Francisco, 1986).

7 Grover insisted that the three sets or triptychs were planned as a whole, which given their eleven-year time-span must count as one of the most long-range pieces of planning, or slowest realisations of a plan, in the history of music, second only to Wagner's rather more substantial *Ring.*

8 Gianpaolo Romanato, *Vita del Papa Sarto* (Milan, 1992). Things had at one stage been no better in France: 'We can nowadays hardly imagine the extent to which the theatre dominated [French] musical life, nor was it always the best theatre music that found its way into the churches.' Jean-Michel Nectoux, *Gabriel Fauré: A Musical Life* (Cambridge, 1991). But thanks to the innovations of Louis Niedermeyer and the participation of prominent composers, the half-century before Pius x's *Motu Proprio* had already seen a marked improvement there.

9 Pius x wrote in a 1908 Apostolic Exhortation, *Haerent Animo,* 'the most principal cornerstone for the profession of virtue is the daily dedication of part of our time to meditation on the eternal things'.

10 English conductor and composer, 1885–1963, whose major works, mostly from his final twenty years when growing deafness had ended his conducting, are a Mass in C from 1948 and a Requiem from 1957.

11 Aficionados of *A Dance to the Music of Time* might like to know that Rubbra also mentioned a Scott song to a text by the now totally forgotten nineteenth-century poet Baron de Tabley, whom Charles Stringham quotes at his Eton housemaster Le Bas in the first volume, *A Question of Upbringing.* His name is also given to another Bayswater hotel.

12 Recorded speech of thanks to the National Institute of Arts and Letters, New York, after its 1947 award of a grant of $1,000. The English is Schönberg's.

13 The American conductor Bernard Herrmann, who provided the musical score for *The Birds,* was a great admirer of Rubbra, and introduced several of his works to the United States.

14 'J'écoute jusqu'à la souffrance', as the poet Van Lerberghe makes Eve say in one of the poems taken by Fauré as the text for his great song-cycle *La Chanson d'Ève.*

[15] There was one dissenting voice; a year after the symphony's première Anthony Milner reviewed the BBC's radio music output for October 1955 in *The Musical Times*. It was his nature to be full of good will yet quick to find fault; to him, Humphrey Searle's new Symphony was 'certainly the best English symphony of the past year, though that remark is not as complimentary as it might be, since it has had few companions'. So much for Rubbra's Sixth!

[16] Notes I took in the early 1950s as Rubbra analysed the F♯ minor fugue from the second book of Bach's '48' show him commenting on the way Bach held back one note, E, until the second appearance ('answer' or *comes*) of the fugue-subject. The rubric at the end of the preceding fugue, 'Schönberg's 12-tone technique', might *prima facie* seem more likely to stem from a wild student than from a highly respectable teacher, but I knew virtually nothing about twelve-tone music then, and it was his observation, referring to the final cadence where the upper parts move in sixths, something which to him reflected a melodic sixth in the fugue subject.

[17] The source in Thompson was the poem *A Corymbus for Autumn*, the source confirming Rubbra's knowledge of him a lecture 'The Contemporary Composer – Tradition and Environment'. For the term's botanical significance and Rubbra's musical application of it, see pp. 136–7.

[18] This 'retracing of steps' in place of a simple repetition is also found in Schubert's last major religious work, the Mass in E♭ ('Crucifixus').

CHAPTER 7   A Question of Mysticism - II

[1] One of the overtly mystical texts set by Schubert is that of his short male-voice part-song *Das stille Lied*, where he rounds off each strophe with the phrase that began it. In Schönberg's song-cycle *Das Buch der hängenden Gärten*, a crucial work in his career and one whose Stefan George poems show the mixture of erotic and religious imagery found in mystical literature ever since the *Song of Solomon*, there is the same tendency to end songs with the music that began them.

[2] 'Up to a point, Lord Copper': scouring the third section of the 1980/2001 *New Grove* entry 'Symphony' for any reference at all to Rubbra, one finally stumbles across a comparison between his 'tortuous reflectiveness' and 'the least imitable aspect' of Holst and Vaughan Williams. (See Preface, p. vi.)

[3] Koestler, *The Act of Creation*.

CHAPTER 8   The Seventh Symphony

[1] Rubbra's introduction to the recital *Poetry into Song*, a BBC Midland production, broadcast 5 April 1957.

[2] A comparable though smaller-scale procedure is found in the slow movement of Fauré's last instrumental work, the 1924 String Quartet.

3 The middle 1950s were the time when in jazz Dizzie Gillespie was extending the instrument's upward range and its capacity to communicate crazy extremes, but Rubbra's musical sympathies, though wide, are not known to have extended to bebop. In the first movement an idea given out in parallel triads not only by the piano but by a trio of trumpets is a reminder that the years around 1950 were also those when Pete Rugolo's arrangements for the Stan Kenton band took the brassiness of swing music to a new extreme.

4 Benjamin Britten had contributed in that way to the Zorian String Quartet's recording of the six-part *In Nomine* by Purcell, playing the sustained low viola C that runs right through the piece as an inner pedal.

5 Yet again there is a Schubertian parallel, the important running violin figures that help convey the wonder of 'pleni sunt coeli gloriae Tuae', the heavens are full of Thy glory, in the A♭ Mass. For the crucial importance of that music in Schubert's entire output, see Black, *Franz Schubert: Music and Belief*.

6 Given Rubbra's views on Benjamin Britten, he would not have welcomed any comparison between his 'Elizabethan' trio and the courtly dances from *Gloriana* (1953).

7 An expression from the world of psychology, denoting an apparently unmotivated, intuitive succession of thoughts.

8 FAUST Wer bist du denn?

MEPHISTO Ein Teil von jener Kraft / Die stets das Böse will, und stets das Gute schafft.

(Goethe *Faust*, Part 1). Compare quotation from Robert Musil (p. 132).

9 Rubbra's care for the invertibility of his basic ideas (see pp. 19–20) extended to the structure of this passacaglia theme, in which the final element repeats the first's sequence of intervals – semitone, minor third, minor third – but reverses both their order and their direction. Of this fascinatingly 'twelve-tone' retrograde inversion he makes not the slightest use in the course of the music!

10 The A is not technically the final note, being followed by a C; that, however, acts more as a transition to the next statement of the theme, not least by returning to its key-centre.

11 Marion M. Scott's 1934 *Master Musicians* volume on Beethoven construed the scherzo of the *Eroica* Symphony as ancient-Grecian-style 'funeral games' around the hero's grave.

12 A similarly disturbing, if less dramatic, constant 'fade' from major into minor characterises Fauré's 1916 Twelfth Nocturne. The *fons et origo* for such effects is the opening movement of Schubert's G major string quartet, already cited at various points in this book.

13 'And does the request for the mercy of Christ, the Lamb of God, not make sense at that exact moment when he defenselessly give himself into our hands again as Lamb, the sacrificed yet triumphant Lamb who holds the keys of history in his hands?' Ratzinger, 'In the presence of the Angels', in *A New Song for the Lord*.

[14] Milhaud was known to ascribe his interest in polytonality to 'a recurrent, quasi-mystical experience at night in the country, when he felt rays and tremors converging on him from all points of the sky and below ground, "a thousand simultaneous musics rushing at me from all directions"' (1980 *New Grove* entry by Christopher Palmer).

[15] Francis Routh, 'Edmund Rubbra', *Contemporary British Music* (London, 1972), writing before the Ninth Symphony was composed, but when it was known to be 'visualised as a choral symphony'.

[16] William Butler Yeats, 'Sailing to Byzantium'.

[17] The Phrygian mode is reproducible on the piano by starting the scale on E, so that the second degree is only a semitone higher than the first. This gives it a strange, perhaps Oriental quality, shared only by the comparable mode 'starting on B' (the Locrian) – but the latter was hardly ever used since it also contained a diminished fifth (in our case F). A scale neatly bisected by the *diabolus in musica* would have been well out of place in church music ('Nisi Dominus aedem aedificavit' ...!'). One of the prominent figures in the first movement of the Eighth Symphony, Rubbra's tribute to the Catholic theologian Teilhard de Chardin (Ex. 45b*) splits its octave in that way; the work is not programmatic but this figure could perhaps stand for the forces of evil, or at least of Mephistophelean cussedness.

[18] See Clifton Helliwell, *Music in the Air* (Padstow, 1989). Maurice Loban became assistant principal in the Philharmonia and later in the Royal Philharmonic Orchestra, where he shared the front desk with the veteran and notoriously 'difficult' Frederick Riddle. Asked after a while how he coped with that, he said, 'No problem, he hasn't said a word to me yet.'

[19] Pickard's CD note comments on the 1960s-style juxtaposition of irreconcilable works when the quartet had its première at the 1964 Cheltenham Festival, played by the Allegri Quartet (Rubbra's great friend William Pleeth thus figuring in yet another capacity, as the quartet's cellist). It shared the programme with Stockhausen's aleatoric solo-percussion piece *Zyklus*, in the kind of combination that made Robert Simpson nickname his employer's BBC Invitation series 'the kippers and custard concerts'. The present writer, who enjoyed the conceit even as he produced the concerts, provided a note on *Zyklus*; it was un-phoney by the standards of its time, but if Rubbra examined the concert programme he may all the same have feared the worst for his former pupil ('to us in the early days Universal Edition was a bastion of militant propagation of the avant-garde – Edmund used to shudder at the very name' – letter to the author from Rubbra's younger fellow-composer and sometime unofficial pupil Philip Cannon).

[20] Adrian Yardley recalls that during his early years when Yardleys and Rubbras were neighbours at Highwood Bottom, the Yardleys kept chickens. I leave the implications (if any) of that to Rubbra's future biographer. For that matter, Rubbra owned a record of Haydn's Symphony no. 83 (*La Poule*).

CHAPTER 9 The Tide Turns: The Eighth Symphony

1 Among the notable figures in pre-war BBC music, alongside Rubbra's admirers Adrian Boult and Owen Mase, the Schönberg pupil Edward Clark, husband of the pioneering twelve-tone composer Elisabeth Lutyens, had played very much the proselytising role that would fall to Glock in 1959. Lutyens in her final years never tired of reminding her younger contemporaries of that.

2 It's always the totally individual creators, those one would have thought inimitable (Kafka, Schönberg, Webern, Beckett) who end up being most mindlessly imitated, their uniquely personal content generalised and cheapened, their style misappropriated.

3 'Deliver me from the hand of strange children, whose mouth speaketh vanity' (Psalm 144).

4 Alison Garnham's *Hans Keller and the BBC* (Aldershot, 2003) shrewdly notes that after a quite short 'honeymoon period' with the Second Viennese School he tended to leave them to Keller.

5 Personal communication.

6 This proved such a challenge to the vocal consort encumbered with it that six flautists had to be co-opted to keep them in tune.

7 In 1961, for example, there were twenty-six BBC broadcasts of Rubbra's music, three of Boulez', and a single one of Stockhausen's, according to a 1963 lecture reprinted in Glock's autobiographical *Notes in Advance*. Another section of the book is, however, headed by one of his favourite expressions, 'Creative Unbalance'.

8 Having since retirement from the Corporation come to know Rubbra's chamber music, I know I could and should have done more, that being the field in which I predominantly worked. Others who played an active part in the 'new music' movement of the 1960s likewise came to see what a double-edged business it had been. When Peter Heyworth, a leading radical critic from the 1960s and after, reviewed a London festival of Franz Schmidt's music in 1984, he wrote of a 'determinist view of history, that has echoed down our century, often to disastrous effect'.

9 'What has become the fundamental symphonic problem – the definition and large-scale integration of the contrast between statements and developments – glares at us from all our era's symphonic endeavours, and it is only among works of our more conservative symphonists, such as the string quartets and symphonies of Benjamin Frankel, Edmund Rubbra or Robert Simpson, that frictionless solutions have, at times, been found.' (Hans Keller, 'The State of the Symphony – not only Peter Maxwell Davies'', 1978, reprinted in *Collected Essays*).

10 Personal communication.

11 The work's opus number, lower than those of compositions known to date from before 1969, could suggest, in view of Rubbra's practice with such numbers, that he began it earlier and took his time over it, allotting a number while it was still expected to become a harp concerto.

12 Personal communication.

[13] Letter from Kingsley Amis to Philip Larkin, 12 June 1950 (*Collected Letters*, London 2000). Whatever the situation with the written word, one emphatically *can* have counterpointed rhythm in music, as witness the scherzo of the Second Symphony! Hopkins's preferred expression for his stressed but free verse was 'sprung rhythm'.

[14] Schubert's great 1820 song *Im Walde* memorably sets a Friedrich Schlegel text evoking some such epiphany.

[15] Rubbra might or might not have been amused to find himself posthumously knighted in the index of *Notes in Advance*!

[16] In the early 1960s one or two Manchester school members, impatient of their elders' ways, founded a rival Guild of Professional Composers, of which not too much was ever heard.

[17] This indeterminate chord, one of the two classified in Schönberg's *Harmonielehre* as 'vagrant', is naturally subversive, since, like its counterpart the diminished seventh (colloquially known as The Clapham Junction of Music), it can lead in any direction. It consists of two superimposed major thirds, whereas the diminished seventh consists of three superimposed minor thirds; the combination of both types is needed to give the certainty and steadiness associated with the diatonic triad, whether major or minor.

[18] Anthony Bennett, in a personal communication, has commented that this could be 'somehow a 'creation' or perhaps a 'creator' theme – at least in its slower manifestations. Is it something to do with the insistence on the tonic (ground of being?) as the 'central' pitch, together with the energizing dotted rhythm and its 'outward' (in this case 'procreative'?) move to supertonic; and then the settling (which I suspect is precisely the wrong word?) on the dominant with all its potential?' All of which, Rubbra's disclaimer notwithstanding, one may regard as an arguable piece of hermeneutics.

[19] The end of the introduction in the first movement of Schubert's 'Great' C Major Symphony is composed so that conductors need make no perceptible change of tempo (pulse-rate as distinct from speed of movement) as the exposition proper begins.

[20] Grover suggested two possible schemes for this opening movement: A–B–A plus coda, a simple idea complicated by two things – the second A is far longer and includes the interpolated miniature scherzo; or else an 'enlarged sonatina', meaning that there is no formal development section, only an exposition with its two subjects, then a shortened recapitulation, likewise complicated by the interpolation of the scherzetto. It seems the more realistic interpretation, even though the 'recapitulation' contains a good deal of development of the basic ideas.

[21] A coin in the now-abolished sterling currency, equivalent to 2.5p in metric, and therefore small (slightly bigger than the present-day 5p piece), hence the metaphor.

[22] The end of the Credo in Beethoven's *Missa Solemnis* is the *locus classicus* for the use of simultaneous rising and falling scales to suggest infinite space.

[23] T. S. Eliot, *East Coker* (Four Quartets) (London, 1940), section v.

[24] Or Melchior Franck's – the work's attribution is uncertain.

25 Teilhard was one figure in a movement, going back to the years after the First World War, which aimed to disprove the irreconcilability of science and religion. For example, in the 1960s the Munich physicist-philosopher Aloys Wenzel published a widely read book, *Philosophie der Freiheit*, arguing that the determinist world-picture of classical physics, which left no room for God, had been replaced by an open one with room for the new, unforeseen and incalculable.

26 Note for the BBC National Orchestra of Wales recording.

27 Higginson, 'Edmund Rubbra: Teacher & Guide – As I Knew Him'.

28 Something comparable happened in the performing field; while BBC Controller of Music, Robert Ponsonby told me with amusement of a letter received from Sir Adrian Boult, who in the course of a Radio 3 morning had heard half a dozen orchestras, not one of them playing the music of its own country! Some of that had been foreseen. The Austrian scholar Ulrike Anton's work on Britain's refugee musicians from her country unearthed a letter from Vaughan Williams to the immigré pianist Ferdinand Rauter: notwithstanding his support for talented individual refugees such as the young Hans Keller, RVW declined to endorse the idea of an 'Austrian musical circle', feeling that newcomers should assimilate to English culture rather than remain segregated. In the long run assimilation worked in reverse (the word more often used, for the most part fairly, is 'enrichment').

CHAPTER 10 The Last Three Symphonies

1 That and much else of note about the work is set out in John Pickard's 'Redeeming Rubbra: Generic fusion in the *Sinfonia Sacra*', *The Musical Times*, Winter 2001, pp. 34–8. Rubbra drew mostly on the synoptic gospels, passing up the opportunity to exploit the pictorial possibilities of St John's account of the final miracle with the fisher disciples drawing up a net unbroken by the weight of 153 fish, of which millions of people throughout the world will have been reminded or made aware since the televised Enthronement of Pope Benedict XVI in 2005.

2 Grover was in some doubt, unlike Pickard, while Elsie Payne called it 'a statement of his accumulated musical styles and idioms, above all of his symphonic techniques and his methods of setting words to music', concluding that 'in a free, twentieth-century sense, the work may rightly be called a symphony. For it possesses the essential elements of the symphonic genre – at one extreme, event and drama, at the other contemplation and un-event. Plus the necessary moments of relaxation.' That is a specification the reader might care to test on whichever classical symphonies he or she knows and loves best. In his Skryabin talk Rubbra commented that the term 'sonata', which had become synonymous with an extended work in several movements, reverted in that composer's late music to its original meaning of something played. (The Ninth Sonata, with which he concluded his talk, lasts six and a half minutes.) By the same token, one could see the *Sinfonia Sacra* as re-evoking the original meaning of symphony – 'sounding together'.

[3] Those who know Pfitzner's opera well may be struck, early on in the Rubbra Tenth Symphony, by a beautiful falling and rising phrase very like the motif associated in the opera with the composer's sensitive and devoted son Ighino. *Palestrina* was (and remains) so little known in Britain that the similarity is scarcely to be regarded as more than a matter of chance, plus a reflection of comparable elements in the personalities of two otherwise strongly contrasting composers. Certainly Rubbra never wrote about Pfitzner, any more than about Mahler, and in Britain a kinship of spirit with Pfitzner of all people is not going to earn a native composer any goodwill, there being something apparently hard to take about any post-Mozart German composer with a 'z' in his name: why else should Heinrich von Herzogenberg remain so totally unknown? Both composers are our considerable loss.

[4] Charles Koechlin, *Gabriel Fauré*, trans. Leslie Orrey (London, 1945).

[5] Before referring to the score I got to know it, like all its fellows, by repeated listening, and was left with the strangest impression; it was as if I heard a slightly different work each time. One trend in the fateful 1960s was for pieces of music, such as the Stockhausen percussion piece with which the Third Quartet had shared the Cheltenham programme, where the performer was left free to choose the order in which sections were played, so that a work really was 'different' every time; now, in the late 1970s and working in time-honoured ways with the most traditional of materials, one of England's senior composers created something similar, despite the fact that at every performance more-or-less-precisely the same notes, tempi and dynamic markings are involved.

[6] And, to invoke yet again a favourite classical work, the start of Schubert's 'Great' C Major Symphony, where the talismanic theme is given not to one 'horn of elfland faintly blowing' but to two in unison.

[7] Rubbra's archaism here was not unique to him. Hindemith, too, sometimes wrote in parallel fourths, and 'mixture' stops on the organ to this day perpetuate the habit of moving in parallel intervals, which can play hell with one's enjoyment of a melody, making it seem to be going on in two keys at once!

[8] Robert Browning, 'Abt. Vogler'.

[9] 'Edmund Rubbra: A Personal Memoir', *Worcester College Record*, 1987.

[10] Karl Amadeus Hartmann altered the end of his *Concerto funèbre* in a strikingly similar way when he revised it after the war, four years before he died. Hartmann, however, went on to produce a further symphony, his Eighth.

[11] Information from Adrian Yardley.

[12] Finzi to Cedric Thorpe Davie, quoted by Banfield.

Bibliography

Anon. 'Portrait Gallery'. *The Sunday Times*, 6 October 1957.

Banfield, S. 'Edmund Rubbra, Symphony No. XI, Op. 153' [music review] *Music and Letters*, vol. 64 (1983), p. 144.

—— *Gerald Finzi, An English Composer.* London, 1997, *passim*.

Black, L. 'The Rubbra Sixth'. *Isis*, 23 February 1955, p. 15.

British Composers in Interview, ed. M. Schafer. London, 1963, pp. 64–72.

Edmund Rubbra: Composer [symposium], ed. L. Foreman. Rickmansworth, 1977.

Grover, R. S. *The Music of Edmund Rubbra.* Aldershot, 1993.

—— 'Rubbra, Edmund'. *The New Grove Dictionary of Music and Musicians.* London, 2001, vol. 21, pp. 835–9.

Hamburger, P. 'Cheltenham Festival (Second Week, July 10–15)'. *Music Survey*, December 1950, p. 121.

Jacobson, M. 'Edmund Rubbra'. *The Monthly Musical Record*, February 1935, pp. 32–3.

McVeagh, D. *Gerald Finzi: His Life and Music.* Woodbridge, 2003.

Mellers, W. 'Rubbra and the Dominant Seventh'. *The Music Review*, August 1943, pp. 145–6.

—— *Music and Society: England and the European Tradition*, 2nd edition. London, 1950, pp. 169–80, esp. 172–4.

Ottaway, H. 'Rubbra's Sixth Symphony'. *The Musical Times*, October 1955, pp. 527–9.

—— 'Rubbra at 75'. *The Listener*, 3 June 1976, pp. 710–11.

—— 'Rubbra, Edmund'. *The New Grove Dictionary of Music and Musicians.* London, 1980, vol. 16, pp. 292–4.

Pickard, J. 'Redeeming Rubbra: Generic Fusion in the "Sinfonia Sacra"'. *The Musical Times*, Winter 2001, pp. 34–8.

Routh, F. 'Edmund Rubbra'. *Contemporary British Music.* London, 1972, pp. 70–9.

Rubbra, E. 'An Analysis by the Composer of his Fifth Symphony'. *The Music Review*, February 1949, p. 220.

—— 'A Composer's Problems'. *Music Magazine* (1953), pp. 42–5.

—— 'Letter to a Young Composer'. *The Listener*, 13 September 1956, pp. 379–80.

—— *Counterpoint: A Survey.* London, 1960.

—— 'Edmund Rubbra Writes about his Eighth Symphony. *The Listener,* 31 December 1970, p. 925.

—— 'Edmund Rubbra, Now 70, Looks at his Eight Symphonies'. *The Listener,* 27 May 1971, p. 690.

—— 'Edmund Rubbra Writes about his "Sinfonia Sacra"'. *The Listener,* 15 February 1973, p. 220–1.

Background

Blavatsky, E. *Isis Unveiled.* New York, 1875.

Helliwell, C. *Music in the Air* Padstow, 1989.

Keller, H. *Essays on Music.* Cambridge, 1994.

Koechlin, C. *Gabriel Fauré.* London, 1945.

Koestler, A. *The Act of Creation.* London, 1962.

Musil, R. *Tagebücher, Aphorismen, Essays und Reden.* Hamburg, 1955.

Ouspensky, P. D. *Tertium Organum: The Third Canon of Thought: A Key to the Enigma of The World.* New York, 1920.

Powell, A. *A Dance to the Music of Time* [series of twelve novels]. London, 1951–75.

The Protestant Mystics, ed. A. Fremantle. New York and London, 1964. [Introduction by W. H. Auden.]

Ratzinger, Joseph Cardinal [later Pope Benedict XVI] *The Feast of Faith.* San Francisco 1986.

—— *A New Song for the Lord,* Oxford 1995.

Schönberg, A. *Style and Idea.* Expanded edition, London, 1975.

Scott, C. *The Philosophy of Modernism in Relation to Music.* London, 1917.

Teilhard de Chardin, P. *passim.* [Rubbra had nineteen works by this author in his library, notably *The Phenomenon of Man* (London, 1959).]

Underhill, E. *The Essentials of Mysticism.* London, 1920.

Webern, A. *The Path to the New Music.* Philadelphia and London, 1963.

Discography

Symphonies

⧵⧵ Complete Symphonies

Nos. 1–11. BBC National Orchestra and Chorus of Wales, Lynne Dawson, Della Jones, Stephen Roberts, Richard Hickox. Chandos CHAN 9944(5).

⧵⧵ Original issues of these recordings, still available:

No. 1, with *A Tribute* op. 56, *Sinfonia Concertante* op. 38. Chandos CHAN 9538.
   Only possibility for No. 1.

Nos. 2 and 6. Chandos CHAN 9481.
   Handley well worth considering as an alternative in No. 2, Del Mar in No. 6.

Nos. 3 and 7. Chandos CHAN 9634.
   Del Mar and Boult both had the measure of Rubbra's majestic side.

Nos. 4, 10 and 11. Chandos CHAN 9401.
   Only possibility for No. 11. Del Mar excellent in No. 4. Schönzeler sympathetic in No. 10.

Nos. 5 and 8, with *Ode to the Queen* op. 83. CHAN 9714.
   Barbirolli in a class of his own in No. 5; Del Mar good in No. 8.

No. 9, with *The Morning Watch* op. 55. Chandos CHAN 9441.
   Only possibility.

⧵⧵ Recordings by Lyrita, reissued by Nimbus

No. 2, with *Festival Overture*. New Philharmonia Orchestra, Vernon Handley.
No. 7. London Philharmonic Orchestra, Sir Adrian Boult. Lyrita SRCD 235.
   Boult historic as Rubbra conductor, Handley as next prominent advocate in composer's lifetime.

Nos. 3 and 4, with *A Tribute* op. 56, and *Resurgam* op. 149. Philharmonia Orchestra, Norman del Mar. Lyrita SRCD 202.

Nos. 6 and 8. Philharmonia Orchestra, Norman del Mar. With *Soliloquy* op. 57. London Symphony Orchestra, Rohan de Saram, Vernon Handley. Lyrita SRCD 234.

※ Other recordings of the symphonies

No. 5, with *Farnaby Improvisation* no. 4 (op. 50/4).
Halle Orchestra, Sir John Barbirolli (1950). EMI CDM 5 66053 2.
  Periodically available

No. 5. Melbourne Symphony Orchestra, Hans-Hubert Schönzeler.
Chandos CHAN 6576.

No. 10, with *A Tribute* op. 56, and *Farnaby Improvisations* op. 50.
Bournemouth Sinfonietta, Schönzeler (1978). Chandos CHAN 6599.
  Schönzeler has the Bruckner-conductor's spaciousness, better in place here than
  in No. 5.

Other orchestral

Brahms–Handel Variations (orchestration, op. 47).
—— Cleveland Orchestra, Vladimir Ashkenazy. Decca 470519-2.
—— London Symphony Orchestra, Neemi Järvi. Chandos CHAN 8825.
—— NBC Symphony Orchestra, Arturo Toscanini. Arturo Toscanini Society
ATS 1003-4.

Soliloquy op. 57. Rafael Wallfisch, BBC Concert Orchestra, Vernon
Handley. Sanctuary CDWHL 2153.

Piano Concerto. Denis Matthews, BBC Symphony Orchestra, Sir Malcolm
Sargent. EMI CDZ5 74781 2.

Sinfonia Concertante op. 38, with *A Tribute* op. 56, *The Morning Watch* op. 55,
Ode to the Queen op. 83. Howard Shelley, BBC National Orchestra of Wales,
Richard Hickox. Chandos CHAN 9966

Viola Concerto, with *Meditations on a Byzantine Hymn* op. 117 (solo version).
Lawrence Power, BBC Scottish Symphony Orchestra, Ilan Volkov.
Hyperion CDA 67587.

Violin Concerto, with *Improvisation* for violin and orchestra op. 89, and
Farnaby Improvisations op. 50. Krysia Osostowicz, Ulster Orchestra, Takeo
Yuasa. Naxos 8.557591.

Chamber

Piano Trios nos. 1–2, *Meditazioni sopra Cœurs Désolés* op. 67, Phantasy op. 16, Oboe Sonata op. 100, Duo for cor anglais and piano op. 156, Suite *The Buddha* op. 64. Endymion Ensemble. Dutton CDLX 7106.

String Quartets nos. 1 and 3, Cello Sonata op. 60, Cello Improvisation op. 124. Dante Quartet. Dutton CDLX 7123.

String Quartets nos. 2 and 4, *Lyric Movement* op. 24, *Meditations on a Byzantine Hymn* op. 117 (two-viola version). Dante Quartet. Dutton CDLX 7114.

Violin Sonatas nos. 1–3, *Four Easy Pieces* op. 29, *Variations on a Phrygian Theme*. Krysia Osostowicz, Michael Dussek. Dutton CDLX 7101.

Violin Sonata no. 3. Albert Sammons, Gerald Moore. Dutton CDBP 9765.

Choral

Missa cantuarensis op. 59, *Magnificat and Nunc Dimittis* op. 65, *Missa Sancti Dominici* op. 66, *Tenebrae Nocturns* op. 72, *Meditation* for organ op. 79, Prelude and Fugue for organ op. 69. Choir of St. John's College, Cambridge, Christopher Robinson, Robert Houssart. Naxos 8.555255.

5 Motets op. 37, *Missa a tre* op. 98, *Lauda Sion* op. 110, *The Beatitudes* op. 109, 5 Madrigals op. 51, 2 Madrigals op. 52, *St. Teresa Mass*, 4 carols. Voces Sacrae, Judy Martin. ASV CDDCA 1093.

Missa Cantuarensis, Missa Sancti Dominici, Dormi Jesu, That Virgin's Child so Meek (Op. 114/2). St Margaret's Westminster Singers, Ian Watson (organ), Richard Hickox. Chandos CHAN 10423.

Magnificat and Nunc Dimittis op. 65, 9 Tenebrae Motets op. 72, *Salutation* op. 82, *Missa Sancti Dominici* op. 66, *Festival Gloria* op. 94. Gloriae Dei Cantores, Elizabeth C. Patterson. Gloriae Dei GDCD 024.

US recording, but available in UK

General Index

Entries in square brackets [ ] indicate that the topic is not actually named on the page in question.

(Rubbra, Edmund: Lectures, broadcasts, writings)

contributions to *The Listener*, printed after broadcast talks

ER, Now 70, Looks at his Eight Symphonies 41, 44, 49, 50, 59, 212*n*5, 212*n*14

ER Writes about his Eighth Symphony 164, 173, 209*n*9, 201*nn*15–16

ER Writes about his 'Sinfonia Sacra' 177

ER Writes about the Development of his Choral Music 121

Letter to a Young Composer 11, 23, 101, 174

Rubbra–Gruenberg–Pleeth Trio 176

rugby football, fly-half in 146

Rugolo, Pete 217*n*3

Sachs, Hans (in *Die Meistersinger*) 51, 94, 139, 161

St Cecilia Festival 85

saltarella (= saltarello) 37–8, 49

Sammartini Hall, Milan 32

Sammons, Albert 34

Sargent, Sir Malcolm 65, 117, 120, 121, 136

sarod 136, 153

Saxby, Joseph 114

Saxton, Robert 37, 57, 58, 64, 65, 77, 82, 131, 142, 148, 185, 187, 209*n*1

Schafer, Murray 34, 50, 159–60

Scharrer, Irene 73

Schiller, Friedrich 167

Schmidt, Franz 111, 143, 219*n*8

Fredigundis 214*n*6

Symphony No. 1 143

Symphony No. 4 143, 197

The Book with Seven Seals 178–9

Schnabel, Artur 160

Schoeck, Othmar 160

Schönberg, Arnold 9, 12, 14, 33, 55, 64, 65, 87, 100, 101, 104, 109, 147, 160, 198, 201, 212*n*9, 214*n*6, 215*n*12, 219*nn*1–2

Das Buch der hängenden Gärten 216*n*1

Chamber Symphony No. 1 183

discordant intervals 117

(Schönberg, Arnold, *cont.*)

Erwartung 198

Five Orchestral Pieces, Op. 16 191

Harmonielehre 159, 220*n*17

Moses und Aron 154

ostinato 12

score markings 9, 97

Three Piano Pieces, Op. 11 138

twelve-tone technique 11, 19, 48, 193, 203*n*8, 216*n*2; *see also* twelve-tone composition

Verklärte Nacht 203

Schönzeler, Hans-Hubert 93

Schopenhauer, Arthur 106

Schubert, Franz 47, 50, 55, 64, 65, 72, 83, 123, 124, 133, 183, 213*n*3, 214*n*2

Cantata: *Lazarus* 179

Choral pieces

Das stille Lied 216*n*1

Nachthelle 172

Mass in A♭ 131, 217*n*5

Mass in E♭ 216*n*18

Piano music

Fantasy in C major ('Wanderer') 183

Moments musicaux 212*n*12

Songs

Der Tod und das Mädchen 200

Geheimnis (D491) 213*n*18

Im Walde (D708) 214*n*3, 220*n*14

Der Wanderer (D489) 183

Das Zügenglöcklein 172

String Quartet in A minor (D804) 47

String Quartet in C Minor (unfinished, 'Quartettsatz', D703) 47

String Quartet in D minor ('Death and the Maiden', D810) 47, 200

String Quartet in G major (D887) 47, 48, 217*n*12

Symphony in C major ('Great', D849) 56, 124–5, 141, 220*n*19, 222*n*6

Symphony in B minor ('Unfinished', D759) 212*n*6

Schumann, Robert 75, 133

Symphony No. 1 in B♭ ('Spring') 210*n*10

Schwarz, Rudolf 153, 182

Scott, Cyril 22–6, 32, 100, 154, 201, 211*n*9

Cavatina 116

Society 24

Index of Rubbra's Works

Pages on which works are considered at length are shown in **bold**.